Little Angels Don't Cry

Copyright © 2005 Martha Bertrand
All rights reserved.
ISBN: 1-4196-1782-6

To order additional copies, please contact us.
BookSurge, LLC
www.booksurge.com
1-866-308-6235
orders@booksurge.com

MARTHA
BERTRAND

LITTLE ANGELS
DON'T CRY

2005

Little Angels Don't Cry

TABLE OF CONTENTS

To My Children.

CHAPTER I

Asudden muffled noise towards the door stirred me out of my baby sleep. My little hand searched for something to touch and immediately hit against the tall cold bars of the cot. Curious, I turned my head towards the noise and saw a large dark shadow moving swiftly towards me. Gradually, the silhouette came into focus and this smiling face with a huge white thing stuck on top of her head bent over me, cooing in a series of high-pitched sounds. Her two firm hands propped me up and sat me on the white sheets. I looked around but all I could see was a forest of white iron bars. There were other babies too. I could not see them but I could hear them as one by one, they woke up and cried, fearful of the strangers that seemed to float ominously around them in loose dark robes. Very soon, more dark shadows followed. Their hands clasped together, their heads tilted to one side, they clucked and cooed adoringly at the little crunched faces of the bewildered babies who could think of nothing else to do but cry. I looked at the cot next to mine and saw another little baby looking back at me. She was not crying. Puzzled, I glanced around the room again and wondered why the other babies cried.

After a while, the dark shadows departed, leaving behind a stirred-up atmosphere filled with the anguish of little lost souls longing for something familiar to grip and to hold.

It is in this fraught atmosphere that I spent my first

waking hours, just sitting, staring and waiting—waiting for what, I did not know, but I did not mind. I liked passing the time watching the other babies. Sometimes, I tried to reach out to the baby in the cot next to mine with my little arm stretched out to its limit in an attempt to bring myself closer to the other little being who often stared bewildered at me. The big dark silhouette with the white flapping wings on her head must have noticed our need for interaction, for, occasionally, she would grab me and deposit me gently in the other cot where the little being and I sat gurgling and babbling away at each other, shaking a rattle, or dribbling over some other toy. Fortunately, I was soon able to crawl and my little heart fluttered with excitement at the exhilarating sensation of feeling the cold tiles moving underneath my tiny hands as I began to explore the space around me. It was such a wonderful discovery to know I could go wherever I wanted to go, sit wherever I wanted to sit, and choose which toy I wanted to play with. I liked red, so I went for anything of that colour, even if I did not know what it was. I also liked toys that squeaked, and every time I managed to make a toy squeak at me, I would squeal with delight and squeeze the toy over and over again until it was eventually snatched from me by another little being or taken away by the dark shadow. When that happened, I would look for another red toy or one that had a picture on it, and I would happily spend several long minutes simply squinting at it in an attempt to figure out what exactly I was looking at.

For some time now, I had noticed a noise that purred gently in the background. I did not know what it was and never really had time to find out because so much was happening around me. Now, as I began to explore further a field, I found myself looking at something transparent, full of water, with creatures wriggling about inside it. The dark shadow picked me up so that I could have a closer look.

"*Poisson...poisson.*" She said, pointing at the orange things.

Immediately, I turned my head away. I did not like the look of them and panicked when she brought me closer to the water to satisfy my curiosity.

Right now, I was at the stage where time and space were just a blur filled with noise and subdued colours. The empty hours rolled by unnoticed, and I languished in my cot, fiddling with my tiny fingers and trying to bite my big toe. Slowly, however, a distinctive pattern seemed to emerge and shaped the days. There seemed to be an order of things all built around feeding time, washing time, and sleeping time. I was beginning to understand why the dark shadow came at certain times, but not who this elusive creature was, and while I was gradually getting used to a semblance of a routine, every now and again, everything would stop and I would find myself alone, all the other children having disappeared though I did not know where. When this happened, everything fell silent with nothing stirring in between the forest of white iron bars. No sound, no cries...just me and the goldfish. It was quiet...all so quiet. To pass the time, I would sit up in my cot and listen to the gentle whir of the fish tank that purred soothingly in the lonesome silence.

I do not recall how I learnt her name, but *Sister Bénédicte's* name was the first two words I was able to understand. One particular day, when everyone had gone away, I watched her pale chubby face advance towards me. Gently, she took me out of the cot and took me to the washroom to change and dress me. Her joyful voice echoed all around the bathroom tiles as she cooed admiring words at my pretty little dress. I liked it when she smiled, so I smiled back, engaging in this way in a dialogue more eloquent than if it had words, and I could tell it worked, for every time I smiled, her voice instantly rose to a crescendo of high-pitched notes cascading from her lips in a harmony of maternal bliss. She talked non-stop and today, she was going to teach me how to walk. With a loving smile and admiring words falling from her adoring lips, she propped me up on the tiled floor and called out to me. I stood there, wobbling on my two feet, watching her waving her arms at me, knowing what she wanted from me, but as yet unable to do it. However, when I felt steady enough, I put a foot forward, but soon discovered that I could not move further, as my other foot was stuck underneath my little body like a counter-weight. Her arms outstretched, Sister Bénédicte kept urging me with a flow of encouraging words. I liked to see her smile, so I stuck my tongue out, took a deep breath, and shifted my foot from underneath my body. Alas, with one foot in the air and the other on the move, I simply could not keep my balance and I toppled backward, smacking my head heavily against the cold tiles. Sister Bénédicte picked me up in a panic and pressed my head hard against her well-padded chest while she soothed my worries with gentle strokes. I could sense the high level of anxiety through her voice and her strokes, but I was not hurt, so I did not cry. She was recovered now, so she set about to make me try again. This time, I managed two tiny steps before floundering into the voluminous dark layers of cloth sprawled across her lap, spilling over the floor all around her. Overjoyed and elated, she grabbed me and held me aloft, calling St. Vincent as her witness, reassured that, had she not received *the call* to dedicate her life to God, she would have made a good mother after all.

These precious moments of close intimacy were scarce for, if it was Sister Bénédicte's duty to care for her little charges, it befell on God and God alone to love us all. Having been spared this emotional burden, Sister Bénédicte moved swiftly through the primary stages of our early development from a watchful distance and with calculated reserve.

In her own words, it was always time to grow up and to move on. And so, not long after I had learnt to get dressed, do up my shoelaces, though only just, and use a fork and a spoon, I was moved out of the baby section to the floor below.

Its layout was identical to the floor above, down to the fish tank, which purred quietly away in the same corner of the room, right there between the two picture windows. As I explored the familiar set-up, looking for something new, something different, I stopped in front of one of the picture windows in the playroom and, for the first time, I noticed the view outside. A series of elongated gardens, rolled out like a set of mismatched carpet runners, layered the landscape right up to the redbrick factory which stood imposingly against the greyish horizon, with its line chiselled by the factory's serrated roof. Its red-brick chimney, so tall that it almost touched the sky, regurgitated clouds of white steam high up into the molten atmosphere.

What I could not see, however, was the stark landscape in the midst of which our building lay, its red bricks darkened by the soot of nearby coalmines and the steam of the local textile factories. The town itself was called Tourcoing, a conurbation which entwined round the industrial jungle of Northern France like thick layers of cold black lava, barely indistinguishable from the dark mountains of slag heaps steaming with sulphurous plumes of acrid smoke. Nobody came here for the view, but at least, it was a country at peace.

In this grim darkened land, impoverished by the devastating effects of the Second World War, children by the thousands were systematically being given up to the *Assistance Publique*, the State's welfare organisation which helped fill orphanages all over the country to save thousands of hapless children from a life of poverty, hunger and misery. The *Institution Saint Vincent de Paul* was one such orphanage, a word that carried with it pity and the loss of human dignity. It was the last post beyond which lay a land barren of human emotions and human feelings, but where life could still evolve in an oasis of human solidarity. Adults themselves did not like to use the word 'orphanage,' and if they ever had to mention the place, they would simply refer to it as *Saint Vincent,* practically whispering the name and drowning the words with a little nervous cough.

The institution was divided into three sections, known simply as the Baby Section, the Junior and the Senior Sections. Understandably, whilst the country was still convalescing from the devastation inflicted by two consecutive world wars, no undue sentimentality had been wasted on choosing more appropriate names that might mislead anyone to believe that this was the ultimate refuge for little lost children. There had simply been no time, especially as the rest of the country was involved in a vast programme of reconstruction and recovery. However, to a trained eye used to dealing with human tragedy, the institution *Saint Vincent* was a self-made island built on the consequences of man's reckless behaviour. Nobody seemed able to remember the last words bewailed by Louis XIV as he lay on his deathbed. In his final hours, the magnificent splendour of his bank-breaking palaces, the costly legacy he was about to bequeath to the nation—but first to his numerous mistresses— were far from his mind, and all the Sun King could do, as he prepared to meet a power greater than himself—a thought that would surely have panicked him and quickened his death—was to use his last breath to confess how much he regretted all the follies of wars for which he was responsible. For their part, none of his faithful ministers present to record his last sighs had had the courage or the wisdom to whisper in his ear: "alas, Sire, it is the children who are the bearers of all our deeds."

Inside the institution, the house rules were starkly delivered, never in anything other than black or white; everything was right or wrong, good or bad and your only choice was: you live or die.

The wing where we lived was the newest, a large extension that had been hurriedly built with a pile of breeze blocks stacked up to the hilts to make a tall tower, three-storey high, interspersed with big wide windows. What made it the envy of all who lived in the orphanage was the fact that the Baby Wing had a lift. It did not matter that it reeked with the pungent smell of industrialised rubber; it was a welcome luxury, just like the central heating was.

Still staring dreamily out of the window, a girl came to me and confided in a tone full of awe:

"There's a witch who lives in the second garden...over there..." She pointed.

I looked at the girl wondering whether this was some kind of invitation to join in her imaginary games or whether she truly believed her incredible words.

"A witch? A real witch?" I asked, half excited, half disbelieving.

"And she's got a stick!" She warned, scowling in awe.

Her breathing quickening with excitement, she revealed how this old lady sometimes ventured out in her garden and when she did, she always carried with her a walking stick.

"And if you're naughty, you'd better watch out, because, sometimes, she shakes it in the air."

I looked at Aline, unsure what to make of her. Through the thick lenses of her plastic glasses, her eyes appeared abnormally dilated and emphasised the look of panic painted all over her face. How else could she interpret an old lady brandishing a stick? To the old lady herself, it was probably nothing worse than a friendly greeting, but to us, ensconced in our childish universe filled only with characters that were either good or bad, she was quite simply a baddy, and being an old woman, she had to be a witch. If only she had known, but fortunately she did not, and the poor old lady probably went to her grave not knowing that she had been incorporated in our infantile games in which ugly witches often ruled, but where the most unlikely looking princesses always prevailed.

All the living areas were connected by sets of double doors with, on one side, the dining area, the dayroom, and the dormitory, and on the other side, the washroom, the cloakroom, and the landing. This was perfect chasing ground, as we could run round and round and still not catch up with each other.

Off the dining area, there was the dreaded *cagibi*, a dark windowless storeroom that doubled up as a punishment area. It was a room which I only visited voluntarily, although sometimes I wished I had been able to shut myself away there and use the room as my own personal retreat.

The dormitory was divided into two by a low partition to make the room appear smaller, thus less daunting at night. The light on the ceiling was encased in what looked like a wicker birdcage, and at night, its subdued glow projected playful patterns on the bare walls, creating the illusion of a presence forever there to protect us from the curses of darkness.

Still deliberating over the likely existence of the mysterious witch, I made my way to the sleeping quarters, hoping to gain a better view, but the garden wall stood too high for me to catch a glimpse of her back door. On the other side, the view was blocked by a huge long wall, completely covered in ivy, which separated our building from another world forever closed to my eyes, but left wide open to my starved imagination. It was a magnificent wall with green leaves shimmering in the light breeze, bringing its awesome arms right up close to me. Staring at it, I found that I could lose myself in a world where the days passed unchecked, measured only by the electronic bell of a neighbouring school, the air raid siren, which howled at midday exactly every first Thursday of the month—just to make sure it was still working, should there be another war— and by the colour of the ivy on the wall, which turned crimson red every passing autumn, and I was quite content to accept that this was my life and this was my home.

Sister Bénédicte was assisted in her mission by Mademoiselle Alice, a petite woman, so petite that even to us, she appeared small. Her smooth and shiny skin was tightly stretched across her face and extended her smile beyond the reaches of her heart. There was something unusual about Mlle Alice though, and with the tactless curiosity of little children troubled by anything that looked different, we could not avert our gaze away from her hands.

"Why don't you have any thumbs?" A girl asked, rather boldly I thought.

"Because...because God was so busy, he forgot..."

"And that thing...on your back...does it hurt?"

Mlle Alice shrugged her shoulders uneasily, crunched her thumb-less hands nervously, and replied with a quirky smile:

"No, of course it doesn't...Now, off you go or I'll throw you in the closet!"

Then her smile turned into a nervous giggle while we took flight, squealing in pretend fear, knowing that she was unlikely ever to carry out her threat.

I, myself, would never have dared ask those questions

so directly, although I listened avidly, staring at her hands, fascinated by the way she had learned to balance her knife and fork between her forefingers, and how she cleverly clasped her first and second fingers of both hands around her cup of coffee so that she could lift it without spilling its content. Untroubled by what she had, or had not, Mlle Alice always had a ready smile and often set off in one of her little giggles that shook her ringlets of mousy hair around her shiny doll-like face. Whatever challenge God had sent to try her, she took it with a fortitude hidden behind a permanent smile that narrowed her eyes and made her see nothing but the goodness of untainted hearts which inhabited all the little angels she had in her charge. Even our persistent misdemeanours could not bring her to show real anger; instead, she would close her eyes to efface the dark patches she had detected on our angel faces, wag her finger and shake her head, letting loose her unruly locks of hair before asking us not to do it again, because more than anything, Mlle Alice really could not bear to see any of her little angels cry.

In the early years, the regime was strict but not unduly harsh. I wanted for nothing. My aspirations and dreams never extended beyond hungry wishes for sweets.

I continued to move freely in the communal space of the second floor, barely aware of the other girls. Sister Bénédicte, keen to spread a mantel of fairness in equal measure over her children, treated the whole community as one entity, where individuals were not picked out to receive special attention. As a result of this limited interaction, I developed no wish or desire to speak to any of the adults who hovered around us like ephemeral shadows, appearing in short glimpses and moving swiftly on the edge of our universe, rarely interfering. Still, I evolved fairly normally. I was in good health, played nicely with the other girls, and never complained.

Once I had mastered the complicated art of tying shoelaces,

other little victories came more easily. Mornings were often a race as the first girl all dressed and ready was allowed to carry out the very important task of switching the light on in the dining room. Standing on a chair in order to reach for the switch, I scanned the little round tables with a regal air, feeling so important, so grown up and so clever.

Soon after, Mlle Alice came to prepare breakfast. With my hungry eyes popping out in anticipation, I watched her disfigured hands rack the butter *or* jam on thin slices of bread, meticulously scooping out bits that had escaped through the holes of the soft dough, before asking: "butter or jam?" I always chose butter because jam was sticky and messy and I could not be bothered to wash my hands afterwards. Almost snatching my one piece of bread that was the breakfast ration for all, I would go and sit at the table chewing avidly the little I had to eat, but no matter how hungry I was, I could never bring myself to drink the hot milk to which a few drops of burnt coffee had been added to mask its revolting smell. The slippery skin rippled sickeningly through every single taste bud I had and made me want to retch. If I had not been able to get rid of it by sharing it out with the girls at my table, Sister Bénédicte would pinch my nose, forcing me to open my mouth, and press the bowl against my lips to tip in its fowl content. It was her duty to do so and I never begrudged her this little ritual that blighted every single one of my mornings in the Baby Section.

By now, I was gradually becoming aware that I seemed to be part of a small group of girls, all with straight dark hair and brown eyes, some more slanted than others, except for Nadine who surprised everyone by sporting a mane of blazing blonde hair and huge blue eyes. I did not know what our common denominator was and never asked.

*

11

Suddenly, out of the blue, my nights became disturbed. I kept seeing these people: men in uniform fighting in open fields. I could not see their faces and I could not hear their screams, but I could feel the intense terror that veiled their faces as they fell, dying. The first time it happened, I stumbled brutally out of my dream and woke up...terrified. The visions returned with terrifying regularity, turning me from a normally placid child into a nervous twitchy toddler. Each time they occurred, I would pull the blanket over my head and wait in a semi-conscious state for dawn to come, as I fought hard any urge to go back to sleep.

One night, as I woke up in a post-traumatic trance, I heard this strange noise; it was the reassuring sound of people chatting and laughing, accompanied by the clanging of dishes as if they were in the middle of doing the washing-up. I got up in search of the happy people who would help me forget about my bad dreams. I crept out of the dormitory, crossed the empty dayroom, and glanced at the gold fish tank as I made my way to the washing-up area next to the dining-room. There was nobody there. Still hoping to find some cheerful company, I proceeded onto the landing and looked out of the big square window.

The playground was alive with shadowy patches moving furtively in the silent wind. The sandcastles stood guard, still intact in the sandpit overshadowed by a row of tall poplar trees that swayed gently in the invisible breeze. To the left of the playground, the long refectory of the Middle Section stood eerily empty. No matter where I looked, everything remained in complete darkness with not even the warm yellow glow of a small light that would have reassured me that I was not alone. I lingered on at the window for a while, shivering in my nightie. As I was about to return to bed, I heard a series of muffled footsteps rise from the stairwell, squeaking each time they moved. My heart leapt. I was not all alone after all. I stood at the top of the stairs eagerly waiting to see who was coming. A large amorphous figure slowly wound its way up, its dark shadow creeping silently along the walls. Then, I saw the familiar shape of a large white hat with flapping wings on either side. Sister Bénédicte was on her rounds, and when she saw me standing completely still in my white nightdress, she had such a fright that she nearly fell down the stairs. Even little angels can sometimes look rather frightful and at such an ungodly hour, I must have looked rather ghostly. Thankfully, with God standing firmly by her side, Sister Bénédicte soon recovered from her shock. She scooped me up gently in her arms and carried me back to bed, believing that I was sleepwalking. As for me, I was careful not to say anything lest I got into trouble for being out of bed in the middle of the night. Back in the warm comfort of my soft bed, I quickly dropped off to sleep, exhausted by my unscheduled nocturnal escapade.

Alas for me, the voices returned with singular regularity to come and haunt my dreams. Most of the time, I tried to ignore them, but when I needed to escape the horrors of war, I would get up and play hide and seek with the happy people who remained invisible within the Second Floor walls. As for Sister Bénédicte, she never once mentioned my night errands and, in the mute world I had created around myself, the traumatic war scenes of my dreams and the elusive cheerful voices that kept me awake at night remained a secret to all but me.

In these early years, very little happened to excite me. I was caught in the perpetual motion of a dull routine with other children sharing my space. Apart from a handful of them, they would all disappear at the end of each week, with just me and the goldfish forming the two permanent features of the Second

Floor. Sometimes, I actually wished that everybody would go. It would have been such fun to have had the whole place all to myself.

Then one day, Sister Bénédicte gathered us to say that she had a special announcement to make. She extended her hand and touched several heads, including mine, and said: "You… you…you…you…"

I could not wait to hear what she had to say, but she seemed to enjoy keeping up the suspense for as long as she could. Finally, she came out with it: "You're going to the circus."

The girls who had been chosen jumped and shrieked with excitement. I observed their reaction, unsure of how to welcome the news, since I did not know what a circus was. But they all looked excited, so I joined in. I screamed and jumped and pretended to know why I was feeling so excited. Then, I looked around to see who else had been selected, and I could not help noticing that all the girls belonged to our little group: Marie, Michèle, Claire, Nadine, Marceline, Dominique and me, of course, Martha Bertrand.

Soon the calm returned and the days continued to disappear, swallowed up by a timeless routine that blended evenly into days, weeks, and months.

Then one day, the atmosphere changed. Sister Bénédicte's mood seemed perkier than usual and Mlle Alice's smile beamed brighter than ever, if that was at all possible, as they fretted to collect our coats. It could only mean one thing: the big day had finally arrived.

Darkness and night were about to bring a brand new light. Chatting excitedly, the nuns squeezed their large cornets into the cars and drove us in a fleet of blue and grey 2CVs. The cars bobbed merrily along the cobblestones and we shook merrily on the back seats. Sitting on the edge of the seat, I tried to pull myself up in order to see out of the steamed up window. As we approached the Big Top, I blinked at the bright lights and winced at the noise. The nuns led us inside the giant marquis where a toy soldier showed us to our seats, the best in the house, right next to the ring. I scoured the arena, stared at the gleaming pieces of metal hanging from ropes high above my head and wondered what would happen next. I did not have to wait long. The lions came, roaring at the crowd and strutting their muscular hinds with their heads held up high. Immediately behind, a shy tiger followed grudgingly, keeping its beautifully marked head close to the ground. Despite the huge protective iron cage, I could hardly breathe for the fear, and wedged my tiny bottom right on the edge of my seat, ready to flee. When the lion tamer finally cracked his whip for the last time, I sank back into my seat and let out a huge sigh of relief...until the elephants came...and the white horses...Still, they were not quite as scary. Soon after, a net was stretched right across the arena and a troupe of acrobats came bounding in, churning the sawdust with their huge sparkling capes. They moved so fast and so high that I could hardly follow the daring vaults they performed high above, close to the heavens. After they had bowed low to the overawed audience, they somersaulted their way out of the arena. At last, the moment that all the children had been waiting for arrived with a bang and the screeching sound of a trumpet being blown out of tune. The brass band blasted a cheery tune and the ringmaster, dressed in top hat and tails, shuffled in, his arms outstretched towards the roof. With his voice reaching the pitch of a town crier, he joyfully proclaimed the imminent arrival of the Gossini Brothers and their Pierrot-dressed minder. No sooner had he left the ring than these three characters burst into the arena, shouting and laughing, blowing their trumpets and throwing firecrackers around. Instantly, the whole audience erupted and shook with laughter.

Excited youngsters whistled and jeered while I tried to muffle the noise by covering my ears. The brightly dressed clowns did their funny tricks and the big drum in the music stand exploded, each time the more serious clown kicked their huge baggy bottoms. I wanted to laugh too, but the clowns' painted faces with fake tears rolling down their laughing cheeks contorted by the most tortured expression petrified me.

Then, all went quiet. The lights were dimmed, and the naughty clowns were relegated behind the curtains while Pierrot, their master, stayed in the middle of the arena, tuning his trumpet, ready to blast a lonely tune. A single beam of white light shone on his silvery costume. His white face and his ghostly silhouette set against the pale beam of light reminded me of the faceless soldiers I had seen dying in my dreams. I was terrified, so terrified that, after checking that no one was looking, I slid off my chair and hid behind the parapet where I stayed for the remainder of the act. At long last, to my great relief, the ringmaster shuffled in once more to announce the end of the show. But the clowns re-emerged and, this time, refused to go away. Instead, they lingered on, chatting with the audience and giving out small presents to the delight of the lucky few children who grabbed them excitedly.

One of the naughty brothers spotted our little group and taking great strides, he began to make his way towards us. As soon as I spotted him, I quickly jumped off my seat and hid behind the parapet. The cheerful clown chuckled loudly and began his approach, swinging his bright red chequered arms and waddling along in his oversize shoes. Too late, he had seen me. Standing by the side of the arena in complete terror, I watched his two ghostly hands reach out for me and, with a swift movement, he lifted me into his arms. I was so petrified that I could not even scream. Taking no notice of my face crunched with fear, he spoke soothing words and tickled my chin to make me smile, but I remained frozen in a moment of sheer terror. Even when he produced a magnificent toy in the shape of a gleaming red ocean liner, I refused to smile, and kept the same terrified look while I stared in complete horror at the scary lines on his brightly-coloured face. Then, I felt the tears welling up, my bottom lip began to quiver, and when I could no longer hold up, I let out such a loud cry that Sister Bénédicte felt obliged to rescue me. She thanked the clown profusely, apologised for my behaviour and whisked me away with no further ado. Back in the car, I continued to snivel, clutching the ocean liner tightly against my little body and wishing I was already back at the only place I knew, with its warm glow of light and secured atmosphere. The cars journeyed back in the dark, rolling smoothly over the cobblestones and lulling us in a bewildered slumber.

The minute we arrived back, we ran up the stairs and threw open the playroom's double doors, holding aloft our precious toys.

When Sister Bénédicte eventually caught up with us, she calmly took all the presents from us and said: "They are for everybody to play with".

Stunned, I let her take my ocean liner away and watched her put it in the toy cupboard with all the other toys. This was the first toy, the only toy, I had ever had, but in the righteous words of Sister Bénédicte, I had to learn to share. Instead, all I learned was not to care.

If my waking hours were dull, unexciting, and uneventful for most of the time, my nights were full of adventures, which often took me on a mysterious journey into an unknown world full of actions, sensations, and emotions I was unable to control. To make matters worse, since my visit to the circus, I now had new enemies. The clowns had joined in to torment me in my dreams, jumping out of dark corners, chasing me and scaring me out of my wits. Alongside them, the faceless soldiers continued their relentless fight for a cause I did not understand in a country I did not know; and what made it worse: they always died.

CHAPTER II

Too young to go to school, the only events to punctuate the passing of each year were the changing colours of the ivy and the birth of Baby Jesus. Everything else disappeared into the abyss of time, unnoticed, unmarked, and unrecorded.

Then one day, a young woman slipped into our lives, as silently as if flown in by invisible angels, to relieve Mlle Alice of her never-ending duty—temporarily at least, for the last thing we wanted was to see Mlle Alice go. I cannot even remember what colour the ivy was when she was first introduced to us. Her name was Mademoiselle Hildegard and she was a young student. Our little group always attracted most of the attention, perhaps because we looked different, and we soon became her firm favourites.

One winter, around Christmas time, when the ivy on the wall was completely bare, she took three of us, Marie, Claire, and I, back to her house with her. It was a cold night and snow lay on the ground, frozen. The three of us sat huddled together on the back seat of her car. As the wheels crunched their way through the frozen landscape, the speeding streetlights splattered their orange glow in luminous patches over the snow. Wide-eyed and mouth gaping, I watched each light disappear into the night, never knowing I could be so close to the stars.

The journey ended when the car reached the last house of a small housing estate, at the end of a cul-de-sac. Half asleep, we shuffled along the seat to get out of the car and, with Mlle Hildegard holding our hands, we walked to the front door where her mother waited to greet us. Standing next to her, a tall young man was smiling. His name was Michael and he was Mlle Hildegard's brother. As soon as we came within his reach, he lifted two of us and paraded noisily outside. His mother called out to him.

"It's freezing! Bring the little girls in!" She shouted, but oblivious to her pleading cries, he performed a few quick steps, did a twirl, and finally brought us inside the house where a wave of warm air engulfed our cold faces.

Once inside the house, the first thing I spotted was a huge Christmas tree scintillating in the subdued light of a big room, just off to the right of the corridor. Fretting with excitement, Mlle Hildegard's mother herded us gently towards the big room. There, she walked towards a table, which had been pushed against the wall, lifted a large tablecloth and unveiled the biggest doll house I had ever seen.

"It's all for you!" she declared with a broad smile.

All three of us gasped at the same time. Mlle Hildegard looked happy and so did her brother. As for Madame Hildegard—for we did not know what else to call her—she was…well, extremely emotional. As soon as we had recovered from the delightful surprise, we rushed to the beautiful wooden house and began to play straight away. Later that evening, Mme Hildegard brought us our supper and allowed us to eat it right next to the doll house. I remember glancing at it repeatedly, thinking that this would never have been allowed back at *Saint Vincent*. On the table, the sweet aroma of steaming cups of cocoa mingled deliciously with the comforting smell of pieces of ham mixed with mash potato, and I was convinced this was the best food I had ever tasted.

After supper, we carried on playing, but by now, something else had attracted my attention. The little figurines put aside, I went to stand in front of the fire, totally captivated by the flames jiggling and dancing, while I listened to the cheeky sound of the burning logs hissing, crackling and spitting. For the first time, I discovered the warm atmosphere of a happy home filled with gentle people who spoke to us, interacted, and even played with us. Suddenly, without my being aware of it, I began to open up and speak freely to the adults in the house, expressing words I had never felt before. Later that evening, after she had made sure that we had brushed our teeth, Mlle Hildegard tucked all three of us in a big bed. I snuggled myself in the middle of it, between Marie and Claire—because the littlest always slept in the middle—savouring a wonderful feeling of pure joy, while clutching a teddy bear I had found among the toys. That night, no clowns came running into my dreams, no soldiers came rushing to their deaths, and the war cries remained totally and blissfully silent.

The following day, the whole family took us to a park where the pond had frozen over. Mme Hildegard gave us pieces of stale bread to throw to the ducks and we giggled and giggled as we watched the waddling birds sliding and skidding towards us in their hurry to grab their share of crumbs. Late afternoon, as the night drew in, Michael dusted and padded out a large rucksack. Then, one by one he put Claire and me inside it. Never before had we lived such a fantastic adventure, and we squealed with excitement the moment Michael stepped outside. We squealed even more as we watched our breath escape from our excited little mouths into the starry night. The more Michael wanted us to be quiet—so as not to disturb the neighbours—the louder we squealed. However, nothing he said could contain our joy, and Michael finally retreated back inside the house, lest he got into trouble for creating so much noise.

That same evening, as we were finishing our supper, the doorbell chimed. Mme Hildegard rose to answer the door and was greeted by a chorus of carol singers wrapped up in woolly hats, woolly scarves, and winter coats. She promptly invited them in and, standing in front of the Christmas tree, the whole family listened to the carol singers, muffled in comfort and joy, singing high and low to the angels above. The candlelight threw a warm glow on their flushed faces and glittered in their smiling eyes like little stars. Standing by the roaring fire, totally mesmerized, I flew into a dream world that smelt of hot cocoa and sweet pies.

Alas, the pleasures of life are always a moment too short. Happily, we were to return two or three more times until one day, Mlle Hildegard completed her studies and moved away. I have no recollection of her leaving or even feeling sad when I was told she would not be coming back, because, in those tender years, I had not yet developed any concept of permanency that makes something last forever or someone disappear forever. I lived firmly in the present, with very little notion of the past or the future ahead. She kept in touch for a long while after that, writing long letters and sending us treats. Even when I was old enough to read, I still insisted that the nun or one of the supervisors read the letters, so that someone else could share the excitement with me. Eventually, Mlle Hildegard faded away in the midst of time never to return. I do not remember what she looked like, but the happy memories she left behind remain sharper than ever.

CHAPTER III

B y now, I had lost interest in toys and preferred to sit on my own, dreaming over any picture book I could lay my tiny hands on. But that was not enough. My curiosity awakened, I wanted more and I knew exactly how to get it. Throwing surreptitious glances around, I began to stalk the playroom like a pre-school predator, my little feet barely touching the ground, eyeing any books that were left lying around. After a furtive look to check that the path was clear, I would pounce on them, tuck them firmly under my arm, and quickly walk away. Luckily, it was a pastime that not many others wanted to share and, unlike the few dolls that had been hung, drawn, quartered, dismembered, and discarded by a horde of possessive mini mums, my books were rarely fought over and had managed to survive relatively intact, apart from the odd missing cover that had once been used as a mini sledge to slide with on the tiled floor.

Hence laden with an armful of picture stories, I had taken to retreat to the cloakroom, which was lined with rows of wooden lockers and where I knew I would be able to remain undisturbed and undetected. Once I had made up my mind which locker I was going to snuggle in, one preferably near the light, I would wrap myself up in someone else's coat and leave the door slightly ajar so that enough light could fall on the pages and thrill my imagination. Then, cosily ensconced in my little hideaway, with my little index finger, I would follow scrupulously each and every picture in order to bring alive the dream world I inhabited. As a rule, I did not talk, because I was too busy shaping letters together, forming words that I could not read or comprehend, which really was the best part of the fun, for the simple reason that I could apply my own meaning, my own understanding, and change the story at will. Locked away in my little world and separated from the childish clatter of the other girls at play, I evolved in an eloquent dimension, free from the boundaries of words, expressions and exclamations. One day, I would discover that the sky has no limit, but words do.

As summer approached, my horizon was about to be further stretched by my first trip to the large holiday home situated in a tiny seaside village called Sangatte, just a few kilometres southwest of Calais. The '*Colonie Saint Joseph des Flots*' was the very last building on the outer edge of the village with beyond it, nothing but the meandering road that took the occasional travellers perilously close to the white cliffs of its jagged coast.

On the day of departure, we crowded on the landing, our noses squashed against the large window overlooking the playground while we gesticulated and squealed with excitement, waiting for the arrival of the lorry. Piles of linen and clothes, and other essentials like cutlery and crockery had been packed in boxes, ready to be collected.

The arrival of the lorry was greeted with loud squeals of delight.

"*Le camion! Le camion!*"

Then, some girls formed a spontaneous circle and chanted: "*Le camion est arrivé! Le camion est arrivé!*"

It was a big grey lorry whose loud engine shook its large pointy nose. Its sides were lined with long wooden planks that had been bolted together. We watched it being piled high, and when the men had finished, it waddled precariously out of the porch and onto the cobbled streets. Fortunately, the men of the lorry had thrown a huge piece of tarpaulin over the top and secured its bulging load with ropes that they tied with several knots around the planks of wood. Even so, the huge hunchback of the rickety lorry looked frightfully unstable. As the lorry departed, huffing and puffing, rattling noisily and bouncing perilously over the cobblestones, we gave a resounding cheer to greet the beginning of the long summer holidays, and I knew from this moment on that for me, this would be a new and wonderful adventure, my first real glimpse of the outside world where I would see things I had never seen before.

Later that day, a coach transported our excited crowd to the station. We walked to the platform, hand in hand, and all of a sudden, the squeals of excitement stopped. There, standing high above us in all its might on the busy platform, a huge jet black locomotive, with wheels taller than us, rumbled and grumbled like a great big daddy bear with a sore head. Overwhelmed and scared by the awesome sight of this huge roaring beast, some of the girls who, like me, had never seen a train before, began to cry. Anxious to restore some kind of peace, the nuns darted around our little group, fretting in an attempt to appease the fraught little children. Suddenly, the monster roared, spewed out a jet of white steam, and let out a strident screech with its whistle. Instantly, the cries turned into screams and the nuns were caught in a frantic run to comfort the panic-stricken girls whose tears had turned into hysterical screams. In the middle of this pandemonium, the station guard appeared. He quickly herded us to our carriage where we settled down, feeling a little more subdued, but relieved at the thought that at least, sitting safely inside the belly of the monster, we could no longer see it.

I managed to get a seat by the window and spent most of the journey drifting away with the clouds and the fast changing landscape, only to be drawn out of my reverie by the occasional cry of wonder.

"Regarde! Les vaches!"

"Y'a des moutons aussi!"

"Oh! Des cochons! Y'a des cochons! Regarde les cochons!"

"Ils sont gros les cochons. Regarde les gros cochons!"

No child can ever mention the word 'pig' without making a joke of it and we were no exception. Now the insults were flying.

"Toi, t'es une grosse cochonne!"

"Et toi, t'es plus grosse que moi!"

Once we had exhausted all the comparatives and superlatives to decide who was the biggest, the fattest, and the dirtiest pig, we settled back on the bench seat, crossed our arms in a more subdued pose, and waited expectantly for the next joke, but the fields had nothing else to reveal that would appeal to our childish sense of fun, and we were reduced to simply watching the rich tapestry of their changing colours and patterns, with the occasional cows blotting the landscape and staring at the train with their huge brown eyes as if busy counting the number of carriages.

However, eager to extend the fun, we soon found a new game. Each time the train stopped at a station, it jolted violently and we decided to use its momentum to pretend that we had been thrown brusquely out of our seats, and crashed purposely into one another. After each carefully calculated collision, we collapsed in laughter until Sister Bénédicte turned up scowling and requested a bit more silence, *s'il vous plaît!* Still giggling, we settled back in our seats, choosing instead to do the roll call of all the livestock that flew past the window. This was less fun, but at least we found out who was the best at counting...unless she was making it up.

When the train pulled into Calais station, straight away I detected a different smell. The air was cool, crisp, and free from the sooty particles that hung everywhere around the orphanage, darkening the streets, the clouds, and the sky. I took a deep breath and filled my nostrils with the clean fresh air, while high above in the sky, huge white and grey birds swooped, squawked, and dived on discarded litter, scavenging for an easy meal. These were the biggest birds I had ever seen, and although I was not prepared to admit it, I was...well...a little scared.

"*Ma sœur, ma sœur*, what are they?" I asked, my arm half lifted ready to shield my face.

"*Mouettes, ce sont des mouettes*," Sister Bénédicte replied knowledgeably.

A coach stood just outside the station, waiting to take us to the holiday home. Calais was only a small town and soon we were back in the countryside staring at more fields and more cows with black and white patches and the same ogling eyes.

Tired out by our earlier misdemeanours, we were gently dozing off when suddenly, the excited voice of Sister Bénédicte perforated my sleep.

"Sangatte! We're in Sangatte!" She hailed.

The coach hurtled through the tiny village until we reached the other end where a big sign spelt the name 'Sangatte' in large bold letters crossed with a thick red line to indicate that 'you are now leaving Sangatte'. Just before the sign, on the right-hand side, stood an enormous whitewashed building and as we were herded through the double gates, I discovered that it was facing the sea with only a thin wire fence separating the main lawn from the beach.

Straight away, our little crocodile file was taken to the top floor, to the vast dormitory crowded with little beds and where we had been told to wait to be allocated a place. I could not wait to explore. The room was bright and airy with dormer windows on both sides, one facing sunrise and the other sunset. At the far end, there was a door leading to the attic, which had been transformed into a washroom filled with three large square stone baths. There were no toilets however—they were all outside—so at night, white plastic buckets with lids were placed along the dormitory at regular intervals.

Despite the cold white walls framed by plain green curtains, the excitement of being somewhere new made the whole place feel warm and welcoming. It was a sight that I would forever associate with the word 'holidays': cool, bright, and breezy, a place where we would be awaken by the bright, almost blinding, sunrise and lulled to sleep by the spectacular sunsets slowly sinking into the North Sea. Peering through the small windows, I stared in wonder at the vast expanse of sand rolling into the endless sea, my eyes ogling at a brand new universe that was filled with bright light, fresh air, and infinite space. Here, there were no dark corners for witches or ghostly soldiers to hide, and despite being surrounded by the same people and obeying the same rules, I knew instinctively that the holiday home would offer a welcome respite from my nightly terrors of war.

The days were spent usually playing in the small play area with its large sandpit, adjacent to the main lawn but separated from it by a wire fence, or on the beach. My favourite pastime was on wash days when I sat on the small wall by the sandpit and watched the nun and the supervisor hang miles of crispy white bed sheets on endless rows of washing lines, adding an extra brilliance to the stark luminosity of the bright sunshine.

And the smell…I loved that wonderful fresh smell that made everything else look so pure, so clean. Soon, the rows of fresh laundry were transformed into a maze where we happily played hide and seek until the voice of Sister Bénédicte shouted out: "Get your dirty little hands off my clean sheets!"

The beach, however, was by far the best territory for new discoveries. I could not walk two metres without asking: "What's that?" And, while my head swooned with new words and new phrases, I trickled whole fistfuls of fine sand through my fingers and ran about to make prints in the wet sand with my feet. We nagged the supervisor to let us paddle in the icy cold sea or chase the waves, promising every time that we would not get wet. As we trudged along the beach, without straying too far, I horded new objects in my little arms, proudly repeating to myself all the new words I had learnt: seashells, seaweeds, seagulls, jellyfish, mussels, scallops, *la digue* (seawall) and the awesome rows of *brise-lames* (storm breakers).

Just across the road from the beach, our walks took us near pastures and fields where we touched the ripening barley, picked wild flowers to bring back with us in order to brighten up the small refectory, dodged the odd rickety tractor, and ran after anything that moved: mostly butterflies, grasshoppers, frogs, toads, and small lizards. The countryside smelt of hot hay mixed with the occasional whiff of overripe manure, which made us pinch our noses and giggle in disgust.

"Yuk! It's horrible!"

"It's disgusting!"

"It stinks!"

"Now then, watch your language!" The supervisor boomed.

And, as if to tease us, she would take a deep breath and declare with a big contented smile, "Ahaaa…the sweet smell of the countryside. Lovely! This is good for you!"

Her words were greeted with more cries of disgust, but ignoring our spurns, she added cheerfully: "Come on, take a deep breath; you'll see, it's very good, the best way to purify the lungs."

And, we giggled all the more as we pinched our little noses even more tightly.

The sun shone most days, but on the odd occasion, the rain had taken us by surprise and we had to run back to the *colonie* dripping wet and laughing in the rain. At mealtime, Sister Bénédicte had included the farmers in our prayers, and as we joined hands together, we prayed to God to protect the crops and the hay and asked that the harvest be rich so that we could all have food to eat, especially the poor farmers and their families.

"When is the sun going to shine again?" One girl asked.

"Oh...but the sun always shines," Sister Bénédicte affirmed.

"So where is it then?" I demanded to know.

"It's above the clouds. If the sun weren't there, it would be all dark. You see...it's thanks to the sun that we have daylight."

I looked askance at the nun, wondering if this was another little fib that adults tell in order to get away from children's relentless barrage of questioning. I figured that only my childish logic could establish the true facts and as far as I could tell, the sun was not shining; therefore, it was not there.

After many weeks of living in close proximity to God's almighty powers, admiring his wonderful work, and fearing the might of his powerful storms, we returned to *Saint Vincent*. As we journeyed back, it occurred to me that I felt different, for this time I was returning with a baggage full of new words and a head crammed with all the new adventures we had squealed through. As I watched dreamily the now familiar landscape roll backwards on our way to the station, I felt a pang in my little heart. I knew already that I wanted to return, but how soon? A year equates infinity in a child's mind and stood well beyond my grasp of time.

*

One September, after another summer holiday had whizzed by and the train had thundered back into the familiar darkened land, some of my little friends seemed more excited than usual. They appeared at breakfast wearing different clothes, dark-coloured clothes that all looked the same. What did this mean? I wondered as I glowered at them.

"We're going to school!" Michèle boasted, parading in front of me.

To school? They're going to school? What about me? I wanted to go to school too.

"You can't! You're not grown up yet!" Claire retorted, striking a grown-up pose.

Not grown up yet? What for? I thought school would do that for me. After all, that was where all children went to learn to do grown-up things like read. I stood there, aghast, watching the girls line up for their first big adventure while I stayed behind, dressed in my toddler clothes and dangling a picture book between my baby fingers. I so wanted to go to school, but what would I need to do to convince everybody that I was grown up enough to cope?

I watched them depart in a crocodile file, their heads held up high and their chests swelled up with pride. Once their happy chatter spilled out onto the playground, I dragged my feet back to the playroom feeling utterly bored and dejected. It was time for me to retreat to my favourite place. In a huff,

I picked up all the books I could find and stole myself away in my usual hidey-hole, pouting my lips and scowling at the goldfish as I passed the tank in a truculent mood.

I had, however, noticed that all-important announcements were usually made in the last week of the holidays, while still at Sangatte. I had, in fact, already spotted the signs. When the sunset seemed to come closer to the shore, announcing the end of the summer, I knew we would be leaving soon. From thence, I observed Sister Bénédicte ever so closely, watched her face intently, tested her daily moods, and followed the movements of her hands avidly to see if she was about to pull out an important list from the many folds of her well-padded chest. I, for one, did not like the way she knew things without letting on. I resented the fact that she behaved like the keeper of a hidden chamber full of secrets, open only to those worthy of her wisdom, and unwilling as she was to share her knowledge with the rest of us. In this manner, she created a great divide between the world of grown ups and us little children to whom, in her considered opinion, not all should be revealed. In our eyes, levelled only with Sister Bénédicte's flowing dark robes, keeping us in suspense, seemed to be some kind of grown-up's game—and it probably was—but it is only years later, after my eyes had been opened to the servitudes of the real world, did I finally concede that Sister Bénédicte may have been right after all: children do not need to know everything.

But, curiosity in little children is insatiable and indomitable, and the minute the nun appeared, she was instantly assailed and besieged by our impatience to know. Some girls insisted and asked persistently, while pulling on her long skirts:

"Is there a letter for me?"

"Have I got a parcel?"

"Did my mummy call?"

There was only one question I wanted to ask: *"Ma sœur, ma sœur!* Am I going to school?"

Sister Bénédicte raised her arms as if surrendering to our pleas and begged: "Patience, children, patience."

Then, she stopped to look at our expectant faces, trying to pick out who would be the most worthy to get her first answer. Then, in her usual manner, she extended her arm and touched one head at a time before replying:

"Yes, you have…No, nothing for you…Yes, your mummy called and left a message…and you…I can't remember…"

I pushed my head forward and repeated anxiously:

"What about me…am I going to school?"

She looked at me with a frown, showing that she was thinking very hard. My heart sank. Her facial expression seemed sombre and did not look hopeful. Then she smiled and said, "Yes, you are…"

The effect was instant. I jumped and screamed with joy. In this wonderful moment, I did not care if I got into trouble for being too rowdy, I just could not help myself. I was so excited that I wanted to hear her say it again.

"Am I?…Am I really going to school?"

"Yes, Martha Bertrand, yes, you are…"

"And my sister…?"

Sister Bénédicte stopped dead in her tracks and stared at me with an enigmatic look.

"What sister?"

In a very matter-of-fact way, I shrugged my shoulders and replied, "My twin sister…I have a twin sister."

The nun looked at me, clearly puzzled, until the penny dropped. Sister Bénédicte was used to little children making up stories on the spot, and although she had never known me do this in the past —only because I was stubbornly extremely uncommunicative—I was no different to any other child. She smiled, gave me a patronising pat on the head and said, "Of course you have, my dear, of course you have..."

Her lack of reaction and protestation completely floored me. I did not want her to believe me and expected some kind of response, even if it was just a rebuke, because I was playing games with her just as she played games with me. I wanted her to know that I was only trying to get my own back, but she was not interested and had already moved on to answer another girl's question. I carried on for a while, insisting that I had a twin sister, but nobody seemed willing to take any notice of my invisible sibling, so I got bored with the pretence and soon left her to spirit away in my fantasy world.

CHAPTER IV

L a rentrée! C'est la rentrée!"

How I had longed to hear those words. At last, I was getting ready to go to school. Good-bye toddler clothes and baby books. I was going to have proper books now with lots of writing in them, and instead of a supervisor, I would have a proper teacher and I would become a pupil. Wow! I could hardly wait.

On the first morning of my new life, as soon as Mlle Alice switched the lights on, I jumped out of bed. I quickly slipped into my new outfit, which had the number 24 sewn on it. Once ready, I asked Mlle Alice to check me over and begged her to do my shoelaces.

"You'll never grow up if you don't learn how to tie your shoelaces properly."

"I know how to do them. I just want them to be perfect on my first day!"

She looked up to me with one of her wonderful smiles, patted me on the bottom and said: "Off you go now!"

She did not say 'little rascal,' but I could see the words edged on her shiny lips.

Finally, the moment came to line up in pairs, ready to leave. I was so excited that, for the life of me I cannot remember whose hand I was holding or what the weather was doing, except that it did not rain, not that it mattered anyway; my mind was wholly focused on one thought and one thought alone: my first day at school.

After a short walk, we arrived outside *'Ecole maternelle Sainte Germaine'*, a red brick building with windows so high that it was impossible for me to glimpse inside the place of my future happiness. After we had crossed the threshold, we were led through a narrow corridor which emerged into an enclosed playground completely covered in tarmac and sheltered by rows of overhanging glass panels. Suddenly, the quiet and subdued atmosphere was filled with the screams of a little boy who would not let go of a woman. She was having a hard time trying to dodge the little boy's angry kicks. One of the teachers rushed to help, but she got kicked too. The noise and kerfuffle unsettled me for a few seconds, but I soon recovered and shifted my thoughts back on the exciting day ahead.

The bell went. Immediately, the older children lined up along invisible lines before filing in silence into their respective classes, some on the ground floor, some upstairs, while we, the youngest pupils, were taken to the *jardin d'enfants*, a large playroom, right next door to the head teacher's classroom.

I was disappointed. I did not want to spend my days playing shop, ringing the till, and handing out plastic fruits and vegetables. Nor did I want to walk around the playground with a small beanbag perched on my head. I wanted to be on the other side of the wall, learning how to decipher all the books I had hidden in one of the lockers, back at *Saint Vincent*.

Suddenly, it dawned on me how quiet everything was. What were the pupils doing that they were sitting so quietly? I had to see. I pulled up a chair towards the partition which had clear windows halfway up, and peered inside the classroom next door. From my precarious perch, I was able to see rows upon rows of little desks with children, their heads down, studiously copying from the blackboard beautifully formed letters in their neat exercise books. Mlle Agnès, my teacher who, I soon discovered, never did anything without throwing a threat first, grabbed my arm and wrenched me off the chair, shouting at me a stern warning. I rubbed my arm, determined not to cry despite the pain, and wandered aimlessly from corner to corner, not feeling in the least attracted to any of the other children and totally uninterested in any of their games. Eventually, I picked a chair to sit on, let out a big sigh, and wondered what I should do next.

The time passed at the painstaking speed of a snail on a funeral march. I was pining for proper lessons with lots of work to do. I wanted to return to *Saint Vincent* and brag about the huge amount of homework I had to do, just like the older girls did. I wanted to show that I was just as good as them at learning the little fables by Monsieur Jean de la Fontaine, reciting by heart the tales of *The Crow and The Fox*, *The Cicada* and *The Ant*, or *The Hare and The Tortoise*. I was dreaming about the days when I would have a school report to testify on my hard work and effort. But until such day arrived, I would have to wait...patiently...too patiently. I gave another cursory glance around the dark playroom where the sun never shone and sighed. I was bored, so bored.

At the end of the day, we were herded back inside the narrow corridor to wait for the grown ups to collect us. Mlle la Directrice, the head teacher whose real name we never did find out, posted herself by the double doors. As parents came to collect their children, she shouted their names. When Mlle Alice arrived, I saw the corners of Mlle la Directrice's bright red lips curl downwards and her face take an air of utter disdain, as if she was about to ask: "Did anybody forget to flush the toilets?" Then, pursing her lips, she stiffly called out: "*Les orphelines!* "

The word screeched down the corridor and whistled

through my ears, crushing my pride and denting my self-esteem. I cringed in horror. Only a minute ago I was standing proudly in the queue; now, all I could think of was to creep at the back of the corridor and disappear out of sight. I had never heard that word before, but the strident sound carried with it a nauseous reaction of utter revulsion, so powerful and overwhelming that even Mlle la Directrice found it impossible to hide. What should have been the most exciting day of my life had become a huge disappointment, but somehow I sensed that this was only a small setback. Surely, I tried to convince myself, it would not be like this every day…It could not be…The older girls had always returned from school in a jolly mood, feeling happy and excited, so why shouldn't I be? After a few moments of reflection, I concluded that perhaps Mlle Agnès was not the right teacher for me and that I would have to bind my patience until I moved out of her class and started doing some proper work. How long would that be, though?

In the meantime, despite my forebodings, I adjusted to my school routine very easily. I tried to enjoy playing with the other children, scribbled on pieces of paper instead of drawing, and listened attentively to the various stories the teacher read without falling asleep. There was even a little boy I quite liked. His name was Bruno Lemaire and he was the best pretend cowboy in the whole class. I became totally captivated by his imaginary games and watched him in complete awe, flick his invisible revolvers and shoot from both hips at the menacing Indians that were galloping forth mercilessly to cut our throats or scalp our heads. He looked so strong, so invincible and…so handsome when he fell mortally wounded on the tarmac after being hit by a poisoned arrow. I wanted to be his friend, but he was always too busy fighting and did not have time for girls. After all, where did they fit in his manly games? Were they cowboys or Indians, goodies or baddies? He did not know and, quite frankly, he did not care. To my long-lasting regret, I never did manage to befriend him, and at the end of our pre-school year, I lost him forever, as he moved on to the boys' school across the road where, surrounded by other boys, he would carry on his valiant battles and die in blazing glory, while on this side, I tiptoed nervously into the awesome class of Mlle la Directrice.

At least, I had something to distract me from the loss of my little friend. After months of waiting, I was finally going to learn to read. My fingers tingling with excitement, I opened my first reader and, mouth gaping, I stared at the various groups of letters which would clear once and for all the mystery of words. The further I looked in the book, the longer the words were, and I could not wait to be at the stage when I would be able to close the book, knowing that I was capable of deciphering every single one of its words.

The first excitement over, I could now pay more attention to my new teacher. Mlle la Directrice, the head teacher, was tall and slim, and shaped like a ruler. Her blond hair was tightly pulled into a bun held together with metal clips that disappeared deep inside her thick coiffure. Her arctic blue eyes, sharp and discerning, scanned the room and filtered her charges into groups of favourites and non-favourites. Her pupils, permanently frightened by her blistering moods, lowered their heads in total submission and flinched apprehensively every time she spoke to them to blast out her commands, firing blunt words from her red painted lips. As a woman who still remembered dodging flying bombs, she was rarely seen without the blackboard pointer in her hand, which she brandished menacingly towards us as if we were the enemy.

The proof of her ruthless approach came several days later

when Mlle Agnès next door, angered by a small child's cries, began to lash out on the poor child screaming: "Are you going to stop crying now?"

And as the blows rained on the helpless victim, Mlle Agnès could not think of any other way to deal with it than by hitting harder each time. We could hear the little body bounce off the flimsy partition after each blow; we could even tell that now the teacher had resorted to using her feet to hit the child. I felt my little heart beat faster. I held my little pencil even more tightly to stop myself from shaking, and I even managed to raise my eyes ever so briefly to see if Mlle la Directrice was going to intervene. She did not. The terrified child carried on screaming, and in the end, Mlle Agnès threw the hysterical brat out of the classroom and into the playground. Gradually, peace returned. We sat in a terrorised-silence, prepared to do whatever Mlle la Directrice wanted us to do. Right now, if she had asked us to jump over a cliff, we would have jumped, obediently and without even thinking. As if to signal that the unpleasant incident had now come to a close, she turned to us, pursed her lips and declared coldly: "Let it be a lesson to all of you."

Everything seemed contrived to put me off school, but I managed to overcome my fears, telling myself that I would be all right as long as I kept my head down and steered away from trouble. Despite this traumatic beginning, or perhaps because of it, I made rapid progress. I endeavoured to lose myself in my work and even drew a great deal of enjoyment from it. I loved to copy the beautiful letters in my exercise-book and conquered the enigmatic relationship of numbers using brightly-coloured plastic counters, but copying the date from the board at the beginning of each day provided an exciting glimpse of time which had eluded me so far. With the notion of time came the cyclic intervention of the seasons, the ritual death and revival of nature, and, most importantly for the adults, the solemn dates of the Catholic calendar. It was a perpetual story that we relived year after year with chronological accuracy.

At the end of that particular school day, we lined up in the corridor in a subdued silence, but this time, there was an added edge to our silence, as we could not wait to see who had been beaten to a pulp. Unsurprisingly, it was a girl from the Second Floor. Any other child, and the teacher would have had to face the wrath of her parents but with us, the teacher was safe; she knew that there would be no retribution...ever. As we walked back to *Saint Vincent*, we jostled and shoved each other to walk next to the battered girl, so that we could stare at her face, all black and blue, and admire her stoic silence.

"Why did you cry?"

"Does it hurt?"

But all the girl did was to shrug her shoulders and continue to walk with her gaze fixed in the far distance, as if in a trance, determined not to relive the brutal moment that had blighted her school day.

What would Sister Bénédicte say? I wondered, but later, as the nun examined the disfigured swollen face, holding it by the chin, she made no comment...but we children were not content with her silent verdict. We needed some kind of response which would have taught us what was right and what was wrong, and which would have satisfied our sense of justice, but in the absence of a final verdict, we decided that 'she probably deserved it,' because in our misguided opinion, that was what Sister Bénédicte would have said, had she allowed herself to express her thoughts. The nun probably never thought that; in fact, she probably felt sorry for the girl. In her heart of hearts, she would even have liked to console her and soothe the pain with comforting words and a reassuring hug, but whichever way she felt, she physically blocked any show of feelings, declaring no concern, no sympathy, and refusing to utter a single word that would abnegate the teacher and absolve the girl. As a result, we were forced to conclude that the girl had to be guilty as charged.

*

Anyone with a scant knowledge of French history would have been able to tell that Mlle la Directrice liked Napoleon. Taking a leaf out of our history books, she displayed the same ruthless ambition and applied the same strict code of conduct and discipline to rule her classes, but without the Emperor's fairness or integrity. Just like her favourite hero however— who himself had borrowed the idea from Caesar—she had introduced a popular system of rewards to compliment hard-working pupils, or those who simply happened to be in her group of favourites, which was a great advantage, as you were less likely to be hit on the back of the head when you least expected it, as she strolled around the rows of desks, preying on us like a starved hawk. She awarded medals for the best effort, the best disciplined, the most worthy, and the golden palm for the best performing pupil. The latter should have been mine by right more than once, but she always seemed unwilling to reward my good work, and on one occasion, when I mustered enough courage to ask why I did not get it, she remarked scathingly: "You may have the best report, but so-and-so worked a lot harder than you…"

Armed with sudden courage, which the teacher might easily have read as effrontery, I stared back at her so as to study the cold, detached expression on her face, and I remembered then the look of disdain that contorted her lips every time she had to blast *"Les orphelines!"* down the school corridor at the end of each day, and it became plain to me that as far as she was concerned, fairness and justice could only be applied if the young individual was worthy enough of her esteem and touched sufficiently her adult sensitivity.

This baffled me a little bit because some of her chosen favourites seemed to us the most unlikely of candidates. Indeed, after I had been at *Sainte Germaine* for a while, this girl named Josette turned up. With her beady little brown eyes and oversized grainy cheeks, she did not look in the least attractive. What's more, she was huge for her age and always looked scruffy, no matter how hard she tried to make herself look neat. One Monday morning, she even turned up to school wearing a bright pink puffed-up dress that made her look like a wobbly blob of blancmange. In her limp mousy hair, she had a big pink bow and on her arm, she was clutching a white handbag. And lo! On her feet she was sporting a white pair of high heel shoes. Mlle la Directrice gave her a quick once-over and noted rather bemused: "You look as if you've been to a wedding."

"I have, miss, I have..."

While Josette showed off her new dress, we cupped our hands in front of our mouths to snigger discreetly at her strange turn-out. But that was not all. Josette behaved differently from the rest of us without ever getting into trouble. She would frequently speak out of turn, or in the corridor when we were not supposed to, in a loud voice, even swelling her oversized chest and tucking her precious handbag firmly against her side. Worse still, she would ask the most personal questions to Mlle la Directrice, like: "Did you have a nice weekend, miss, what did you do?" or "I like your hair, did you have it done yesterday?" but instead of getting cross with the girl, to our amazement, Mlle la Directrice would always humour her, jolly her along, and take her arm gently and say: "Now, we're going into the classroom, so you'll have to be quiet…There's a good girl!"

And Josette, unable to understand the basic rules of discipline, would carry on her easy chatter, telling everyone what she had done over the weekend, and who was at the wedding, making us snigger and laugh even more. At the sound of our muffled laughter, Mlle la Directrice made a sharp about turn and darted fiery glances at us; then I got into trouble because I just happened to be the one standing right next to her. What I could not fathom out, however, was that, despite Josette's somewhat unruly behaviour and the fact that she could hardly hold a pencil, let alone write anything comprehensible, Mlle la Directrice seemed to have a particular liking for her and was always prepared to make huge allowances for her shortcomings, which meant that, without fail, at the end of each week, Josette always went home with a medal.

Back at *Saint Vincent*, as I was eating my lunch absentmindedly, churning all sorts of thoughts, but still feeling excited about school, I was quite unprepared for the special piece of news that Sister Bénédicte had for me. She entered the room, positioned herself strategically in front of my table, making sure that she was facing me, and announced in a plain voice, "Martha Bertrand, today you're five…"

Then, without waiting for my reaction, she swiftly moved on to another table.

I was stunned, so stunned that I could not even think what colour the ivy was on the wall. I was confused too. If I was five now, then I must have been four before…What was I like when I was four? Trying hard to work out the meaning of her unusual statement, I found myself lost in the nebulous mist of time. All of a sudden, I had been thrust onto a time scale that so far I had no idea existed. By telling me how old I was, Sister Bénédicte had unwittingly pushed me onto a timeline that was divided into numbers, and today, I had reached number five. Five! That was a big number.

Not long after this extraordinary announcement, one Sunday, Sister Bénédicte came to me with a new set of clothes on top of which sat a beautiful bright red coat with gold shiny buttons. I wanted to ask why I was getting new clothes, but my new coat held me spellbound. I simply loved it and insisted on wearing it straight away. Observing my reaction, Sister Bénédicte pre-empted my question.

"You don't have to put it on straight away, but you'll soon need it as you're going out with these very nice people."

These very nice people? I thought. What very nice people?

"They're called *M. et Mme Cateau*."

It did unnerve me a bit the way Sister Bénédicte sprung out unexpected truths without ever explaining anything. In actual fact, I was not exactly over the moon at the thought of being taken away by complete strangers, but that was no concern of hers.

When M. Cateau came, he exchanged a few words with Sister Bénédicte and together, they led me to his car. I clambered into the old 2CV like a docile lamb, unknowing of its fate. I curled up deep into the soft canvas, too small to see out of the window and too cold to want to sit up. Away in my little dreams, I listened to the wheels rolling noisily over the cobbled streets. I did not wonder where I was going or even who these people were. All I wanted to know was how long it would be before I was back in the only place where I had ever wanted to be.

A short while later, the car pulled outside a tall and narrow terraced house with long thin windows painted in red and black. A woman wearing a small pinny tied around her waist was waiting expectantly on the threshold. The stranger picked me up to introduce me to his wife. His small eyes behind his steel rimmed glasses seemed to smile, but I turned my head away when he tried to kiss me with his prickly lips and his tobacco-smelling breath. To make matters worse, I did not understand a word he was telling me. My delicate ears were totally unfamiliar with the low gravel voice of a man and were incapable of distinguishing its gravelly tones. It was as if he were speaking a different language from mine. Having failed to befriend me, M. Cateau quickly put me back down and left his wife to take over. With a no-nonsense tug, Mme Cateau pulled me firmly inside the house. She took me straight into the kitchen where she served me *un bouillon*, a clear stock with large circles of fat floating smoothly on the surface. Then she left me so that she could rejoin a small group of grown-ups assembled around the dining table inside the small conservatory to the left of the kitchen.

While I waited for the soup to cool down, using my spoon, I chased the glistening circles, bouncing them against each other, breaking them into smaller circles which escaped to the edge of the bowl. A few minutes later, she returned to check on my progress and, seeing that I had finished the soup, she pushed a plate with several cakes in front of me and urged me to take one. Naturally, I chose the biggest one, whether I liked it or not. Afterwards, Mme Cateau propped me up on a chair and proceeded to undress me for my afternoon nap. I fought her back because, by now, I had grown accustomed to doing everything for myself and I had no intention of letting a complete stranger do it for me, but the woman did not understand. She thought I was refusing to get undressed, so she raised her voice, pushed my hands out of the way, and shook me out of my clothes before thrusting a night dress over my head. Her task completed, she tucked me firmly under her arm, took me upstairs and put me to bed.

The room was cold and dark. I did not want to sleep in a strange bed in a strange house, so I lay in the dark wide awake, looking at the bright halos that swept across the walls every time a car happened to pass by. Perhaps the view out of the window would offer something more exciting to look at, so I got up and sat on the windowsill.

The pane of glass misted over as I watched the occasional car thunder over the cobblestones, flashing its yellow lights down the deserted street. Feeling the cold, I pulled my night dress over my feet and lingered on, perched for a few more minutes on the edge of a world I did not want to inhabit. When it got too cold, I went back into bed. It seemed that I had been there for hours when Mme Cateau returned. Propping me back on the chair in the kitchen, she performed the same ritual in reverse, after which she left me alone in the kitchen so that she could carry on with whatever adults have to do. I made my way to the front room where M. Cateau was watching a football match on a small black and white television, engulfed in a thick haze of pipe smoke. I sat down for a few minutes, but unable to make out what I was looking at, I soon left the room and wandered aimlessly in search of something a little more interesting to do. Finding the women still chatting merrily, I approached the dining table cautiously, quite prepared to be dismissed on the spot, but one of the women picked up the small porcelain cup she had in front of her and showed it to me.

"Look," she said, showing me a black liquid. "It's coffee."

Mme Cateau picked up her cup and said: "Come here and try some."

She brought her cup to my mouth while the other women waited with a quirky smile fixed on their lips. Just as they expected, I pulled a face as I tried to spit out the bitter liquid. Instantly, the women burst out laughing.

"Don't give it to her like that," one of them said, "give her a lump of sugar to dunk in the coffee."

Mme Cateau reached out for an oblong blue box in the middle of the table, took a white grainy lump out of it and gave it to me. Then she took my hand and firmly dunked the sugar in her coffee.

"Now you taste it…Nice? Off you go now."

Summarily dismissed, I went back to the smog in the front room. Perhaps, there would be something else to watch now. Alas no, the hardly distinguishable figures were still chasing a ball around. With nowhere else to go, I sat down again. At the end of the match, M. Cateau got up brusquely and said it was time to drive me back. I was so relieved.

At long last, the car stopped just opposite the electronic doors of the orphanage. Before crossing the road, Mme Cateau handed to me a bag of sweets and a bar of chocolate, but still held on firmly to them.

"What do you say?"

I returned an awkward glance and whispered a shy 'thank you'. M. Cateau took me across the street, rang the buzzer, and the door clanked loudly. He exchanged a few words with the nun who was sitting at the reception desk. I did not hear what he said because I was already rushing towards the Second Floor of the Baby Section, clutching proudly my bag of sweets and the chocolate bar.

At bedtime, as we all lined up ready to go to bed, Mlle

Alice gave out the sweets and said that today these very special sweets were from me. I felt so proud to be able to give something for once.

My outings to the Cateau's house lasted over several Sundays, during which I was left on my own in a lonely room in a strange house with nobody to play with...except on the rare occasions, when M. and Mme Cateau's daughter was home. The first time I saw her, she was sitting on her bed reading something. Her bedroom door had been left ajar, so I stopped on the stairs and stared at her. Sensing my presence, she lifted her head.

"Hi, what's your name?"

"Martha."

"My name is Charlotte and I am fourteen."

Wow, I thought, I have never spoken to a girl that old before. Charlotte tried her best to strike a dialogue with me. Little did she know what a difficult task it would be. Suddenly, she had a thought.

"Can you ride a bike?"

"No."

"Come with me, I'll show you."

She took me downstairs to the garage and got this rusty old bike out, clearly a vestige of her own past. We moved on to the pavement where she wheeled me a few times; then suddenly, she let go. As soon as I felt the wheels move freely, I could hardly breathe for the excitement and I pedalled with my mouth wide open in complete wonder at this new toy. It was such a thrilling sensation to watch the paving stones whiz by that I felt as if time and space were moving at the same time. The cold air brushed against my face as the exhilarating path to freedom opened up in front of me. I felt free, so free.

I was beginning to look forward to my weekends, especially

as another young woman occasionally appeared. I guessed she must have been M. and Mme Cateau's older daughter. I never learnt her name, but she was nice and friendly, so I began to open up a little. Unfortunately, I did not see Charlotte or her older sister often enough to get me into the habit of talking. M. and Mme Cateau were beginning to show signs of exasperation. They did not want to dish out their charity on a child who stubbornly refused to speak. Something had to be done. And so, one Sunday afternoon, Mme Cateau put my red coat on while M. Cateau went to open the door to let me into the car. I clambered inside, fixed in my usual muted silence. The streetlights shone on the droplets of rain that hung coldly on the misted windows. Somehow, I sensed the finality of that last journey. When the car pulled outside *Saint Vincent*, M. Cateau got out of the car with me. He gave me the usual bag of sweets and the bar of chocolate but this time, he held on to them and said rather sternly, "If you don't say anything now, you're never going back to our house."

I kept my eyes firmly fixed on the sweets, wondering what he possibly wanted me to say. I heard Mme Cateau shout, "Ask her what colour her coat is!"

So, her husband duly repeated his wife's enlightened question.

"What colour is your coat?"

If I had not sensed the seriousness of the situation, I would have burst out laughing. I mean, what kind of question was this? I was five and at five, I expected to discuss something a little more advanced than the plain colours of the rainbow. I looked at the sweets, then at the familiar building across the road. The warm yellow glow in the winter night beaming through its windows beckoned to me irresistibly, and in that tense moment, it all became clear as to what I should or should not do. I did not laugh, but I did not say anything either. Mme Cateau bristled on the car seat, muttering to herself and expelling a lot of exasperated air, while M. Cateau reiterated his final ultimatum, "If you don't say anything now, you'll never come back, and if you don't come back, you'll never have any sweets again."

This was a very tempting proposition, one that made me dither for a brief second; sure I wanted the sweets, but I did not want to return to their cold unfriendly home, so I did not budge. At the end of his ultimatum, M. Cateau took the sweets back and crossed the street with me for the last time. He rang the buzzer and pushed me inside. I do not know what happened next for the door clanked heavily behind him, separating our worlds and shutting him out of mine forever and ever.

CHAPTER V

The matter was closed. Nobody said anything, not even a word that would have admonished M. and Mme Cateau or absolved me. I had been reprieved.

Approaching my seventh year, Sister Bénédicte was now concentrating on our religious awareness. Seven, she told us, was the age of reason, the age of understanding, but above all, the age when we suddenly became enlightened with the power of God, the goodness of Jesus, and the wickedness of Man. To press the point further, she herded us towards a large picture of Pope John XXVIII, which hung majestically over the stairwell wall. I had often stared at the picture of the Pope sitting on a large ornate chair in some kind of field, his arms reaching out to a group of small children, not much younger than myself and surrounded by a halo of purity and innocence that only the perspicacious eyes of the Holy Man could detect. At the bottom of the picture, Sister Bénédicte read the Holy Man's most celebrated words: 'Let the little children come to me'. These little people looked like me, but were not me — they looked too happy and carefree — therefore the holy message was meant for them and not for me. Nevertheless, I still thought how good of the Holy Man to make his mission to protect the children of the world, but whether it included us, I was not sure. Still, I could now look at the holy portrait and understand the picture. I was no longer looking at a stranger with a warm welcoming smile, but at the portrait of the revered Pope dressed in long white robes and coifed with a little round hat perched on the crown of his head. He had been chosen by God because he had worked out that the only way to absolve man's wickedness and sins was to seek redemption through the purity and innocence of little children whose souls were closer to the celestial angels and more significantly, closer to God than any other being on earth, and I felt so proud and lucky to be on his side. The story fascinated me because, above everything else, I wanted to be good just like baby Jesus. Thankfully, Sister Bénédicte assured us that we all had a guardian angel to help us along the way and keep us on the right path.

"And...How do we know we are on the right path?" Aline asked judiciously.

"You have to learn to listen to your guardian angel."

"Does he speak like us?"

"Not exactly; he has a special voice that only the good can hear."

Well, so far, I had never heard the voice of my guardian angel and wondered what it sounded like. If Sister Bénédicte was right, I had clearly not paid enough attention so, I vouched, I had better start listening and listening well, but first, I had to learn how. I followed Sister Bénédicte's religious instruction avidly and began to read picture books about saints and martyrs. Alas, shocked by the horrid pictures depicting how they invariably came to a cruel and gruesome end, I decided that perhaps I did not want to be as good as a saint after all. I had enough gore to cope with in my nightmares. No, on second thought, from now on, I would stick to just being good. I piled up the books neatly and left them on the table, knowing that, may it be against God's will, these saintly books would never find a place in my special locker, and I was ever so relieved.

Having mulled over the good words of God and Jesus, the

saints and the apostles, there was something in particular that puzzled me. I could not understand the notion of sin. Quite apart from words like 'adultery', 'murder', 'blasphemy', and 'jealousy', whose meanings escaped me completely, there was scarcely any opportunity to carry out any of those I understood. After all, here in the righteous world of Sister Bénédicte and Mlle Alice, where or how could I go wrong? What could I possibly do that would upset God and make my guardian angel cry? I did not know. Nevertheless, I learnt all about confession so that I could clear my heart, purify my soul, and be ready to receive the Body of Christ. Christ?...Oh heck, I had never heard of Him...Who the heck was he? Nobody had actually mentioned Him before, let alone explained how He fitted in the story of God and Jesus, and at this point, I was left thoroughly confused.

Unfazed, Sister Bénédicte answered my question, in the same way she answered all ecumenical questions, with a patronising nod of the head and a sanctimonious smile: "The key to understanding will come to us all, once we are in heaven".

Hence, assured that I would indeed be going to Heaven, I lay my questions aside and diligently prepared for my first communion.

*

The big day arrived. My very first grand occasion, I thought, and sighed with joy. Sister Bénédicte, with the help of Mlle Alice, dressed us and combed our hair in which she added a beautiful white carnation to complement our white dresses and white shoes. Then, giggling with excitement, we all filed into pairs and walked the short distance to the small chapel. It was packed.

I had long wondered what it would be like to touch holy water. I had imagined that I would sense the gentle touch of God's hand on my shoulder and feel like an angel as he welcomed me into his divine domain, and that I would feel a warm spiritual glow spread all over me as I took my place right next to Jesus. And so, on that bright sunny morning, my chest heaving with trepidation and pride, I prepared myself to undergo the holy metamorphosis that would put me on a par with God and Jesus. As we reached the chapel's double doors, I stood in the queue quietly, eagerly awaiting my turn to dip my fingers into the stone dish perched on the wall. Finally, the moment came for me to touch the holy water. It was cold...in fact it was quite cold, but beside that...I felt nothing, absolutely nothing. Something was wrong. Did I use my right hand? I looked at my hand, and yes I had used my right hand. Perhaps I had not dipped my fingers deep enough, or perhaps, in my wild anticipation, I had taken my hand too quickly out of the water...so I dipped my fingers in again. Still, I felt nothing. I was extremely disappointed to say the least.

Worse still, I was a little worried in case God or Jesus, or even Christ, for that matter, had not seen me and had forgotten to send their blessing, just like God had forgotten to give Mlle Alice her thumbs because He had been too busy. Standing tall in the central aisle, Sister Bénédicte had no such qualms. Flushed with pride, she tenderly herded her miniature flock to the front pews, while smiling faces from the congregation followed the little procession with their adoring eyes.

The altar boy rang the little brass bell and the service began. All the nuns were crammed on the pew just behind us and, with their oversized cornets, formed a solid black and white protective wall ready to oversee our first initiation to God. Bending over us, they helped us find the right page in our missals. The mass was said in Latin and I did not understand any of it, but that did not bother me. I was far too excited to be troubled by a small passing detail like this, especially as I did not know how to pronounce the words anyway. Besides, my attention was already taken up by the magnificent pane-glass windows that threw their multicoloured patterns all over the congregation; I spotted a shepherd with a lamb wrapped around his neck and carrying a long staff, was he Saint John the Baptist? I was not sure...I would have to go back and look up all the saints books again to check. On the next window, there was an angel resplendent like a bright new star, and of course, in the middle, there was God with his bright golden halo and his hands opened towards the world, sending rays of hope, warm like love and as bright as a shiny star. The brass bell rang again. My attention returned to the altar. The priest blessed the body of Christ and the signal was given for us to line up in the central aisle. The special moment had arrived for me to take the body of Christ for the very first time. The priest placed the white wafer on my tongue where it stuck. Back on the pew, using my finger and keeping my head low, I scraped the wafer off my tongue to help it go down, then waited for the effect of the holy communion to take hold. Again, I felt nothing...I was beginning to wonder. I suppose I would have to take Sister Bénédicte's word for it and accept that 'God moves in strange ways', but whichever way God chose to move, it clearly was too subtle for me. Despite it all, on this glorious morning, nothing else mattered, because I was now on a par with God and Jesus and seeing for the first time through the eyes of God, everything looked absolutely beautiful and wonderful.

After the service, we were led back to the ground floor of the Baby Section where the communal playroom had been turned into a vast dining room. The tables seemed to glow under their crisp white tablecloths, and in the middle of each, someone had placed little vases filled with pink and white carnations. The glasses, the cutlery, everything sparkled in the glorious sun of this very special day, and I felt sure I had never seen anything look so magnificent, so resplendent.

Immediately, animated parents, godparents, guardians, and foster parents grabbed their little angels and looked for their allocated tables. Very soon, everyone was seated and all one could hear was a buzz of jubilant voices chatting merrily away, discussing the momentous event of the day.

A few minutes passed while I surveyed the happy scene, standing alone by the door with no one to look after me and nowhere to sit. Eventually, Sister Bénédicte spotted me. She grabbed my little hand and took me to Michèle's table where she asked the happy gathering if they did not mind having an extra little angel at their table. Of course they did not mind, and a chair was quickly brought in and placed right next to Michèle. As I took my seat, Michèle and I looked at each other and giggled. We were now the children of God and we were very happy indeed.

I had barely finished the festive meal when a girl came to say that I was wanted at the parlour. Me? Wanted at the parlour? There must be some kind of mistake. The parlour was only used to receive visitors, so she could not possibly have meant me. She had quite obviously delivered the message to the wrong girl and I had better tell her, but she insisted, and even took my hand to lead me there. I was so curious to find out what this was all about that we both ran. We were soon on the outside of the vestibule door and through the coloured-glass windows, I could distinguish several silhouettes, but could not make out who they were. I stopped for a brief moment to catch my breath, then pushed the door open, not knowing what to expect.

Sister Bénédicte was standing awkwardly between, lo and behold, M. and Mme Cateau on the one side, and on the other, a young coquettish woman with long dark hair, dressed in a smart suit and stiletto shoes. Her slanted eyes, large flat nose, and smooth complexion reminded me of Claire, Michèle, Marceline, and a little bit of Marie and Dominique, but apart from that, I felt sure I had never seen her before.

The young woman was fidgeting nervously with her handbag while talking to Sister Bénédicte. The latter introduced her as my godmother from Indochina. What on earth did this mean? I stood there speechless, at pains to understand what was going on and trying to make sense of the situation. However, now that we all knew who we were, what did they expect me to do? The strange gathering kept staring at me, with quirky smiles in awkward poses and a hunched silence. At last, Sister Bénédicte tilted her head, clasped her hands together and asked: "Who would you like to go out with: M. and Mme Cateau or your godmother?"

I looked at Sister Bénédicte, desperate to tell her that I did not really want to go with any of them. I was enjoying myself, even if joining Michèle's table came as an afterthought, but the intense look in Sister Bénédicte's eyes indicated quite clearly that I had no option but to make a choice. I looked again at the young woman, avoiding any eye contact with the Cateaus, and unequivocally pointed my finger at her. Instantly, M. and Mme Cateau turned their heels and started to walk towards the big clunky doors while Sister Bénédicte followed, whispering heart-felt apologies. When she rejoined us, the young woman, the godmother from Indochina who now lived in Paris, started to go on and on about the car accident she had

had on her way here. Graciously, Sister Bénédicte nodded her head in sympathy and stirred her gently but firmly towards the exit. The door shut behind her with an abrupt loud clunk. Indignant, the godmother threw an angry glance at it, vexed by the swiftness with which Sister Bénédicte had made her exit; then she looked at me with a glare full of reproach.

"It's all your fault!" She suddenly blurted out.

Her words came out so suddenly and so unexpectedly that they nearly blew off the delicate petals of the white carnation, which now drooped sadly on my straight hair.

"If I hadn't come to see you, I would never have had that accident. So you see, it's all your fault! I'm a good driver. I am, I've never had an accident before…and to think it was almost for nothing…Yes, you do realize if you had chosen to go off with these other people, it would have been all for nothing…"

And she had not finished.

"If you don't believe me…I'm telling the truth…the car rolled over several times. I had nightmares all last night. I was even screaming in my sleep, yes…it's true, I was screaming! The man at the hotel was very worried about me. He even knocked on my door in the middle of the night to see if I was all right…and it's all your fault!"

I stood on the pavement, waiting for her tirade to end. There was nothing I could do, but stare back at her with a blank expression on my face, my ears shut to the misery of her whole misfortune. Now that she was stuck with me for the rest of the day, I wondered what she was going to do. She tucked her handbag firmly in the crook of her arm, seemed to hesitate for a moment, then marched down the pavement, her stiletto shoes clacking purposefully on the cobblestones. She sounded just like Mlle la Directrice. Preoccupied with her own miserable destiny, it never occurred to her to ask any questions about me, but then, I reasoned, why should she want to know…I had already done enough damage as it was. At least, she was resigned enough to accept that life had to go on, and so, despite her traumatic misadventure, for which she kept reminding me I was wholly responsible, she felt magnanimous enough to take me to the park. We took the tramway to Lille, crossed a bridge, and walked along the canal for a while. As I watched the ducks resting on the bank, I became lost in my own thoughts and nearly forgot the presence of the cantankerous woman from Indochina standing next to me, who, having stated her case and finding nothing else to reproach me for, finally asked: "What do you want?"

"An ice cream," I replied, not knowing what else I could ask for.

"You can't have an ice cream…it's going to give you a sore tummy."

We walked on in silence until we reached the park. There, she insisted on taking some pictures, which did surprise me somewhat, considering that these pictures would represent a permanent reminder of her accident, but there she was, happy to click away at a face for which she felt nothing but deep rancour.

Later that afternoon, she took me back to *Saint Vincent*, and when the main door opened with a loud buzz and a clunk, I ran inside and promptly disappeared.

As soon as I met up with the other girls, I was besieged with questions.

"Who was she?"

"Was she your mother?"

I did not understand the last question, because the only time I had come across the word 'mother' was in reference to the Mother Superior. So, with a detached look on my face and a cynical grin, I replied that I did not know and I did not care whether she was the godmother from Indochina, Paris, or Timbuktu. Then, I made straight for my locker and spent the rest of the evening surrounded by my books and snuggled up in my secluded dreams.

The next time I saw Sister Bénédicte, I tugged on her long dark skirts and asked: *"Ma sœur, where is Indochina?"*

I expected the normal rebuff, the all encompassing reply which always came out the same, 'Only God knows the answer'; but for once, to my surprise, she gave me a straight forward answer:

"It's a far away country, very far from here in the Orient... That's where you were born."

"Me? I was born in Indochina? Me!"

"Not just you! There are others..."

"Others? Who?" I insisted to know. "Who are the others?"

"Well, There's Claire and Marie, Michèle, Nadine, Marceline and Dominique..."

I had finally discovered our common denominator: we had all arrived together from a far away place called Indochina. I liked the sound of it because it was a nice big long word— but then, the more I thought about it, the more I wondered if this was why we had been treated differently. This would explain the trip to the circus. And what about that trip we had made to the local branch of the *Caisse d'Epargne,* where we had been herded in this magnificent reception room all lit up with enormous crystal chandeliers glittering high above the ceiling? Standing rigidly in two perfect rows, I remember being startled by all the noise and the unexpected snap and crackle of disposable flashes. It had been fun but, as usual, nobody had thought of telling us why we warranted so much attention.

Perhaps, the building society had made a donation to the nuns. And then, there was the yearly visit by Mlle Jacqueline, who, I discovered much later, was the social worker in charge of our welfare and who, in order to perform her duty, had to travel all the way from Paris to visit us and take us, and only us, out for the day. Everything was beginning to make sense.

As the mystery of our origins unravelled, I suddenly felt the urge to seek out someone from our group and came across Claire.

"Did you know you were from Indochina?"

"Yeah..."

"How did you know?"

"My foster parents told me and I've got a mark on my shoulder to prove it."

"A mark?" I exclaimed bewildered. "What kind of mark? Let me see."

Claire pulled her jumper down and bore her shoulder. Incredulous, I stared at the strange mark, a series of lines crossing each other. It looked like a Chinese sign.

"I've got one too," Michèle said.

I rushed to her to inspect her shoulder and saw the very same mark.

"And me..." Marie and Dominique said, joining the inspection parade.

They all had the mysterious mark.

"What about me? Have I got it?" I asked intrepid.

The girls peered at my shoulder, and I stood with my back to them, hardly able to bare the suspense.

"Nope, you haven't got it," Michèle stated categorically.

I did not expect this. Admittedly, I did not look like them, apart from my dark hair and my brown eyes, but here in France, these physical characteristics were hardly unusual; now

I discovered I did not have the mark either. Had there been some kind of mistake? Was I the victim of some mistaken identity? I felt a little distressed. It had always been in my psyche that I was not French, but now, I had to face the evidence that I did not possess any of the characteristics that would set me firmly in any particular group. I did not belong here or anywhere else. I was trapped in between two camps, marooned in no man's land which made me feel at odds with everybody. Then I thought of Nadine. With her blond hair and blue eyes, I wondered how she felt, but I was not going to ask and give her another excuse to sneer at me.

CHAPTER VI

The changing colours of the ivy on the wall were the only reminders that I stood ineluctably on an infinite timeline with numbers as big as five. Twice I had been told where I stood on it, when I was five, and when I did my first communion, although on the latter occasion I had not been specifically told when I had actually turned seven. The sequence of events had taught me that I must be that age; otherwise I would not have gone through the important religious transformation. But, where was I on the timeline now? There was no way of telling, and the only notion of time I had was through the dates that we wrote everyday in our neat exercise books with one particular one sticking in my mind. It was upon our return to school, after the Christmas holidays, and I remember applying myself to use my very best hand-writing in order to draw with care the beautiful capital letters to welcome in a new decade: it was January 1960. I felt a sense of excitement as I wrote the date down and wondered what the new decade would bring. But, apart from that date, all the memorable events that had happened in my life so far had now disappeared in the distant memory of time. Bored senseless by a timeless routine, I was always on the lookout for the next big adventure.

As I pressed my head against the picture window overlooking the witch's garden, I let my imagination carry me beyond the grey horizon. My mind was full of wishes that would take me to far away places where there would be lots of food and lots of chocolate and cakes. And, there would be ice creams too. And there would be a huge park with swings, slides, and lots of other things to go on. And, we would be given a few francs to buy sweets and more ice creams. And, we would scream with delight, jump in the air and laugh until our ribs hurt without being told off. The great fun was that I could fly away anywhere in my dreams...so long as I always returned to *Saint Vincent* with both my feet firmly on the ground.

The witch did not come out, but the sound of a door opening behind me made me turn around. It was Sister Bénédicte.

"Now who wants to come and visit the factory?"

At last, something to do. Without waiting to find out what it meant, I jumped up and down with my hand high up in the air:

"Me! Me! Me!"

"I can only take four," she declared, trying to decide which four of us to select.

"All right, you can come...and you...and you...yes, you Martha Bertrand!"

I was jubilant. At long last, I was embarking on a new adventure. Would it be as exciting as going to Sangatte? I turned to Aline who, behind her thick glasses, always sported the dazed look of a startled little bunny.

"Have you been before?"

"Yeah."

"Is it far? What is it like? What do we have to do?"

"Nothing...We just go around the factory and say hello to these nice ladies, but when we come to the spinning room, you'll have to cover your ears, because it's very *very* noisy."

"Is that it?"

"Oh no. The best bit is that they give you sweets and bars of chocolate."

"Really? Lots of sweets and chocolates?"

"Yeah…"

"I can't wait to go! Will my hands be big enough to carry all the sweets back? Hang on…let me check my pockets…"

I peered at my overalls.

"Great, I've got two pockets!"

"Yeah…but don't forget, you won't be going wearing your overalls."

"*Oh zut alors!* My skirt hasn't got any pockets."

But, I'll manage. Somehow, I would manage. After all, sweets are not so heavy.

A short while later, we piled into one of the 2CVs. Sister Marguerite from the linen room came along too.

The tinny noise of the 2CV rattling along the cobbled streets was in my mind the best sound ever. I was on the move, on my way to somewhere new, hurtling towards a new adventure that was dragging me away from the eternal boredom of a dull life that rarely extended beyond four solid walls.

After the car had rolled along a road lined with plane trees, we reached this enormous red brick building. Sister Bénédicte parked the car just outside the gate and our little group advanced nervously, unsure as to whether we should still feel excited.

Just like Aline had said, we were taken inside where rows upon rows of ladies facing looms or rolls of all sorts of materials sat, their concentration unbroken by the deafening noise that filled the room all around them. I covered my ears.

Aline nudged me.

"No. Not yet…We haven't reached the noisy room yet."

"Haven't we?" I replied, unable to believe that anything could be noisier than this room.

"It's upstairs."

We stuck to the two nuns like fearful little lambs, frightened by the noise and the giant machines. Then, we clambered the slippery steps of a huge iron staircase. As I glared at the wide gap between each step, I gripped the metal ramp as hard as I could. It would have been so easy to slip and disappear through the gaping hole. As we reached the door, I became rather apprehensive and without thinking, I grabbed hold of Sister Bénédicte's skirts. When she pushed the door open, the shock of the deafening hammering noise took my breath away. My heart missed a beat, I felt sure of it. Instantly, I let go of the nun's skirts to cover my ears. We all did, and as we ambled through the long avenues of spinning reels supervised by large ladies perched on adjustable stools, I could hardly bring myself to be civilized enough to greet them politely. Nevertheless, they still gave us sweets and chocolates, and I was forced to uncover my ears in order to accept their small offerings. Very soon, Sister Bénédicte nodded her head and indicated the exit. I could not reach the door fast enough, and we spent a few minutes on the metal landing, stunned, dazed, and shaking our heads with our ears still ringing.

Back in the car, Sister Marguerite spoke first.

"Did you enjoy the visit, girls?"

Still in shock, we could not bring ourselves to answer in words, so we nodded our heads instead.

"Well, you see," Sister Bénédicte warned, carefully squeezing her cornet inside the car, "if you don't work hard at school, that's where you'll end up."

The very thought panicked me. I may only have been as high as three apples, but I knew my mind, and I knew that I did not want to end up working in a textile factory, because labouring away in those unbearable conditions would make me a martyr, and I, Martha Bertrand, was no saint, and I definitely did not want to become a martyr.

CHAPTER VII

Now, I was old enough to move down to the First Floor which was ruled by the firm hand of Sister Thérèse and aided by her assistant, Mlle Pauline. Sister Thérèse was a lot shorter than Sister Bénédicte and, with a pair of small brown eyes set deep within the angular features of her face, she looked as mean as a witch. By contrast, Mlle Pauline was a plump woman, taller than Sister Thérèse, whose gentle disposition was constantly kept in check by the nun's rule of iron.

The first thing I did when I moved down, was to check the locker room and, to my immense relief, saw the same rows of tall wooden doors. I tried a few doors and made a mental note as to which locker would provide the cosiest 'reading corner'. Sister Thérèse and Mlle Pauline must have been warned about my peculiar reading habit, for when they needed to look for me, they always knew where to find me, but, to my surprise, they never expressed any kind of annoyance and, by and large, left me undisturbed, sitting amongst the usual pile of books I had temporarily borrowed.

In the playroom, there was a fish tank in exactly the same place as on the floor above, but here, in the far corner of the room, there was also a cage perched high on a chrome pedestal with a pair of budgies in it. How exciting, I thought. Mlle Pauline was able to bestow all her motherly love upon George and Georgette, although she had no idea which was the male and which was the female, or if indeed they were a matching pair. A big rubber plant stretched its big waxy leaves right into their corner, which must have pleased the budgies, for this artificial jungle must have looked reassuringly like home. I approached the cage to investigate the creatures more closely and, like every child instinctively does, I poked my fingers through the bar to egg them on, when I heard: "Don't put your fingers through the bars, you're going to get bitten!"

Immediately, I retrieved my fingers and wondered how it was possible that these two gentle birds could ever hurt a finger.

Unfortunately, here on the First Floor, the breakfast saga took a turn for the worse. Sister Thérèse had other more important things to do than waste her time waiting for me to drink the sickening milk. The worse incident was when the reviled milk was served up with my lunch and I was told that I was not to touch my food until I had drunk all the milk. I let out a big sigh, sank my head on my hand, and resigned myself to go hungry. The end of the lunch hour was approaching; all the other girls had already left and I could hear them playing happily outside while I was detained at the table, my food still untouched.

In a fit of pique, Sister Thérèse emptied the bowl all over my mashed potatoes and desiccated ham. At that point, I began to wonder about the logic of adults. I looked down at the gooey mess, then at the walls, saying nothing and doing nothing. Sister Thérèse fretted. She had probably read somewhere or been told that a child should never be allowed to win a battle and that lesson she was determined to teach me. No longer content to force feed me, she now resorted to smacking me, which seemed to me a curious thing to do, because my dislike of milk was not an act of defiance, but purely and simply a matter of taste.

Nevertheless, I was subjected to this punishment daily. From then on, every morning, from the moment I woke up, I tensed my muscles and psyched myself up to undergo the harsh ritual. Once, however, I decided to go to the nun without my head bowed low. As the nun was about to carry out the punishment, I stared back at her with a stance full of defiance. Deciphering her facial expression was almost as exhilarating as solving the mystery of words. For the first time, I felt like a little rebel and I had not even said a word. To my surprise, instead of seeing a look cold and cruel, I detected a degree of resignation in her eyes, almost as if she herself thought it all pointless, but it was her duty to uphold the all-important notion of discipline without which no social group could evolve effectively. Discipline and manners were spelled out in her rigorous set of rules which she had inscribed in her own code of conduct and to which she adhered like an ultimate act of faith. This made life difficult for her and unpleasant for me, and if either of us was going to give in, it was not going to be me, for I profoundly disliked milk; I detested it with all my senses and nothing, absolutely nothing, could be done to alter that particular taste.

Life resumed its slow labouring pace with only Christmas to break the sheer dullness of the daily routine. Christmas had always been and always remained the beautiful story of baby Jesus and the only event I had to really look forward to.

From the confines of my secluded locker, I sensed that the atmosphere was changing, more gentle and gay. Was it already time to make up the nativity scene and put up the Christmas tree? I pushed the locker door to see if anybody else was getting excited.

Mlle Pauline had moved George and Georgette out of their leafy corner to make room for the Christmas tree. Exceptionally, we were allowed to decorate the lower branches of the tree with mirror baubles and little candles while Mlle Pauline, perched on a wooden pedestal, tried to fix Angel Gabriel on the very top. As she wrestled with the prickly branches, a girl pointed out: "It's not the Angel Gabriel...It's a fairy!"

Mlle Pauline was quick to retort: "It may look like a fairy but it's the Angel Gabriel."

"But it's got wings!"

"Angels have got wings too, you know..."

Now, she was busy crumpling the dark brown paper pockmarked with specks of white paint to imitate the stars. Then, she set up the nativity scene opposite the fish tank, pushed the mini-wooden shed inside the fake sky and placed it on top of the straw, carefully filling the surrounding space with little porcelain figurines. Only the main characters had been left in their boxes to be gradually added later as the story of Christmas unravelled. In the evening, we said our prayers assembled around the beautiful display. Our angelic faces glowed in the suffused candlelight and my little heart heaved with contentment at the sight of the whole scene, a picture of sheer comfort and pure joy. If we had been good, we might even get to add one of the figurines, and when my turn came, I was very careful not to upset anything with my little ox because when Aline added the ass, Joseph fell into the empty crib and a sheep landed on the floor, shattering into thousands of minuscule pieces. We were bursting to laugh but, mindful of the solemnity of the moment, we quickly muffled our giggles in the cotton sleeves of our neat overalls.

In the middle of the Christmas Story, I had heard of a mysterious character. Here at *Saint Vincent*, I had never heard of him but some of the girls here and at school became extremely agitated at the mere mention of his name. I would simply have to find out who he was.

When the nun came on her next round, I grabbed hold of her and asked eagerly: "Who is Father Christmas? Does he really exist?"

"No," she replied rather dryly. "Only pagans believe in Father Christmas."

Good, I thought. As the good Christian that I was, I really did not want to do anything that would upset Baby Jesus. My mind set at peace, from that day on, I listened to all the excited children reciting enormous lists of glittering presents that the *Petit Papa Noël* would bring, and while their eyes sparkled with dreams of wonderful wishes, I wondered if God had enough room in his purgatory for all the children who had been led to believe in a pagan dream. What was Christmas about anyway? Wishes for the rich, dreams for the poor...Was this the voice of my guardian angel? Was he trying to speak to me? No, this was not my guardian angel speaking because I had always known that Christmas was all about the story of Baby Jesus and that was all I cared about.

*

At school, Mlle la Directrice continued to dissect each and every word before chanting her dictations. Each Monday morning began with the reading of a moral lesson, so that we could tell the difference between a primitive ape and a well brought up child. Sometimes, I found it extremely difficult not to giggle at her exaggerated metaphors, but the sight of the menacing blackboard pointer, always close at hand—if not *in* her hand, was enough to keep me in check. The compulsory P.E. lessons were conducted in the playground or in the gym if it was raining. These usually started with a quick march to the tune of *The Bridge over the River Kwai*. She was so fond of this whistling tune that she even had us learn the lyrics which we had to sing louder and louder still:

Hello, le soleil brille, brille, brille
Hello, il reviendra bientôt
Là-bas, dans ton village…

as we swung our arms high and stamped our feet hard on the wooden floor.

To my personal delight, Josette was still there, causing chaos by constantly challenging Mlle la Directrice to rethink her educational strategy and forcing her to bend her previously inflexible rules. In the days when all knowledge was acquired through rote learning, I often had to hide my face to smother an irresistible urge to laugh every time Josette stood up and asked: "What was I supposed to learn, miss?" or simply stated without a hint of fear in her eyes: "I could not do my work because I went to see granny…"

Or better still, when we were asked to produce our exercise books to have our work marked, Josette would asked candidly with a blank look on her face: "Homework, miss? What homework?"

Sometimes the whole class erupted and Mlle la Directrice would reach for the blackboard pointer and bang it noisily on her desk screaming: "Silence! Silence!".

Occasionally, we still had to walk around the confined playground with a bean bag perched on our heads, and when we did, I made sure I did not walk behind Josette or I was sure to get into trouble for laughing too much and dropping my beanbag once too often. As a matter of fact, it became a potential risk to be anywhere near Josette, because, if anything happened in a dispute or a fight, she would relate the events back to Mlle la Directrice exactly the way they happened because, with all her innocence and naivety, Josette did not have the intellectual capability to distort the facts in favour of a particular girl which meant that, if we had done something wrong and Josette had seen us, we knew straight away we were in trouble! The best thing to do, we convened, was to check where Josette was lurking before we even thought of putting a foot wrong.

One day, I saw a girl leaning against the doorway leading into the playground, nonchalantly blowing huge sticky bubbles. Curious, three of us walked up to her.

"What are you eating?"

"*Un malabar,*" she replied, feeling a tad superior because she had something we did not.

"What is it?"

"It's a chewing gum...They're the best to blow bubbles with. My brother blew one that was as big as his head!"

"We don't believe you."

"Yeah, he did!

Croix de feu, croix de fer

Si je mens, j'vais en enfer!" She chanted beating her chest, vouching that, were she to lie, she would go straight to hell.

"If you put two or three in your mouth," she added, "you can make really big bubbles!"

"Where did you get it from?" I asked, knowing that we had no access to sweets, least of all chewing gum, which was still a fairly new invention that had only just reached these parts.

"I found it on the street..."

"On the street?"

"Yeah, there's loads of them on the pavement."

"Really? So we could find some too, then!"

"Yeah...if you walk at the front, you'll get the first pick."

From that day on, as we walked back and forth to school, we shoved each other and jostled our way to the front of the crocodile file so that we could enjoy the rich pickings of chewing gum that had been discarded and flattened by rubber soles. The supervisor was quite revolted by this new craze.

"This is absolutely disgusting! Imagine, you don't know where it's been…A dog could have peed on it!"

But her warnings fell on deaf ears. We wanted chewing gum because we wanted to blow bubbles, and in our blind determination, we really could not care less where or how we got them.

By now, Nadine had joined us. She was in the class below me while Marie was in the class above, but we were all taught together by Mlle la Directrice in the same classroom. I never paid too much attention to my progress, as I passed through every new learning phase with quiet confidence, but sitting at the desk next to me, Nadine could not help but compare our work and our marks, and in so doing, introduced a competitive edge which satisfied her pride and forced me to take notice of how I was doing. She took particular pleasure in boasting about the medals she got and I did not, and almost blinded me with the golden palm which shone on her proud breast and sent cutting rays into my dejected eyes.

I had no interest in competing with anybody, especially as nobody had ever commented on my reports but, back at *Saint Vincent*, Nadine would corner me and boast: "I'm top of the class this week…Are you?" knowing full well that I had no medal, least of all the golden palm to vouch for my good work.

Still, I was resigned. If the teacher could take the honours away from me, no one, not even Nadine, could ever crush the glory and the huge satisfaction I drew from my work. When other girls came back from school comparing their awards and arguing which medal was the most worthy, I would throw my head back, shrug my shoulders and walk away as if I did not care. Only Nadine was insistent enough to pursue me. Fortunately, I had my secret retreat and I was able to escape her puppy bites while safely hidden in my reading locker.

Alas, I could not always avoid the mortification that came with coming back to *Saint Vincent* empty handed. The worst time came after prize giving at the end of the school year. Nadine returned from school boasting about the book she had received, a 'Junior Encyclopaedia' and, of course, the minute she saw me, she squared me up and sneered: "You didn't get anything, did you?"

Having failed to get any response from me, she dug the knife in deeper.

"Anyway, teacher says you're lazy, that's why…"

Soon after, other girls arrived, some of them waving their precious prizes. I watched them aghast. I felt mortally wounded, fuming with anger at the injustice of it all. I could not stand it anymore, so I went to look out of the picture window in the playroom, willing the witch to come out of her little hole and cast a spell that would frazzle their hideous little brains. Then, after a few minutes of reflection, I turned round and looked at the proud girls with a cynical smile knowing that, at some stage or other, most of their books would eventually end up in my locker, where they would remain…temporarily borrowed…

The first signs that I was growing up came when I began to lose my baby teeth and grow new ones. I took the habit of looking at myself in the mirror more frequently to watch for other signs that I was growing up. One day, Sister Thérèse caught me inspecting my face even more closely than usual, and riled *en passant*:

"Don't look at yourself too much in the mirror…One day you might see the devil!"

Another sign was that, at the end of the summer, some girls would be moving on to the Junior Section. In our little group from Indochina, all were selected except Nadine, who was younger and had not done her first communion, Marceline, and me.

"Why not me?" I asked rather miffed, "I've done my first communion."

Nadine, who never missed an opportunity to sneer at me, retorted with glee: "Because you *still* don't like milk, so you're *still* a baby!"

"*Mince alors,*" I thought. Was I doomed to stay in the Baby Section forever while those moving on already contemplated a life of plenty.

"We'll be able to eat all the bread we want at breakfast!" Dominique boasted.

"Yeah! I'm going to have two slices…or even three! With butter *and* jam!"

"And we'll have more time to play."

"Yes, and the playground is a lot bigger."

Listening to them gloating over the new exciting life ahead of them was becoming quite unbearable. So, as soon as Sister Thérèse reappeared, I stopped her.

"*Ma sœur, ma sœur*! Why am I not moving to the Junior Section?"

"Because you're too young."

"But…I've done my first communion…Everybody else who's done theirs is going, so why not me?"

"Because, Martha Bertrand…you are still…a little too immature."

While Sister Thérèse was talking, I could hear Nadine snigger behind my back, and as soon as the nun left, she chanted mockingly: "Ah! Ah! You're too immature!"

Then sitting astride on the bench in the cloakroom, she resumed her reading, leafing the pages of her Junior Encyclopaedia with great affection, lingering on any big word she could read loud and clear, just to show how much more clever she was than me.

After the summer holidays, accompanied by other girls, Marie, Michele, Claire, and Dominique all moved out of the Baby Section, while I was left to contemplate life as one of the oldest girls in the Baby Section, and the only one left who had done her first communion. Sister Bénédicte and Sister Thérèse may have tried to convince me that everything was preordained, that our fate was in the hands of God—*c'est le destin! c'est le destin!*—but in my view, all the unfair decisions were entirely people's doings and had nothing to do with God. While I harboured dark thoughts and ruminated over my undeserved destiny, unbeknownst to me, my little guardian angel was working harder than ever on my behalf. However, too busy sulking over my unjust fate, I did not hear his soft whisper whistling in my ear and spelling out my good fortune. With a heavy frown, I watched grudgingly the older girls walk across the playground towards the Junior Section, with the sudden urge to scream at them: "You know! Not liking milk doesn't make me a baby!"

But, who could I scream to without getting into trouble? I stormed off the landing and threw myself into the unreachable depths of my off-limit, out of bounds, secret locker.

Despite my disgruntled look, life was improving. Adults were beginning to notice me and, as a result, I became a little more communicative, but only just. Sister Thérèse had even stopped smacking me every morning for not drinking my milk, and once even, when I was not well enough to go to school, instead of being left alone in the dormitory, Mlle

Pauline stayed with me for a while. She read me some books while I sat snugly on her lap. Then, she taught me how to tell the time, and sang my praises to Sister Thérèse who, pretending not to believe her, asked: "Mlle Bertrand, what's the time?"

I looked at the clock and replied with a big grin on my face: "*Il est midi et demi.*"

"My good Lord!" She exclaimed with pretend admiration, joining her hands together and looking up to the ceiling in an exaggerated show of beatitude. "She *can* tell the time!"

The one drawback to having done my first communion was that every Wednesday morning, Mlle Pauline would wake me up at the crack of dawn to get me ready for chapel. It was not something I was desperate to do—not that I was reluctant to go and greet the Lord, far from it—but it was so incredibly hard to get up in the middle of the night, a real sacrifice, especially in winter time when I could hear the smooth regular breathing of the other girls still asleep in their nice warm beds. However, there were compensations. Once dressed, I would sit at the grown-ups' table to have breakfast. When Mlle Pauline presented me with a bowl of milk, I looked at her with pleading eyes. She understood and, without saying a word, took my bowl, tipped half of the milk out, and poured instead strong black coffee and added extra sugar. To thank her, I smiled. It was delicious, the best breakfast I had ever had. Then, she spread one slice of bread with butter *and* jam, and gave me some biscuits too. I felt so special.

However, after breakfast, the long lonely walk through the orphanage beckoned. The dark passage which separated the Baby Section from the Junior Section was full of ghostly visions filled with scrawny witches and blood-thirsty bats. Snow White had not yet eaten the poisoned apple, but I knew I was not strong enough to fight off the evil hand. It seemed that on my way to Heaven, I would have to pass the hissing gates of Hell, and I would be forced to stare at them, unable to avert my gaze, just like curious crowds are irresistibly drawn to the scene of an accident, only to run away screaming after having witnessed unmentionable horrors. At this very moment, a rush of sinister thoughts made me all jittery and I looked around for something...anything that would reassure me, but in the tenebrous obscurity, all I could see was the devil and his horns, and sneering witches with long hair, warts and hairy chins. I was so scared that I could not hear my guardian angel urging me to quicken my steps and run into the loving arms of Jesus. Whether I was responding to his call, I know not, but I suddenly broke into a sprint and ran like hell.

As soon as I emerged from the dark passage, my heart lifted and any lugubrious thoughts dissipated in the instant I saw the warm yellow glow of the main building in front of me and the illuminated stained-glass windows of the chapel, high above my head to the right. I was now running along the deserted playground. Then, winding my way up to the first floor, I entered the chapel, dipped my fingers into the cold holy water, walked down the aisle with my head held up high— despite being overwhelmed by a sudden bout of shyness—and sat right at the front where I knelt in front of the solid row of nuns, all gripped in the same state of beatitude. I felt so grown up, so important and so glad to meet up with Baby Jesus again. I liked God too, but He kept stirring my conscience...No wonder I was scared of Him...a little bit...sometimes.

At the beginning of the school year, a new girl joined us. Her name was Maryse and, being of a similar height as me, I guessed that she must have been roughly the same age, except that she had not done her first communion. She had noticed the way I gathered all the books and paraded with them tucked under my arm. How boring, she was quick to tell me, you can do other things apart from reading them.

Really? Like what? I wondered, mightily puzzled. Not one to delay the chance of a good laugh, one evening at playtime, she suggested that we lay them out on the tiled floor and see how many we could clear in one jump. Interesting, I thought, watching her lay the first book down. She jumped and I jumped. That was easy. She then put two books down. She jumped and I jumped. Still easy. She continued the same process until we had a whole line of books laid out neatly right in front of the radiator. When the last book was carefully lined on the tiles, I prepared to jump first. I heaved up my whole body and, as I landed, my heels clipped the binding of the last book. The hard cover slid on the slippery floor and continued its vertiginous run until my head smacked against the sharp edges of the radiator. At that moment, everything stopped. Dazed, stunned, and in shock, I struggled to get up. I knew instantly there was something wrong...very wrong. I felt all the blood drain off my face and began to feel woozy. I could not speak. I held my head with my hand and went to stand in front of Mlle Pauline. She raised her eyes from her newspaper and looked at me with a puzzled look. Then it came: a warm thick liquid trickled over my face. Mlle Pauline gave a loud gasp and nearly screamed in horror. In a swift movement, she swoop me off my feet and rushed me to the infirmary, leaving a trail of blood behind her hurried steps.

Minutes later, several nuns rushed in, like a formation of dark clouds foreboding an approaching doom. One of them with nursing skills, started to cut my hair around the injured area, tended to the wound and began to wrap my head with meters upon meters of a soft stretchy bandage while the others murmured words of praise and admiration.

"She is being so brave…" The nursing nun commented.

"She's not even crying…" Sister Thérèse added, clearly impressed.

I may have looked worried and unhappy, but inside I was smiling. Their lavish praises for my courage and stoicism were readily absorbed like a soothing ointment and made me revel in my own glory. If only they knew that the only reason why I was not crying was simply because I could not feel anything.

"Well, that's you off school for a few days," the nurse mused. "And if this doesn't heal, we'll just have to get you a new head!"

A new head? I did not want a new head. I was quite happy with this one, I thought. As for missing school…No, I could not possibly miss school. Mlle la Directrice would be so angry; she'll call me lazy and blast "daydreaming again!" as she'll slap the back of my head. Ouch! My head! I'm scared…She's going to hit my head…I don't want her to hit my head…All right, I will have to miss school after all. She might punish me and call me lazy again, but at least it won't be as painful as a blow on the head.

Then, I caught sight of the nurse approaching my head with a menacing safety-pin. I cringed and sank my head into my shoulders in a vain attempt to avoid the sharp point.

"Don't worry," she said in a calm voice. "It's only to keep the bandages in place."

After the nurse had finished putting my head back together, Mlle Pauline carried me to bed, followed closely by Sister Thérèse. There, they gave me an aspirin for the pain, which I did not feel, and ordered the other girls to tiptoe to bed ever so quietly so as not to disturb me.

After a short period of convalescence, I returned to school. I sat at my desk fidgeting nervously, with the top of my hair standing hirsute, as I waited for the onslaught. I could not even bring myself to look at Mlle la Directrice, but like the Napoleonic armies along the Berezina, she had already began her imponderable march towards me, clacking her stiletto shoes on the hard floor, and I quivered apprehensively under her icy glare. When she came level with my desk, fearing the worse, I instinctively flinched.

"I'm not going to hit you, you stupid girl...I just want to say that you are not to go out during break. You need to rest."

"For how long?" I managed to stutter, thinking that she would probably say five minutes or ten at most.

"For a week," she replied as if delivering a sentence.

"For a week!" I exclaimed, slumping my head on my fists and sighing loudly as I saw the same words flash in front of my eyes: I AM BORED! BORED! BORED!

When the bell rang, I watched all the girls file out and soon, the walls echoed with their excited cries while I sat at my desk, swinging my legs in sheer frustration and fidgeting with anything I could lay my hands on. A few minutes later, Josette appeared in the doorway.

"Miss, I don't want to go out today, it's too cold..."

"You need to go out; fresh air is good for you," Mlle la Directrice replied comfortingly.

"Yeah...but I've got me chest, you see..." she said, patting her ample chest as she spoke. "I've got a weak chest, miss..."

Mlle la Directrice responded with an incredulous look and a wry smile.

"I'm gone cough all night and me mum will be worried..."

"All right, you go and sit down, but I don't want to hear you."

"That's all right, miss, I want to practise doing up my shoe laces."

I watched the scene flabbergasted, amazed at how easily Teacher had given in. I scrutinised the girl ever so closely to try and understand why she was being treated so favourably; why she could never manage to do anything and yet still get lots of praises for nil accomplishment; and why we, her classmates, instinctively knew not to make fun of her despite being witnesses to her daily blunders. I watched her again, sitting at her desk with her tongue sticking out, as it often did, and her chair half turned towards the aisle so that she could fiddle with her laces with more ease. She may have been Teacher's pet but I certainly did not envy her.

Years later, I was still pondering over Josette, and it is only after I had left school and came to mix with a greater variety of people that I discovered what the matter with her was. It was quite simple, really. Josette had Down's Syndrome and I understood then why Mlle la Directrice felt so protective towards her, and despite begrudging her for never awarding me a medal—least of all the golden palm during all my time at *Sainte Germaine*—it suddenly dawned on me that Mlle la Directrice, for all her misplaced prejudices, was not the complete fire-spitting dragon I had always perceived her to be.

CHAPTER VIII

A t the end of the summer, just before we left Sangatte, I looked over towards the sea, and this time, the horizon appeared like a neat line drawn right across a page with below it gentle waves scribbling an illegible story that I could not wait to read. Jumping ahead of time, a whole year on, I imagined myself playing on the main lawn, standing against the wire fence, and watching dreamily the green and dark blue ferries travel back and forth like colour pencils drawing scribbling lines to retell mysterious adventures of the kind I had never read before. And as I followed the white wake trailing behind, I saw myself lounging on the main deck, sunk deeply into a *chaise longue*, wrapped up in an expensive blanket and surrounded by a mountain of grown-up story books. Then after a while, I would close my eyes and let my imagination run wild while the gentle caress of the sea breeze brushed my pale cheeks and the heady smell of fresh iodine air scented my dreams.

The coach arrived to take us back to the station. The Junior Section beckoned. During the whole journey, all we could talk about was the list of all the extras we would be able to enjoy: the extra bread at breakfast with as much butter and jam as we wanted—the extra playtime in the bigger playground, and the extra fun we would have, and with Maryse by my side, it was definitely going to be a lot more fun.

The momentous day arrived. A tremor of excitement made

me shiver just like on my first day at school. I was enthralled at the prospect of beginning a new page, a new chapter. It was a new day and just like with any book, I could not wait to begin.

Hand in hand, we were led across the playground towards the red brick building, the one that I had often peered at in the dark from above the Baby Section and where I had often hoped to find the happy people merrily chatting together. I was so excited that I forgot to check what colour the ivy was on the wall, and if I had, I would have seen that its magnificent mantel had begun to die.

We entered through the back door where a small corridor led us straight into the refectory. The room felt cold and reeked of the stale smell of food. Undeterred, I was ready to mingle amongst the Junior Section girls, all so much taller than me. At last, I was standing on the other side of the plain net curtains which had so expertly hidden its secrets from me. I paused for a moment, seized by a sudden feeling of foreboding. Looking all around me, I was not sure whether I liked what I saw. At the back of my mind, I had the sneaky suspicion that I had been tricked, that I had been fooled by girls who were too scared to tell the truth. I felt cold. I looked around again for some source of warmth but only saw a small coal burner, hunched up in its own darkness, tucked half way along against the refectory's naked wall. Two rows of tables skirted with long wooden benches divided the room into two, and on the floor, the dark red tiles made the room appear darker than it should be. I was no longer feeling excited. Perhaps I was just feeling a little nervous. After all, the older girls who had made the move the previous year had had such pleasure in taunting *me*, the oldest baby of the Baby Section, about their new and exciting life. So really, I was probably worrying over nothing.

All the girls were standing casually in the central alley and the sound of their easy chatter reassured me a little. I looked around eager to find familiar faces and spotted Michèle and Claire, but, standing tall in their own importance, they threw a cold glance at me and carried on talking while completely ignoring me. Fortunately, I still had Maryse who kept following me like a lost puppy. Suddenly, a woman came in and shouted: "Line up in order of height!"

Maryse and I looked at each other.

"Why do we have to line up?" I asked.

"Silence!" The woman barked.

A girl whispered: "We're going to be given our uniforms."

There was a general hustle and bustle while girls pushed and shoved each other to arrange themselves in order of height. I stood back to back with Maryse while another girl decided who was the taller and decreed that we were both the same height.

I jostled her behind me claiming: "I have to go in front of you because my surname starts with a B whereas yours starts with a G."

Maryse shrugged her shoulders and complied.

When I arrived at the front of the queue, the woman looked me up and handed over a pile of clothes.

"Uniform no. 111," she said dryly to another woman who wrote the number down on a long list of names.

Afterwards, we were told to line up again.

"In a neat line!" one of the women spat out.

At her signal, we had to make an about turn and remain still, standing very straight and in complete silence. Then, after another signal, we were marched out towards the stairs where we wound our way up along the wooden steps in a neat crocodile file right up to the top floor where the dormitory was situated.

"No talking!" The same woman barked again.

I, for one, was not talking for at that point, my nostrils were assailed by an unfamiliar powerful smell and I was too busy looking around to figure out what it was. It suddenly clicked: wood polish, it was wood polish and its gluey sticky aroma hung everywhere we went.

"Always walk along the wall on the way up and always go down the stairs on the side of the rails."

Girls who had been walking in the middle quickly shifted themselves along the plain white wall.

At the top of the stairs, the crocodile file stopped while the woman opened a large cupboard and, leaning over the banister, declared: "No one should walk in the dormitory without wearing carpet slippers!"

She showed us flat pieces of a strong material just big enough to cover the sole of our shoes, held on with a wide elastic band. As we reached the top of the stairs, we took a pair each before gathering at the dormitory door. There, the woman held up a list and began to call out names.

The smell of wood polish followed us inside the dormitory. The dormitory itself was an enormous room parcelled off by low partitions into smaller dorms, each holding between four and eight beds. Immediately, by the door, there was a single cubicle where the supervisor on duty slept, and next to it, there were two others with two beds in each, and despite being located right next to the supervisor's cell, these two small rooms were highly coveted. For a brief moment, I dared hope that I could steal myself away in one of these, but when my name was finally called, we were standing at the far end of the dormitory. I threw an inspectorial glance around the room, counted six beds and three wooden lockers. The iron beds had long ago been painted in a creamy kind of colour and, along the years, unsightly dark patches had begun to appear. At the foot of each, a metal stool stood against the beds' metal railings. I felt cold just looking at them. There was not even a door to create the illusion of comfort, just a plain green curtain that drooped unevenly on wooden rings. Natural light came in through a series of tall windows that ran the whole length of the dormitory on both sides, and set so high up the wall that it was impossible to see anything from them except the dull grey sky. When night fell, the light was provided by long strips of neon tubes strategically positioned above each partition so as to light up two dorms at once.

I remembered then how Sister Bénédicte had raved about them when this latest invention had reached the doors of the orphanage. The neon light was so white and so bright that it would be just like daylight in the middle of the night, she had effused. It was a miracle of science, she had exclaimed as we had watched her face beam with a whitish glow.

When everybody was allocated to a bed, we were ordered to get into our uniforms. I had never taken much notice of the clothes I wore before, until that very moment. I lifted one item at a time and stared at them in dismay. The worse items by far were the pants which were of a colour I could not even describe, and which were so misshapen that I had to toss them around several times to work out which were the holes for the legs. Underneath the pants, I had found a pair of limp grey socks, all shrivelled and distended by their loose elastics. The rest of the dark-coloured uniform looked passable, but when I finally brought myself to put the pants on, they felt rather draughty as they hung so loose on me. I supposed it was something I would have to get used to—and that was not all. On top of the pile, I had picked up this thin cardboard looking thing. I held it up to examine it more closely, then turned to Roberte, a sickly looking girl with short blond hair who had the bed next to me.

"What's this?" I asked, intrigued.

"It's a false collar."

"A what?"

"Put your jumper on and I'll show you how to put it on."

As soon as I had slipped my jumper on, she grabbed me by the neck.

"See the holes here on the collar? They go on the buttons at the front and back of the jumper's neck."

"But I can't see what I'm doing...there's no mirror in here."

"I'll help you...but don't worry, you'll soon get the hang of it."

After we had changed into our uniforms, we, the new girls, were shown the washroom while the others had to sit in complete silence on their metal stools. Before we entered, the supervisor stopped and showed us the dorm to the right, nearest to the washroom.

"This dorm..." she explained, raising her nostrils above the pungent atmosphere with an air of disgust, "is called '*les pichoux*'. If you wet your bed, that's where you'll sleep."

The minute she said it, I too could detect the faint aroma of stale urine which filtered through my delicate nostrils, and suddenly, I felt grateful that my dorm was a good distance away from the rather unpleasant fumes.

The washroom was lined with rows of washbasins and along the far wall, there was a set of showers, five in all.

"You will shower every Wednesday and Sunday," the woman declared. "You will get a clean pair of pants on each shower day and your uniform will be changed every Sunday."

When we returned to our dorms, the supervisor whisked away our old clothes so fast I did not have time to realise that, with a swift action of her arm, she had taken away the memories of a more gentle world with its warm smell still hanging onto every fibre softly woven into a childhood that had ended too soon. I sat on the metal stool staring at the blank space in front of me feeling all numb inside. Maryse was not with me. She was probably sitting on her metal stool in the dorm right next to the washroom, waiting for me.

A while later, we were taken downstairs again and ordered to go outside into the playground. Still holding a list in her hand, the supervisor announced that we were going to be split into 'ranks'. She began to call out names again.

"Line up here the following…"

Row by row, we lined up as we were told. There were six rows of ten girls, perhaps slightly more, and as we stood in silence, the woman proceeded to spell out the rules.

"Before each roll call, you will have to line up in silence. You will have to stand in your own ranks, and no swapping is permitted. You will remain silent at all times in the refectory, in the corridors, in the dormitory, in the washroom, and during study time. If you are caught talking, a cross will be put against your name, each cross represents a paragraph to be learnt by heart; ten crosses means you will not be allowed home at leave-out weekends."

I stood to attention in my new rank, trying not to smirk.

"If you misbehave in the refectory, in addition to getting a cross by your name, you will have no pudding."

No pudding? That was the best piece of news so far, I sniggered under my breath. Who on earth wanted those revolting milky puddings anyway?

At that point, I lost interest and stopped listening. I did

not like puddings and I had nowhere to go on weekends. I was, effectively, unpunishable. In my head, I was already anticipating, better still, reeling with pleasure at the thought that I would be the only girl in the Junior Section able to outdo the adults. While others would wince and cringe, and even cry, I would stand firmly in my rank, my head held up high, my arms pressed rigidly against my flanks, and my eyes looking fixedly in front of me, for I, Martha Bertrand, was untouchable. And when names would be called, matched against the inevitable punishments, I would smile at the silly rules that stifled our existence, at the po-faced supervisors who thought of nothing better to do than make our lives utterly miserable. And I would smile again at all the future victories I would score against them, but the sound of my name shouted above the rows of still heads brought me rudely back into the cold yard.

"Martha Bertrand! Are you listening? What did I just say? I'll soon wipe that stupid grin off your face...you just wait!"

My inner voice rose and began to take over. I heard it rile cheekily: "Not me, *Mademoiselle*, *you* shall have to wait..." as I tried in vain to keep a straight face. I bit my cheeks, straightened myself, and hoped that I looked contrite enough to avoid my first cross.

Once the rules had been spelled out, we filed back in silence into the refectory, rank by rank, and while I settled happily on the wooden bench, I looked at the adults' table with a stare full of contempt. There were four women there who, as I was about to discover, spent most of their time standing around us like rigid posts of a ring fence deeply set on the periphery of hatred and contempt.

One was talking more animatedly than the others.

"Who's that?" I queried in a whisper.

"Annie Brenn," the girl sitting next to me replied.

"Annie Brenn?" I repeated, surprised that she had not used the usual prefix *Mlle* in front of her name.

"Everybody calls her Annie Brenn," she explained, shrugging her shoulders.

I looked back at Annie Brenn and wondered why. As I scrutinised every fold and crease in her ageless face, I saw a look I had never seen in an adult before. Mlle Alice had always looked blissfully happy, Sister Bénédicte righteous and sanctimonious, Mlle Pauline permanently gripped in the throes of pity and sadness, and often on the edge of tears. Sister Thérèse again looked righteous, but Annie Brenn had a look so vacant and so vapid that no one, it seemed, took her seriously. Her only saving grace was the fact that she was taller than anybody else, and from this accidental physical attribute, she drew an immense feeling of superiority which she did not hesitate to use in order to bolster her weak cerebral powers.

Suddenly, the refectory fell totally silent. There was a short shuffle and I heard a door close. Standing erect at the front of the long refectory, Sister Marie-Catherine heaved her chest and scowled at the faces in front of her. Nobody moved. I glanced discreetly around the room, wondering why the sudden change of mood. Every single girl sat up straight, as if all of a sudden they had been turned into stone at the mere sight of the nun. I did the same, just in case.

"Mlle Brenn," the nun asked dryly, "could you do the roll call? I want each new girl to stand up and say 'present' when her name is called."

The named supervisor jumped out of her seat and, clutching nervously the list of names, hurriedly made her way from the back of the refectory to the front where she stood next to Sister Marie-Catherine, practically trembling. Then, she began the roll call, jerking her head slightly after each name, as if suffering from a nervous tick. A few feeble 'present' echoed down the refectory. Sister Marie-Catherine let out an exasperated grunt through her dilated nostrils, clutched her hands together, and squeezed them even tighter than before.

"Louder, girl! I can't hear you!" She spluttered.

So, when my name was called, I made sure I stood up and said 'present' loud and clear. The nun leered at me with a suspicious look, not knowing whether I was complying with her wishes or looking for trouble. The atmosphere was tense. Nobody made eye contact with anyone else. If I had been able to read the other girls 'minds at that point, I would have seen the same question etched on their minds: what would her reaction be this time? But all Sister Marie-Catherine did was to take a sharp intake of breath; then, she racked her throat, turned to Annie Brenn and begged her to continue. Desperately trying to stop herself from shaking, Annie Brenn stretched the piece of paper in front of her again and completed the roll call.

Then the refectory fell silent again. Sister Marie-Catherine jerked her cumbersome cornet sideways a few times and began her welcoming speech.

"You all know the rules by now, but remember, I want manners, orderliness, obedience...but above all, I want... discipline!"

A few girls cringed in fear. I even thought I saw those nearest to the nun duck as she spluttered her stern words all across the refectory. Then, her shoes squeaked and she left the room abruptly.

The deathly silence continued for a while until, whisper-by-whisper, those who dared began to talk again.

"Silence!" One of the women blasted.

"Who's gonna get the first cross?" Another threatened.

After an interminable wait, Mlle Bernadette got up and walked to the front of the refectory.

"Line up in the central aisle!" She ordered.

Like puppets on springs, we all stood up.

"In silence! Or you'll stay behind!"

Then, we were led outside, back into the courtyard that was to be our playground. At long last, we were able to speak, but I was so numbed by my first introduction to the Junior Section that I could not think of anything to say. Maryse stood beside me, quiet too. After a cursory glance at our new surroundings, we noticed an old woman on a decrepit wicker chair sitting outside the main kitchens. Having regained her usual cheerfulness, Maryse grabbed my arm and led me towards her.

"Let's go and say hello."

We straddled across, hands in pocket, feeling brash and confident, and went to stare at the woman who was busy pealing potatoes.

"What's your name?" Maryse asked with childish aplomb.

The old woman scrutinised us for a moment, her grey wiry hair ensconced in an old scarf.

"Mlle Agnes," the woman replied with a toothless grin.

At the sight of her lips collapsing on her empty jaws, we both burst out laughing, but aware that our reaction could have hurt the old woman, Maryse made a huge effort to regain her composure and asked another question.

"Are you the kitchen maid?"

"I'm not the kitchen maid, I'm the kitchen helper…anyway, nice to see young girls like you bothering with old folks like me, especially as I'm often sitting out here…on my own. It's nice when someone comes and says hello. You will come and say hello again, won't you?"

"Of course we will, miss," Maryse replied cheerfully, dragging me away with her.

"Did you notice?" She immediately said.

"What?" I asked, having seen nothing except her chin, long and curved with prickly short hair standing at the end of it.

Maryse giggled and, cupping her hand over my ear, she whispered: "She's got a moustache!"

"She hasn't got a moustache!" I refuted loudly.

"Yeah she has...come and see."

Again, Maryse dragged me back towards the kitchen. Just as we were beginning our approach, the old woman chuckled: "I didn't expect to see you back so soon!"

Then she rose from her seat and began to waddle across the playground. We both stopped to stare at her.

"See...see..." Maryse pointed, snagging my arm.

When the old woman walked passed us, she let out a little snigger through her collapsing lips. In Maryse's very own universe, women beyond a certain age could never be spared.

"I tell you," she insisted, "she's a witch!"

Our irreverent laughter must have attracted some attention because almost immediately, a girl with a bowl hair cut came over to speak to us. I recognised her straight away. She was Roberte, the girl from my dorm.

"So...you've just come from the Baby Section?"

"Yeah..." Maryse and I replied as one.

"The playground isn't that much bigger," I remarked.

Roberte looked a little puzzled by my remark, then she pointed at three perfectly square patches of lawn symmetrically placed one after the other.

"We can play over there too if we want...but only on Sundays...when there's not so many of us, so we can't do too much damage to the lawns...and by the way, you're not allowed to walk on them, and if you're caught, you're in real trouble." Then she paused to catch her breath, clearly flustered at the thought of getting into trouble. "And look, right over there by the back gate, there's an old pigsty where the nuns used to keep pigs..."

"Real pigs? They used to keep real pigs?" I asked astonished.

"Of course they were real! And they used to kill them themselves. You could hear the pigs squeal and squeal all over the orphanage!"

"How did they kill them?"

"Cut their throat!" Roberte replied sharply, slicing her throat with her thumb.

"Have you seen them do it?" Maryse enquired, sniffing a tall story.

"No...but my big sister has...she's left now."

Maryse and I threw a dubious look at each other.

"Can you show us the pigsty?"

"Not now, but on Sunday after church, I'll show you..."

Our conversation was suddenly interrupted by someone shouting:

"*Rassemblement!*"

"It's roll call. We've got to line up," Roberte translated as she ran off.

"Into your ranks!" Mlle Bernadette blasted.

We quickly lined up in silence. Those who could not remember which rank they belonged to simply lined up anywhere, so long as they were lined up somewhere, they would be all right. Mlle Bernadette frowned at the sight of the third rank which seemed to have fifteen girls or more.

"All right, who's in the wrong rank here?" she scolded.

As she checked her list, the shadow of Sister Marie-Catherine emerged from the main building. Everybody froze on the spot.

"Are they not in their ranks yet?" She asked impatiently.

"Some of the new girls could not remember which rank they were in, Sister..."

"Well, I'll make sure they remember! Stand straight!" She shouted while walking in and out of the ranks, holding a long ruler which she pressed hard against the backs of girls she considered not straight enough.

"Shoulders back! You're drooping, girl, you're drooping!"

Blowing hot air like an enraged bull, she moved swiftly back in front of her troops and gave another inspectorial glance at the ranks.

"I want straight lines in the ranks. Stretch your right arm in front of you and form a straight line."

We quickly shuffled our feet into the correct position, tucked our arms rigidly against our sides, and waited for Sister Marie-Catherine's verdict.

"Now, I want everyone to march. At my signal, you will lift your right leg, then the left, and you will swing your arms, keeping them straight. Right! Heads...up! March! Right... left...right...left..."

Fortunately, I had had some practice with Mlle la Directrice to the rhythm of her favourite tune 'The Bridge over the River Kwai', but there were some girls who simply could not keep to the rhythm and whose feet bounded on the ground at the wrong time and in the wrong place.

Sister Marie-Catherine was swift to intervene. Using her ruler, she hit the right leg of a girl while at the same time screaming in her ear:

"Right!...Right!...Right!..."

Crippled by the pain, the girl tried to rub her leg, but she could not reach because Sister Marie-Catherine kept hitting harder and harder until the stinging pain became too much and, just as the girl was about to collapse in a heap on the ground, the nun caught her by the shoulder and threw her unceremoniously out of the rank.

"To the back of the rank, you useless girl!"

Fighting back the tears, the girl limped where she had been told to go. Then, Sister Marie-Catherine resumed her position at the front.

"Heads held up high! Higher the arms, higher!"

After a few minutes of this, she tapped her ruler in the palm of her hand and declared haughtily: "That's what I call discipline! *Au repos!*"

This meant that we could stop marching. We stood as still as our fears would allow us to in our respective lines, almost afraid to breathe, waiting for the next command.

"Entrez maintenant!"

At last, we were finally allowed in the refectory and one rank at a time, we filed passed the nun, always watching her hands to anticipate the moment she would hit you at the back of the head snapping: "Your socks!...Yours laces!...Look at the state of your overalls, you little scruff!"

The evening meal was brought table-to-table. I looked at the transparent Pyrex plate with a small pile of something lost in the middle of it.

"What's that?" I whispered to the girl sitting next to me.

"Don't know. Just eat it."

"Was that you, Martha Bertrand, talking?"

I stared at the supervisor but said nothing.

"All right, that's your first cross."

Knowing that it would not affect me much, I ignored her

remark and tucked into what looked like a mini pile of dung. Whatever it was had clearly been burnt, but I managed to struggle through and finish my frugal portion, all the while picturing in my head Michèle and Claire a year ago boasting about the plentiful and delicious food they were having, while I had to make do with mashed potatoes mixed with desiccated ham. But I liked mashed potatoes mixed with desiccated ham; that was my favourite food. What else did they have that could taste better? It was not long before I discovered the truth behind their boastful taunts. At breakfast, we still only had one slice of bread with, instead of butter, a tiny square of cheap, and at times rancid margarine to spread on it. Lunch always started with a soup that had been dished out before we came into the refectory, which meant that it was invariably cold with a layer of scum floating on the surface. As for the meat, even the supervisors could not cut it. Fortunately, the portions were always small, but the worse day of all by far was Friday.

I remember walking into the building that first Friday and being hit by the most awful stench that had me convinced that a pile of dead rats must be hiding somewhere. As the food was dished out, one table at a time, a ladle of dead fish was slopped out onto my plate. The smell was so revolting that I simply could not look at it, let alone eat it. To my utter surprise—and somewhat disgust—some of the girls ate their food as if they were totally devoid of any sense of smell or taste. I looked at Maryse, who was sitting opposite me, and studied her reaction. With an exaggerated flick of the wrist, she forked her piece of fish a few times to make sure it was dead, and then ate it. I could not believe my eyes. Was I the only girl to find the food utterly revolting? There was no two ways about it; to empty my plate, I would have to do some bargaining.

"Who wants to swap my fish for their potato?" I whispered.

Amazingly, I had several takers. I did not care how small their piece of potato was as long as I was able to clear my plate of this disgusting mound of dead fish.

Afterwards, rank one was told that they were in charge of the washing up and cleaning the refectory, which, with some sixty-odd covers to wash up, was a monumental task, but despite being an unpopular chore, it was seen as an advantage, because girls on duty could stay up longer while the rest of us scraped the blank walls of the stairwell all the way up to the dormitory every evening at ten past seven precisely.

Alas, the day was not over yet. As I was about to get into bed, Roberte warned me that I would probably need to have my hair cut. I looked at her ugly hairstyle from which emerged an unsightly pair of enormous ears, and asked which of the women was in charge of cutting hair.

"It depends…but the worse one is Mlle Pierrette."

"Which one is Mlle Pierrette?" I asked, noting that I had not heard the name before.

"Oh, you're all right…she's not there."

At that moment, Chantal, another new girl, returned from having her hair cut, her right hand holding the back of her neck.

"Who cut your hair?" I hastily asked.

"Annie Brenn."

"Did she cut you?" Roberte asked in a matter-of-fact way.

"Yeah…right there," Chantal replied, showing us a thin red line on her smooth neck.

"Is it sore?" I asked rather worried.

"Of course it's sore!…it stings!"

Roberte inspected the wound and declared: "Well, it's not as bad as Martine C.'s cuts."

"Why, what happened to her?" I enquired, growing increasingly worried.

"Annie Brenn cut her in the ears as well as in the neck!"

"Yeah...but that's because Martine C.'s ears stick out too much!" Chantal replied. "Anyway, it's your turn."

"I don't want to go," I protested.

"You have to. If you don't go, they'll come and get you anyway, so you might as well go," Roberte declared philosophically.

I walked the whole length of the dormitory, with butterflies running riots in my tummy. Annie Brenn and Mlle Bernadette were both busy cutting hair.

"You can do hers," Mlle Bernadette said as soon as she spotted me.

"That'll be easy," Annie Brenn quickly assessed, lifting her eyes from a massacred mop of hair. "She's got straight hair..."

Then, she pushed the girl off the stool and called me.

"Off you go to bed! Here, Martha Bertrand, your turn...sit here," she ordered, showing me the vacated stool. "And you'd better sit very still...otherwise..."

She did not finish her sentence, but I knew exactly what she had meant to say. Then, she grabbed a razor blade and started to cut my hair.

"Ouch! Ouch!" I screamed.

"Stop winging, little wimp, or you'll get cut!"

"But it hurts!"

"It only hurts if you move, so sit still!"

But I could not sit still. It hurt too much. I felt tears well up in my eyes as Annie Brenn continued to chop my hair with a razor blade that must have been quite blunt by now after so many haircuts, but despite the pain, I was determined not to cry. After a few minutes of sheer agony, Annie Brenn decreed: "That's you done! Go back to your dorm now."

I jumped off the stool and ran as fast as I could before she decided that she had missed a bit. Roberte was waiting, sitting up in her bed.

"Well, it wasn't that bad, was it?" she asked.

"You didn't tell me it hurts like hell!" I whinged.

"Did you get cut?"

"I don't think so..."

"Touch your neck, you'll soon find out."

"I don't want to."

"Do you want me to have a look?"

"O.K...but don't touch my neck," I warned her.

"Yeah..." Roberte declared pensively.

"Yeah what?"

"Yeah...you've been cut."

"Where?...Don't touch my neck! Don't touch my neck!" I screamed.

"Right there," Roberte replied with her finger hovering just above the cut. Without thinking, I swiped my hand all along my neck to check.

"Ouch, it stings!" I whinged again. "Razor blades! Why can't they use scissors?"

"It's more hygienic..." Roberte's answer sounded somewhat clinical.

"And why do we have to have our hair cut so short anyway?" I vociferated.

"So we don't get nits...but it doesn't make any difference, we still get them." Roberte said, shrugging her shoulders. Then she added: "You look like a boy..."

"I don't care," I retorted.

"Well, we all do, really, but what does it matter anyway," Roberte said in a resigned way.

I looked at her, impressed by her quiet resolve. Her

short blond hair bobbed in the cruellest of cuts seemed to sit haphazardly on her ears, and her lips, too wide and too full, contrasted awkwardly with the rest of her smooth angelic face. The paleness of her complexion gave her a calm and serene expression that seemed to say that there was nothing to fear, nothing to worry about, and her boyish unruffled looks exuded a peaceful aura that made me feel secure. Somehow, she seemed to be surviving on a double dose of resilience coupled with a good measure of stoicism, and I wanted to be like her. I was so glad to have her right next to me, and if the harsh treatment we received on a daily basis did not bother her, then it would not bother me either.

Suddenly, the strip neon lights went out and I settled for the night, my mind emptied of any thoughts, too frightened to imagine what lay ahead. It was dark...very dark...and as long as it stayed dark, I could steal myself away in a safer world. I closed my eyes and quickly went to sleep.

The faceless soldiers returned, but this time, I saw them marching before dying. I did not know if it was morning or night, but I could tell that the tortured silence in which they fell was something approaching the sound of hell.

However, while I could terminate and jolt out of my horrible dreams, I could not escape life in the Junior Section.

After a night spent in the throes of darkness, a blinding flash of light flooded the room. Startled, I rubbed my eyes and saw that the neon lights had been switched on. I shielded my face, dazzled by the starkness of the strip light. It was a brutal awakening, but there was no point in moaning about it. That was how life would be from now on, I told myself, burying my head back under the blanket.

"And don't be the last to get ready," Roberte warned, "otherwise the other girls at your table will probably pinch your breakfast."

That was enough to get me going. With my eyes half-closed, I fumbled about to find my clothes, still unable to face the light, and all the while wondering why Sister Bénédicte had called those awful neon tubes 'the miracle lights'.

As the days went by, breakfast became my favourite part of the day for it was the only time we did not have to march; but best of all, there was school afterwards. School at last...such a relief...how I longed to be in a place where I could forget my lowly status and mingle freely among other 'normal' children, a place where we were able to run and play, laugh and scream to our heart's content...until it was time to return to *Saint Vincent* where the only noise to be heard was the lonely, hollow sound of our feet marching on the cold ground.

After several days of the strict and rigorous regime, I held my breath and fumed at all the girls who had told so many blatant lies. Just like on my first day at school, the distant promises of a new happiness, a new bliss — and an abundance of food — disintegrated in front of me like the burst bubble of an untenable dream.

Why did they do it? I glowered at them in the refectory in a silent rage that knotted my stomach into a ball of anger. But...with their thoughtless boasts and their silly taunts, my elders had unwittingly spared me a huge amount of worry and anxiety, and Sister Thérèse, for whatever reason, had delayed for one more year the inevitable, the inexorable, and the inescapable moment when I took those steps and walked blindfolded into a dismal future.

Whatever lay ahead, children should be spared the burden of truth.

CHAPTER IX

At least, one thing changed for the better. That year, I left *Sainte Germaine* for good, which was great news for me as it meant that I would no longer have to put up with *Mlle la Directrice*, her blackboard pointer, and her twitchy hands that seemed to spring into action every time she passed my desk. I would no longer cringe every time she shouted: "*Les orphelines!*" But, I would miss Josette. I imagined that, away from my teasing eyes, she would continue to parade in her pink blanc-mange and white candy shoes, and the stiff tension would drop as *Mlle la Directrice* would try to jolly her along to make her do whatever she had to do, even if the poor girl did not understand. Without Josette around, the light would seem dimmer, the atmosphere duller, and the mischievous sparkle that shone in my eyes every time Josette missed her cue would be slowly extinguished. I sighed with a heavy heart...then I remembered *Mlle la Directrice* and her blackboard pointer, and her twitchy hands, and I felt all excited at the prospect of moving on.

I did not yet know which school I would be sent to, and began to ask around.

"We're going to *Ecole Notre Dame...*" Michèle and Claire boasted in unison.

It was a good school with a high academic reputation and that was where I wanted to go too.

"It's too good for you," Claire sneered.

Was she talking about my work or my behaviour? I wondered.

In the past, Sister Thérèse had often decried that if we wanted to know anything, we should go and ask God Himself. Her familiar rebuke was the perfect way to eschew any awkward or difficult question, but I wanted a more tangible answer... and one a little more instant. There was only one thing to do: ask Sister Marie-Catherine...On second thought...perhaps not. I was not brave enough to risk putting my neck on the block, no, not me. Neither a saint nor a martyr be. Her reactions were far too unpredictable. I would simply have to wait and see.

The first clue that I would be attending *l'Ecole Notre Dame* came when I was given an assortment of clothes that looked neater than my usual uniform. Like in all French schools, no formal uniform was required, but in this particular establishment, the rules specified that whatever we wore had to be navy blue or white. The best thing about this new set of clothes, however, was the compulsory navy blue beret we had to wear, and mine gleamed under the shiny chrome badge that it sported at the front in the shape of the school's initials. From that day on, instead of getting on with my chores of clearing the tables and washing the floor, I would parade and posture in front of the refectory mirror, one hand resting commandingly on my hip, and the other gripping the fire poker that now rested on the end of my foot, just like I had seen Louis XIV do in my history book.

My new clothes spelt out the words: 'clever', 'intelligent' and 'good catholic' and I paraded around in a regal pose feeling 'clever', 'intelligent' and ever so 'righteous'. From my new intellectual pedestal, I even began to send condescending stares at the less fortunate girls who had to drudge their way daily to less reputed schools, feeling mightily proud and a shade above everybody else.

Before departing for school, I rushed and jostled my way to stand in line, almost hyper-ventilating with pride. I was holding Maryse's hand, and we both smiled in delight. Very briefly, however, my thoughts were directed one more time— and perhaps one last time—to *Mlle la Directrice*. What moral story would she be reading on that glorious morning? And...most importantly...who would she pick on now that I had gone? Her unfortunate habit had not bothered me all that much really, for I understood the cause of it. Indeed, right until the end, I had remained a total mystery to her, an unfathomable enigma, rather like a mathematical theorem of *Fermat* proportion which, despite all her knowledge and expertise, she had not been able to solve. How could this little snot from the orphanage be doing so well when all she did all day long was to daydream? Mindful of her somewhat violent temper, I never dared say anything back, but I used to look at her with a hint of *schadenfreude* glinting in my eyes, every time she turned apoplectic with anger as my rapid progress, yet again, defeated her worse than low expectations.

*

L'Ecole Notre Dame was a much bigger school with rows of classrooms on each of its two floors. When the bell went, there was an almighty shuffle as everyone hurried to line up inside their respective classes. Unfortunately, nobody had thought of telling me which classroom I was to join, and when all the girls had filed into the building silently, I found myself standing in the playground, all alone...or not quite. Claire was there too, looking equally lost. One of the nuns spotted us and rushed towards us with a big smile. Still wary of most adults, I did not know what to make of her spontaneous smile, though it did reassure me a little. Would this be, at last, the exciting beginning I had expected when I started school back at *Sainte Germaine*?

The nun made her approach in her long black robes that flowed freely around her, but strangely enough, instead of her appearance reminding me of the dark angels—those that work alongside Satan—her whole demeanour put me at ease. Perhaps it was the absence of the cumbersome white cornet that made her look less threatening, for on her head—unlike all the nuns I had so far met—she wore a very long black veil. But, quite beside that, not many adults ever bothered to smile, and I felt her welcome to be truly genuine.

"What are your names?" She asked in a friendly tone.

We duly obliged and gave our names.

"And how old are you?"

I was stumped. I did not know what to say. All I knew was that I was over seven because I had done my first Communion, but it seemed such a long time ago that I was not sure where I stood on the timeline. Which number had I reached? Fortunately, Claire had a better idea, so she replied first.

"I'm nine."

That did not help me. Claire was taller than me, so I had always assumed that she was older, but seizing my chance, I parroted: "I'm nine too…" not knowing exactly how close or far I was to being that age, but that little insignificant detail bothered me much less than having to admit that I did not know how old I was.

The nun consulted her various lists pensively, then finally said: "Come with me."

She led us towards the stairs to the floor above. At the top of the stairs, we came to a long corridor that appeared endless and which smelt strongly of something rubbery, though I did not know what.

The nun caught my puzzled expression and explained:

"We've just had new lino laid down during the summer holidays. It does smell a bit, doesn't it?" She stated with a ready smile.

She opened the first door and ushered Claire in. Then we moved to the next door down where she introduced me to the teacher.

"Mlle Claire, I have a new pupil for you, this is Martha Bertrand."

A sea of subdued faces turned towards me. All of a sudden, I felt rather self-conscious, below task and below par. All the pupils, quietly sitting at their desks in their nice pristine clothes and neat hairstyles, looked too good for me. What if I was not nine? What if I was only eight? I would not be able to keep up and I would end up languishing at the bottom of the class. The thought made me nervous, and the more I dwelled upon it, the more I convinced myself that I was definitely in a class too high for my age and my ability—but it was too late to retreat now.

Mlle Claire raised her head from her elevated desk and stared at me with her small beady eyes. The rigid layout of her angular features, separated only by a pair of thin lips, spelt nothing but strictness and discipline. I watched her scrawny hand point towards the window.

"Thank you, Sister."

Then looking at me straight in the eyes, she commanded: "Go and sit over there, by the window."

I had never felt more awkward than at that moment when I had to weave my way around the tight-fitting rows of desks, under the watchful gaze of my new classmates. From my clothes, they would be able to tell straight away that I was from the orphanage and they would probably not want to have anything to do with me, let alone befriend me.

After I had reached my desk, I threw a quick glance around the classroom. There was no one else in the class from *Saint Vincent,* and strangely enough, this came as some kind of relief for here, lost in the midst of conscientious and neat-looking girls, I would be able to forget *that* tenebrous place where I came from, with all its horrid people.

I had never been in such a large classroom with so many pupils before and, immediately, felt hopeful that in a class of forty, I would not be picked on too often.

Outside, in the middle of the playground stood a magnificent chestnut tree so large that its branches threw their playful shadows right across the yard. If I could no longer seek solace in the comforting presence of the ivy wall, I now had for company a huge, majestic tree that extended its strong, solid arms towards me, and I felt safe. I noticed that the window was held slightly ajar, and in my first moment of inattention, I took a deep breath, taking in as much of the autumn air as I could, filling my lungs with a new bliss and a new happiness, knowing that at last, I had found my very own haven of peace.

Mlle Claire was indeed strict, but she rewarded good work in equal measure. At the end of each day, she named the girls whose behaviour had been exemplary and gave them a token; ten tokens could be swapped for a saintly picture. At the end of each week, she would collect all the tokens back and start the process all over again the following Monday, pencilling in her mark book how many tokens each pupil had managed to win.

The most exciting thing to happen so far was the music lessons that we had once a fortnight, and which was broadcast on the radio at three o'clock precisely. On those days, after the afternoon break, Mlle Claire would bring in her wireless, position it on the edge of her desk, and we would wait with our arms folded on the desks for the lesson to begin. The man's voice would first tell us to sit up very straight and clear our throats in order to *dégager la voix*. Then he would lead us along the musical scale which we had to sing after him, and on hot summer's days, when all the windows had been flung open, all one could hear was the uniform sound of children's voices rising up and down the musical scale in a synchronised harmonious wave. Once we had practised sufficiently, the voice would introduce a piece of music with its composer, and in this way, our ears were cajoled and soothed in a creative euphony that belonged to Beethoven, Chopin, Litz, Mozart, Schubert, Schumann, and many others. It was a favourite time of mine during which everything stood still while the gentle rustling of leaves mingled with the beautiful notes cascading from the open windows into a maelstrom of musical harmony. I was enthralled, transported in a new dimension where music had replaced the common word and created a new form of dialogue totally unfamiliar to me, but which had me riveted and glued to my seat. As I listened to the harmonious notes floating in the peaceful atmosphere, I saw Debussy's Sea with palm trees swaying on the edge of an ocean. I saw pirates and boats and deserted islands, and in the middle of the ocean, I saw Mozart's Magic Flute being played by mermaids, wooing unfortunate mariners lost in the high seas, and I saw Schubert's Trout wriggling about in a fast flowing torrent raging through a thick jungle somewhere, though I did not know where. These were all too rare moments of bliss in its purest form, and if the musical pieces had come with a story, I would have grown, convinced that here, in my new school, I had caught a glimpse of God's paradise.

*

Now, the time had come for our first reports. I dreaded

to think where I stood among the thirty-nine other pupils, all so immaculately dressed and all looking so much cleverer than me. On those Fridays, everybody behaved even better than usual, and in the long corridor outside, there was an expectant hush as we waited for the Mother Superior to arrive in order to distribute the results of our work.

That first time, I watched the Mother Superior float into our classroom, her long black veil skimming along the blackboard. She sat at Mlle Claire's desk while the teacher stood beside her, her hands clasped righteously together. The names were read and the reports given in reverse order of merit. The first twenty names were called; my name was not among them. Thank goodness, I thought. I could settle with being among the top twenty, but not the bottom twenty. Now, I was beginning to fidget nervously. In a sudden flash of bare ambition, I decided that I did not want my name to be called in the next ten either. The Mother Superior continued to reel out the names unaware of my growing anxiety. She had complimented number ten and now she was calling: "*Neuvième*: Martha Bertrand."

I cringed...or I think I did. It was better than I had expected, but still not good enough for me, not when I had hovered between first and third place back at *Sainte Germaine*. Admittedly, there were less of us there, but while I was already picturing Nadine laughing and taunting me, pointing her finger at me and chanting: "You're ninth...you're ninth...and I am first...", I saw Mlle Claire tilt her head and say almost in a whisper: "Well done, Martha..."

I could not believe it. Here was the worse school result I had ever had, and for the first time in my life, I was actually being praised. Adults really did baffle me. I replied with a quirky smile, embarrassed by a compliment I felt I did not deserve. Fortunately, I did not let it go to my head or expect further praises for, as the year wore on and I eventually made it to the top of the class several times over, I never again received another compliment. Was it because I blotted my copybook by not having the right P.E. kit?

"Martha Bertrand, where are your gym shoes?" Was the constant question that rang in my ears every time we had a P.E. lesson.

Unfortunately, I was too embarrassed to admit that I did not have any. So, week after week, I had to play the forgetful, totally disorganised child and reply:

"Sorry Miss, I forgot…"

"Again! Go and stand over there."

And, week after week, I was left to ruminate on the playground bench, looking bored and dejected. The P.E. teacher was a short and dumpy woman with a friendly manner, and if she had to punish me, it was only because she was following the rules rigidly, thereby acting in all fairness towards the other girls who conscientiously followed all her instructions. One day, however, without giving any explanation, she relented.

"You'll just have to do the exercises in your shoes, then…"

She was quite willing to make allowances whenever she could, for in me, she saw a raw potential sharpened by a slight competitive edge which she longed to tame in her after-school gym club, but girls from *Saint Vincent* were not allowed to join clubs. It cost money and who was going to pay? This left me uncertain as to how much I could actually achieve, and despite my glowing reports, I was never exactly sure how good I was. In fact, I had started to believe that the placing system was a bit of a lottery. With nobody to point out to me what exactly I was doing right, I did not understand how I ended up being top of the class. I thought I was just being lucky. Then, one day, in the playground, I overheard some girls boast to each other: "My dad helped me with my maths problem...", "And my mum helped me do my homework..."

The comments, caught quite by chance, made me prick up my ears. From the corner of my eye, I observed the small group and noted that these particular girls were all in the top ten. All of a sudden, I felt absolutely wonderful. Up until now, their neat appearance and cool confidence had always intimidated me. Now, I was able to look at them, face on, feeling oh...so superior. After I had looked them up and down with a condescending glare, I threw my shoulders back and swaggered away from them, hands in pockets and my head held up high, and when I had reached a distance not too far away from them, I sneered under my breath: 'Well, I'm top of the class...and nobody helped me!'

Upon our return to the Junior Section, we would place our reports in a neat pile on the table by the door...and hope for the best, for I soon discovered that Sister Marie-Catherine was obsessed with badness and wickedness. Almost everyday, usually at lunch time, her dark figure would loom in the doorway like the spectre of death. If she was in a particularly bad mood, she would position herself in the middle of the refectory and hail:

"You are all sinners and you must repent!"

So we had to pray. Jerking her wide cornet like a mad hen, she would scour our faces, looking for something bad, something that would make her point the finger, so that she could proceed to thrashing the devil out of our wicked souls. On that particular day, she remembered the reports.

"Yes, the reports!" She exclaimed wagging a threatening finger towards the ceiling as she stormed out, leaving an atmosphere of petrified gloom in her wake.

In the room next door, we could hear her rummage through the pile of reports like a possessed woman, and a few minutes later, she reappeared in the refectory brandishing a handful of shameful results. That was the moment when we would have done anything to disappear from the face of the earth. She had singled out the culprits and, one by one, she grabbed them by the hair and dragged them in the central alley, screaming, shouting and kicking:

"How dare you come back with such a bad report?" She yelled, lashing out at her defenceless victim. "Don't you ever dare come back with such a bad report again, you bad, lazy, useless girl!"

Then, without taking the time to catch her breath, she immediately threw herself onto her next victim and yelled more insults at her.

"I'm going to make an example of you, you cretin, imbecile, stupid girl!"

And as the blows rained together with the insults, the poor victims covered their heads and rolled themselves into a ball so as to protect the more vulnerable parts of their bodies from the punishing blows. Time and time again, they wriggled in pain and whimpered in despair, but no matter how bruised their bodies were, I was amazed to see that they very rarely cried.

The rest of us sat bold upright on our benches, terrorised, petrified, and too afraid to move. I wanted to close my eyes and cover my ears, but the slightest movement would have drawn attention to me, so I sat paralysed on my seat, my gaze immovably fixed on the table in front of me, barely able to breathe.

Once all the lazy demons had been thrashed out of her last victim, the nun straightened herself up, brushed her habit with a swift movement of the arm and declared haughtily:

"Who loves well, chastises well!" putting as much vigour in her quote as she did in her beatings. Then, she flung the door open and disappeared.

The atmosphere remained tense for a good few minutes after her departure. The supervisors paced up and down the refectory, darting aggressive glances at us, with pen and paper at the ready to sully our names with big black crosses.

When we were eventually allowed out, we shuffled past the supervisors as quietly as if we were in a mortuary. Outside, I overheard several girls exclaim: "Phew! She did not pick on me."

I knew that I was not likely to be picked on either, but right now, my thoughts were with Maryse, for if anything did happen to her, I would be totally powerless to protect her.

CHAPTER X

The leaves on the chestnut tree turned a rustic brown, and as they weaved about and slowly fell on the ground sprayed with tepid rain, the autumnal wind swirled and gathered them in small untidy clusters. From the classroom window, I could hear them rustle as they skimmed just above the ground in hurried swirls; and when the brass bell eventually signalled the beginning of morning break, we spilled out of the building and went straight for them, plunging in and dispersing the leaves with our hands and feet—ruining the gardener's hard labour to keep the playground swept clean.

The morning mist was scented with the wonderful smell of burning leaves, and a short distance away, the church carillon chimed relentlessly the passing of time, full of memories that were our lives then, a childhood imprinted on our minds like a distant dream that had been—which could have been better or worse—but which we knew could have been simply wonderful.

School remained my only haven of peace where the loudest noise came from our muffled footsteps on the lino. The nuns moved furtively like ephemeral angels chasing their own shadows, and the teacher's words rang soothingly over our heads, dissecting with relish the more difficult words in the dictations, imparting her general knowledge with care and teasing our brains without ever getting angry. This was like being back in my secluded locker, except that this time, I was sharing my space with thirty-nine other girls. The imposed silence and the pictorial view afforded from the window seemed the perfect backdrop for my perpetual daydreams.

Back in the Junior Section, we continued to march in silence. At times, our steps were muffled by the snow, or clip-clopped in the rain. Sometimes, we had to duck without losing the tempo to avoid bats or swallows swooping low before returning to their nests wedged in the cornices of the first floor, a whiff away from the nuns' living quarters. And we marched… endlessly…mindlessly…and as our feet pounded rhythmically on the ground, we observed each other from the corners of our eyes. Standing close, so very close to one another, we longed for the light touch of a hand, a warm embrace, an affectionate smile, but strictly forbidden to touch, speak or interact, we continued to march in our own little space within its invisible walls where we would remain forever unloved, untouched, and uninvolved…marching…still marching…always marching.

There was, however, the occasional reprieve, and even light-hearted moments which we held on to like life rafts. However, with all the best will in the world, it was only possible to hold on to one raft at a time—and mine was Maryse.

These short reprieves usually coincided with a religious feast during which we were allowed to have a little fun, and behave almost like normal children. The first of these came on the feast of Sainte Catherine. Of all the saints and martyrs I had read about so far, none had been a woman. Now, I was hearing about Saint Catherine who was not only a saint, but she was a martyr too. I did not know anything about her saintly deeds, but there was one thing for sure, I definitely did not want to know how she came to die. Her name, however, made me ponder. Did that make Sister Marie-Catherine a saint too? Was the oppressive regime she had imposed around her a kind of personal redemption, her chosen Calvary along which she would drag us with her towards sainthood? Had she somehow reasoned that there had to be more suffering, more thrashing of souls, in order to begin to qualify as a saint or a martyr? The next time Sister Marie-Catherine swept ominously into the refectory, I studied her face and analysed the tortured expression that contorted her features, and I wondered if she looked anything like Sainte Catherine. I could not tell, but to this day, I cannot hear Sainte Catherine's name without thinking of Sister Marie-Catherine, even if I can no longer visualise her face, and I wonder if she is standing next to God up there in Heaven or rotting somewhere—and God only knows where—in her own hell.

If we, children, did not know how to forgive, we were quick to forget, and on 25th November, we danced with gay abandon to the feast of Sainte Catherine, in the communal playroom, which had now acquired a big black and white television, a gift from the mayor to whom I remember presenting a huge bouquet of flowers—almost as big as me—to say thank you on behalf of the whole orphanage. I had been picked on that occasion because I had been considered the girl the most *dégourdie*.

Saint Catherine's day was a poignant feast to celebrate all the spinsters in the world. Indeed, the supervisors had told us, in no uncertain terms, that if a young woman was not married by her 24th birthday, she would stay an old maid for the rest of her life, and fearing to be left unclaimed, unwanted, and unlocked in some wedding vows, we danced and twirled madly, willing out all the Princes Charming of our dreams to come and rescue us from a fate of eternal dereliction.

The 6th of December, the feast of St Nicholas, was marked by the putting up of the Christmas tree. Sitting on the benches in the refectory, we watched, with envy, the supervisors wrestle with long strips of glittering tinsels, shiny coloured baubles and...real candles—and that was not all. We were treated to a rare trip to the local cinema where we were introduced to the magic of Disney. However, before the film began, a man dressed up as Saint Nicolas walked up and down the aisles carrying a golden shaft closely followed by his sidekick, *le Père Fouettard*, a sorcerer kind of character brandishing a menacing whip which he would not hesitate to use if you had been bad. Marching pompously among the rows, Saint Nicolas would stop at random and ask:

"Have you been good?"

As soon as he stopped, the old man in rags would rush to his side to listen to the answer. If the reply fitted the child's angelic face, they would both move on with a grunt and a nod of the head. However, they were there to entertain, and every now and again, they would pretend to refute a child's polite answer—usually a boy—and the *Père Fouettard* would shake his whip above the boy's head and threaten a good thrashing.

"And we'll be back next year to check that your behaviour has improved!"

The old man's voice thundered as the rest of the audience squealed in pretend fear while the boy shielded his head with his arms and giggled fearlessly. The fear expressed in our playful screams was not entirely faked, for we genuinely believed that the duo would return to ask the same questions to the very same children. So we would have to behave...at all times.

Once Saint Nicolas and *Le Père Fouettard* had departed, the manager of the cinema jumped on the stage in front of the screen and requested complete silence so that the film could begin. The effect was instant, and the auditorium almost instantly fell into an expectant silence. Soon after, the lights went out and the red velvet curtains opened slowly to the music of Cinderella. I was enthralled, spellbound by the beauty, the singing, and all the glitter. I became totally captivated by the characters and the magic of the story. In fact, I was so transfixed by it all that I felt sure I had held my breath all through the film. It was pure magic, and the wonderful memories of the film left me spellbound for days afterwards. Poor Cinderella, so beautiful, so delicate, so defenceless, was at the complete mercy of her stepsisters and stepmother and there was nothing she could do about it until she met the prince. How wonderful. She had found happiness without a single fight or a single drop of blood having been shed. Peace and harmony...That's all I ever wanted.

On our way back to *Saint Vincent*, we managed to piece together all the lyrics because, more than ever before, I, too, hoped that one day, a beautiful prince would come to my rescue. I lingered over the lyrics and sang the songs heartily in a determined attempt to keep the dream alive. From then on, my daydreams appeared more colourful, often wrapped up in a melodious tune surrounded by singing mice, and sprinkled copiously with handfuls of glittering magic sand.

That was not all. A rumour was now flying around that we had been invited to the town hall for an afternoon of entertainment. Sister Marie-Catherine aside, I was beginning to feel that being in the Junior Section was not that bad after all. I could not wait, Maryse could not wait, and at break, we let our excitement burst out into the playground where our squeals of delight echoed all around the walls so raucously that a nun eventually poked her head out from one of the windows on the first floor and pleaded: "Not so much noise, girls!"

Later, when someone shouted: *"rassemblement!"*, we rushed to form our lines, and as we marched on the spot, our heads held up high, lifting our feet and arms vigorously, we let our imaginations transport us away somewhere in a glittering room lit with crystal chandeliers and lined with strong courageous soldiers who would protect us from the evil supervisors. I sighed with joy in anticipation, wondering how long it would be before this extraordinary event.

Sister Marie-Catherine immediately set about to prepare us for the occasion. As we sat on the benches in the cold refectory, we rehearsed the popular carols with which we would greet the arrival of Baby Jesus. I learnt the words diligently, because for me, this was still the most exciting event of the year.

The nun walked up and down the central alley, selecting girls by pointing at them to gather a small group to sing to the mayor and his retinue. Frightened to be picked, girls bowed their heads in the hope that Sister Marie-Catherine would not notice them, or slid right down on the bench to make themselves as small as possible.

But, we could not all escape. As we stood to attention in the small playroom, next door to the refectory, we sang the best we could with Sister Marie-Catherine beating the gentle tempo rigidly with a firm hand. After a few minutes, her eyes flared up, her face froze into a grimace, and her lips stiffened up. Not happy with our performance, she scoured our faces with predatory eyes. She was on the warpath and she was looking for a victim. Suddenly, her long finger jerked out in front of us, nearly scratching the end of my nose, and she screamed: "You!" as she pointed directly in the face of a girl standing two rows behind me.

The victim, a tallish girl with fair hair, had such a fright that she fainted. Not at all put off by the girl's unexpected reaction, Sister Marie-Catherine jostled us brusquely out of the way and fell upon her poor victim like a possessed woman, ranting and cursing at the lifeless body incapable of responding to her threats and her commands.

"You'd better stop pretending right now! You're not fooling me!"

She was shouting, slapping the girl mercilessly. Eventually, the girl came to and began to sob uncontrollably, trying to shield her face to fend off further blows. But, Sister Marie-Catherine was very determined and never defeated. She screamed harder and the louder her voice rose, the louder her victim sobbed. In the end, the tormentor was becoming the tormented and, feeling her strength weaken, the nun rasped: "Take her outside! The fresh air will calm her!" to the two girls who were standing on either side, as rigid as two wooden soldiers.

Without a word, the girls picked up Sylvie and helped her to get back on her feet before dragging her away...gently.

During the whole scene, I dared not move. I only threw a quick glance behind me when I heard the heavy thump on the floor to see which girl had fallen, but from the moment Sister Marie-Catherine shot forward and lunged towards the girl like a demonic shrew, I was so frightened that I only just about managed to breathe.

The calm returned. I fixed my gaze firmly on the red tiles and, with my fingers fidgeting nervously behind my back, I waited for the next command.

"All right! Backs straight! Heads up! Shoulders back and let's start again! This time, I want to hear every single one of you and I want to hear the words...the *correct* words!" She blasted, wagging her menacing finger at us.

I did not want to sing anymore, but fearing the consequences, I sang louder, all the while wondering why in the past Sister Bénédicte had always urged us to 'grow up', pushing us inexorably towards the fierce claws of a lioness out of control. Was she aware of how painful it would be? Did she know how Sister Marie-Catherine went about to make us 'grow up'?

The worse thing about the Junior Section was that there were no hidden corners, no secret hide-outs where I could seek refuge and distance myself from the ruthless regime of Sister Marie-Catherine. Worse still, there was not a single book which would take me away from it all. There was nothing, absolutely nothing I could use as a safe haven, not even the locker room which was just a draughty place, a cold quadrangle stuck on the edge of the building that served as the back entrance to the refectory. I was trapped like a bird without wings, and the only thing that kept me going was the muted solidarity of other girls in the same plight as me. I often tried to catch their eyes in an attempt to guess what they were thinking, and how they felt, but their imposed silence was not always easy to interpret, and whilst everybody else appeared to be a lot stronger, a lot more resilient, I was often left to feel weak and inadequate, afraid to do or say anything, and forced to seek refuge in Maryse's playful cynicism, of which thankfully she had plenty.

*

Outside, darkness had befallen upon the Christmas lights. The pearly strings of multicoloured bulbs guided our steps towards the town hall. In the cold frosty night, we found it shimmering through the warm haze of a yellow glow bursting out of its tall chequered windows and, for a few precious moments, I was able to lose myself in the magic of Christmas. I could feel myself flying to a distant land where I spotted a tiny crib filled with strong-scented straw — just like the straw

I had smelt at Sangatte—where a little baby lay. He looked at me and smiled. I smiled in return, and putting my hands together in awe of the little infant, I murmured softly: "At last, Jesus, you've arrived!"

A sharp nudge from Maryse brought me back abruptly to the town hall and together, we climbed the large open staircase sweeping majestically above the twinkling lights of a giant Christmas tree. The whole building smelt of Christmas: sweet brioches, juicy tangerines, and hot chocolate. The younger girls from the Baby Section were already seated around a long table, busily tucking into a feast of large brioches dipped into generous bowls of hot chocolate. I caught a glimpse of the radiant faces of Sister Bénédicte and Sister Thérèse glowing in the multicoloured lights, while they nodded their cornets excitedly as they exchanged happy words among themselves and the younger children. For a brief second, I had a vision of a vagrant girl dressed in rags looking at a Christmas feast through an illuminated window as the snow fell around her. In another flash, I glimpsed myself back in the Baby Section, my hands together praying fervently to Baby Jesus in front of the nativity scene. It was a wonderful feeling and I stared happily at the glorious scene. Suddenly, someone tugged at my sleeve and the whole vision disappeared.

"Come on, Martha, let's go and sit over there, near the basket of brioches..."

Maryse dragged me towards the middle of the long table covered with a white tablecloth and sprinkled with small Christmas decorations. I had been so used to eating frugal portions that I could finish neither the brioche nor the hot chocolate. My stomach felt uncomfortably full and I slumped on my chair waiting with trepidation to see what would happen next.

The entertainment soon began. A magician made his assistant disappear and we gasped in horror as his guillotine fell with a clacking sound on his assistant's head, leaving it intact, but cutting in half the carrot dangling underneath it. Then the clowns came on. Oh no…not the clowns, I thought, closing my eyes, but I opened them again, purposely diverting my gaze towards the Christmas tree, at the sparkling lights, at the shimmering tinsels, in an effort to fill my mind with blissful pictures that I hoped would return to comfort me in my dreams. When the brightly-coloured clowns left the makeshift stage, their mentor Pierrot returned. As soon as the lights dimmed, he emerged from the blackened wing, blowing a lonely tune on his gleaming trumpet. The spotlight shone white on his sparkling suit, and to avoid his ghostly stare, I closed my eyes, covered my ears, and tried to concentrate on happier scenes…but in vain.

That night, my dreams took me back to the First Floor of the Baby Section where the clowns chased me relentlessly, round and round. I knew I was dreaming, yet I could not escape, because I did not know how to wake up. I seemed to be stuck in a parallel dimension where people existed, but without ever being able to cross the line, trapped as they were in a time warp I could not escape. I heard myself scream: "I want to wake up! I want to wake up!"

But the clowns were right there, standing very close to me. With their oversized smiles, big red noses, and contorted faces, they lurched forward, extending their enormous hands ready to grab me. I screamed…then I woke up…in the big dormitory where I could hear nothing but the regular breathing of the other girls asleep. I got up and went into the corridor where the coal burner was purring gently. I sat in front of the fire shivering, watching the glowing cinders slowly die out and when it got too cold, I went back to bed. As I passed the other girls asleep, I looked at Roberte's angelic face and wondered if she ever had any nightmares.

Father Christmas would not be calling here. Sister Benedicte had declared long ago that he did not exist, so no one even bothered to mention him. By contrast, at school all the girls were beside themselves with excitement, citing long lists of unimaginable treats. I used to stare at their flushed faces and rejoice with them at the impossible wishes they had made, taking comfort in the thought that at least, *they* would be happy.

On Christmas Day, girls were allowed to go home after mass. It was a very quiet day, and the handful of us left behind were allowed to play in the small room next to the refectory. A few toys had been scattered over the floor and we were left to play quietly without having to worry about threats or retribution. I did not see any books, so I picked up a tube of transparent coloured beads, and soon became totally captivated by their sparkle and their crystal-like brilliance. I shone them against the light and studied intently the beautiful rays twinkling in my eyes. They were magic beads, I decreed, the very same that the Seven Dwarves extracted from their secret mine somewhere in a mysterious kingdom—precious stones fit for a royal crown that one day a prince would wear as he walked majestically towards the altar where his future bride waited patiently in her resplendent beauty. The coloured beads had become crystal balls in which I could see beauty shine through an aura of peace and harmony. But, the tableau was not quite complete; there was one vital element missing: music.

Meanwhile, Sister Marie-Catherine was sitting at the big table, in no mood to interfere, and busied herself with writing, mending, thinking, and sometimes, mumbling to herself. I had never seen her in such a light-hearted mood, and I even thought that for once, she looked quite normal.

My own blessing was that so far, I had managed to escape the full force of her uncontrollable rages. My school reports did not justify it, and being small in stature, I could easily make myself invisible, except on occasions when marching up and down the refectory, and in desperate need to vent her frustration and anger caused by some unknown grief, Sister Marie-Catherine's hand would ricochet from head to head, as she slapped whomever happened to be within her reach. To our dismay, she was armed with an inexhaustible source of strength and energy—which she hailed from God, begging Him 'to give her strength'—which meant that she could 'give it' even when there were several of us queuing to 'receive it', as on that occasion when several of us walked back from school without putting our hoods on despite the pouring rain. We wanted to feel the cool droplets run down on our warm skin, and enjoy the smooth sensation of the gentle rain soothe our flushed cheeks. As a result, we got soaked and we got thrashed. That was the order of things with Sister Marie-Catherine, and now, she was standing at the top of the refectory, flanked by two supervisors for extra support, as she proceeded to beat some common sense into our weak and wet bodies.

Assailed by a systematic violence which we did not understand, we had learned to protect ourselves by retreating behind a wall of silence, and during these long silent spells, I was thinking, pondering, questioning the legitimacy of adults' behaviour. If they acted on behalf of God, and this was God's will, then I was not sure I wanted to be part of His flock anymore. Life would be a great deal more bearable without His divine intervention. And, why should He have chosen a devotee like Sister Marie-Catherine to look after the children of

God, so pure and innocent that even Pope John XXIII wanted them and them alone by his side? But, here lay the crux of the matter. In the eyes of Sister Marie-Catherine, we were neither pure nor innocent; her blackened heart could not see the purity in ours. We were all sinners and, for this, we had to repent… daily…physically and spiritually.

In the name of God, we had to suffer…In the name of God, we had to repent…In the name of God, we had to pray to purify our souls of sins we did not understand, and sins we did not commit. And the more they made us feel bad, wicked, and unworthy, the more I felt good, saintly, and beyond reproach. No longer willing to submit to an eternal life of guilt, seeking in vain a redemption we were too wicked to receive, I gradually began to shut my mind to the castigating sermons we were subjected to every day. I no longer wanted to hear about our badness and wickedness; I no longer wanted to be forced to stare at the dark, evil side of ruthless beings intent on invading our innocent lives to present a doomed picture with us in the middle. My only salvation, I reasoned, would be to distance myself from God, because I, Martha Bertrand, was no martyr, and I had no desire to come to a gruesome end.

The warm feeling bestowed upon me by the love of God had gone. In church, I recited the prayers dutifully, but without religious fervour. I became easily distracted. When Maryse pointed at something amusing like a hat sitting askew on an old lady's head, or drew my attention to the frail quivering voices of old spinsters and widows as they sang the hymns on the highest pitch, or when a particular priest tortured by an incredible stutter had to read the lesson, our little bodies shook with laughter. And while we desperately tried to muffle our irresistible giggles in the holy pages of our missals, I could feel Sister Marie-Catherine's hawk eyes drill in the back of my neck.

Noticing a change in my overall behaviour, other girls began to accuse Maryse of leading me astray. But, I was a willing participant, and I would readily watch her and follow her, just so that I could see a brighter, lighter picture, more bearable, more forgiving, more enlightening, and in which someone at least did smile.

Just as I suspected, our misdemeanours did not go unnoticed; at the end of the service, Sister Marie-Catherine came over, and when I spotted her dark shadow looming over us, I looked back at her with a stare full of contempt. For the first time, I felt no fear, because we were in a public place, a place which happened to be the House of God. Surely, she would not dare.

I instinctively flinched, however, when she bent over and whispered angrily:

"You two are staying for the next service!"

I could not believe it. Sitting for an hour in a cold church chanting and reciting words in an incomprehensible language was bad enough, but the next service was the main service and lasted for at least an hour and a half. I could not bear the thought. And...oh no, not the sermon...the sermon was always the worse...we would have to sit through yet another interminable boring sermon, and God...if the priest with the terrible stammer was picked to deliver the sermon, I was finished. I knew I would never be able to keep a straight face, not with Maryse sitting next to me. My soul would be damned forever with no hope of redemption, and I would be banished to Hell for eternity. I sunk in my chair, folded my arms in a huff, and avoided any eye contact with Maryse.

In my more thoughtful moments, however, I had often stared at the pure, white cloth laid out on the altar, at the ornate candelabras casting their golden glow on either side of the cross with their ardent flames reigniting the love of God that I was no longer prepared to acknowledge, and I often wondered how the adults in charge felt every time they went to church and came face-to-face with God. Did their conscience prick a little and did they have the courage to look at Jesus on the cross and pray for their own salvation when they were so busy behind His back condemning us to our own irremediable damnation? I still wonder.

As I walked back from church to *Saint Vincent*, I tried to draw Maryse into the debate of the state of our supervisors' conscience. Did they pray? And, in their prayers, did they feel obliged to ask for forgiveness? Were they acting with full intent or was it a case of, as Jesus stated on the cross, 'Forgive them for they know not what they do'? But Maryse was not prepared to waste her intellectual energy on a matter that was, to her, as clear cut as Judas's treason: 'Let them go to hell with their warts and all!'

That winter was particularly harsh, and the ground was covered with patches of black ice. As we made our way back to *Saint Vincent*, I failed to see a particular patch of ice in front of me and I slid on it and fell. This would have been of no consequence if my missal had not slipped out of my hand and disappeared through the cellar grid of the chemist that stood on the corner of the main street. For a few moments, I stared at the missal wondering how I could possibly retrieve it. With Maryse's help, I tried to lift the iron grid, but it was cemented to the ground.

"What am I going to do?" I asked with anguish.

"You're gonna have to tell Annie Brenn," Maryse replied placidly.

"Are you mad? She'll tell Sister Marie-Catherine and I'll be in real trouble!"

"They're going to find out anyway when they collect the missals and yours won't be there..."

"Yeah...but I still don't have to tell her. They might not even notice."

"They're all numbered, silly, so they're bound to find out. If you say it now, by the time we get back to *Saint Vincent*, Annie Brenn may have forgotten about it."

Maryse's suggestion made perfect sense, so I swiftly moved through the crocodile file and levelled myself with the supervisor who was still wearing the white lace veil she always wore every time she went to church.

"Mlle Brenn...I've dropped my missal and it fell through the grid outside the chemist."

"Oh well, you're in trouble now, aren't you."

"But it wasn't my fault. I slid on the ice and I fell."

"You were messing about as usual! Wait until I tell Sister Marie-Catherine..." She replied with glee.

"I wasn't! It was an accident!"

"She won't believe that. You're always messing about."

"You don't have to tell her." I pleaded.

"I have to. Besides, she'll find out anyway when you haven't got a missal to hand back."

"What is she going to do?"

"It depends on her mood. She might slap you, or make an example of you...in the refectory as usual..."

I could feel cramps beginning to seize my tummy. What was I going to do? I could hide in the locker room or lock myself in the toilets...but I could not stay there forever, and they would be waiting for me to come out...and they would hit harder because I had tried to slip away. No, I had to accept the inevitable truth: there was no way out.

I looked up at Annie Brenn and wondered if she might

just be playing games. There was no doubt in my mind that she wanted to see me quiver and quake in my shoes. She wanted to enjoy the mental agony she was putting me through, and was already relishing the moment when I would have to face Sister Marie-Catherine and tell her I did not have a missal to hand back.

"They cost a lot of money, you know..."

She threw that last salve as if to finish the job, like the final *coup de grace* delivered, not out of mercy, but in cold blood for her own enjoyment, but it missed me by a mile, for I did not know what money was. I had never seen it, although I had heard its light clinking sound tinkling around the church as the collection baskets were passed around to plump up the church's funds. In History lessons, I had learnt that the Church was richer than the State, and while the coins rebounded more heavily in the baskets as they moved further and further away, I could easily deduce where all the gold, jewels and precious stones had come from, but none of these riches could help me right now. Besides, what was the point of all these generous donations if they could not help the children of God?

Back at *Saint Vincent*, the girls dropped their missals on the usual table in the refectory before spilling out onto the playground. As I was about to disappear, Annie Brenn grabbed me by the scruff of the neck and held me firmly in place. Maryse threw a helpless glance at me before disappearing too.

Executing what she felt was her duty, Annie Brenn pushed me towards Sister Marie-Catherine like a hangman forces a prisoner towards the gallows.

"Go on! Tell Sister what you've done!"

In the past, I had been called cheeky, mischievous, insolent, arrogant, and lazy, but I had never committed an offence serious enough to warrant a direct confrontation with the dreaded nun. Now, for the first time ever, I was being held up in front of the enemy. I could feel all the blood in my head drain away and my lips went numb. I looked at Sister Marie-Catherine and stared at her blue eyes, searching for the tiniest hint of mercy that would spare me a good old beating.

Sister Marie-Catherine looked back at me with a bland expression that gave nothing away of the kind of mood she was in; I feared the worse.

"Come on, girl, I don't have all day!" She rasped.

Annie Brenn shook my shoulder even more brusquely.

"You heard, Martha Bertrand, so tell Sister!" She ordered, feeling emboldened by the powerful presence of our common enemy for, even if she was the last to acknowledge it, we all knew that she feared the nun as much as we did. Right now though, she was feeling all jittery, like a shark caught in a feeding frenzy, looking for blood, my blood, which would invigorate and energise her own derisory power.

"I've lost my missal," I finally managed to mumble.

Sister Marie-Catherine waited for a few seconds while she measured the seriousness of the offence.

"No doubt, she was messing about as usual!" Annie Brenn added, disappointed at the lack of an instant reaction from the nun.

I continued to stare at the nun, watching closely the movement of both her hands, psyching myself up for the inevitable blow. Suddenly, quicker than I had anticipated, Sister Marie-Catherine's hand struck, but instead of the painful stinging slap I had been expecting, her fingers seemed to slide off my face in a half-hearted attempt to hit me. She had missed and she was sure to strike again. Annie Brenn waited eagerly for the second blow. Just like the knitters during the revolution armed with their baskets full of provisions to make sure they would last the day, as they watched avidly the heads of the nobles and aristocrats fall amid the cheers of the crowd, the supervisor was determined not to miss the final execution. And, unlike Sister Marie-Catherine, she had all the time in the world.

"Disappear…silly girl…out of my sight!" Sister Marie-Catherine finally ordered, dismissing me with an indifferent gesture of the hand.

Annie Brenn's jaw hit the floor. She had never witnessed a girl being treated so leniently, especially when that girl happened to be that undisciplined, unruly, insolent Martha Bertrand, and she stood there, her mouth gaping wide and her eyes rolling with disbelief while I scampered away like a scared little rabbit, trying to hide a smile that had suddenly broken out. Poor Annie Brenn, she could never get the last word.

*

There was no school on Thursdays. It was the mid-week break for all schools. To keep us occupied and out of mischief, the morning was spent cleaning the dormitory while the supervisors busied themselves, counting how many crosses each girl had. We were given one broom per dorm to sweep the floor, and old rags to dust the beds, the lockers, the top of the partitions, and the windowsills. Only the windows were left for the supervisors to clean, simply because we could not reach them. Once a month, we had to polish the floorboards, and that was quickly turned into a sliding game, but only if 'the coast was clear'. As we became more enthusiastic in our endeavours, giggling away as we scrubbed the floor, the supervisor appeared and blasted: "Don't forget, Martha Bertrand, you've already got eight crosses!"

And of course, no threats of hers could ever tarnish my

good humour for I really could not care less how many crosses I had, and I was always happy to ignore her ineffective warnings, except that one day, when the supervisor spotted me busily sliding on the planks of wood I had just finished polishing. I watched her tall silhouette march towards me and stop only a foot away from me. In a stern voice, she ordered me to go straight to Sister Marie-Catherine. The nun wanted to see me and she was waiting in the refectory. Instantly, my giggling ceased and my good humour disappeared. An intense fear, so familiar, so powerful, gripped me. I was so terrified that I thought I was about to be sick, and so scared that I could not even gather my thoughts. Oh God…what had I done this time? I was only using my carpet slippers to slide on the freshly polished floor; surely, that was not a criminal offence or one of the mortal sins listed in the Ten Commandments.

I grabbed the wooden rail and descended the stairs like a condemned child walking to her death. Worse still, there would be no one to witness my final moment. I was doomed. At the bottom of the stairs, I sat down on the last wooden step, clutching my burning stomach when a nun happened to pass by.

"What's the matter with you, child, you shouldn't be here…"

I rose up slowly, too nervous to acknowledge her remark. I stopped for a few seconds outside the refectory door, took a deep breath, and pushed it open.

Sister Marie-Catherine was standing as usual at the top of the refectory, leaning casually against the wooden sideboard. Her unusually relaxed posture struck me immediately and made me wonder if this was another of the devil's tricks: the malevolent spirit smiles at you, beckons you to approach with your guard down, and makes you believe that he has nothing against you in order to lure you slowly, but surely into his fire.

I continued my approach slowly, all the while studying the nun's facial expression scrupulously. Still on tender hooks, I studied her eyes, her hands, and again her posture. My legs felt like jelly and I feared they would give way any second. Oh no, I'm going to faint…I mustn't faint…

After my doomed walk, I stood in front of her, calculating with precision how much distance I should leave between her and me so that, should her arm spring into action, it would miss me. I stared into her icy cold eyes, trying to anticipate the moment she would strike, but to my utter amazement, when she looked back at me, her features softened, and when she spoke, lo and behold, her voice was totally devoid of its usual threatening tone.

"So, you're doing well at school," she declared flatly.

I was shocked, so shocked in fact that I forgot to flinch. She had put me through this mental agony and called me here just to talk about my school progress? She had put me through this hell just to tell me something I already knew? And why should she talk about my schoolwork when, so far, no one had ever taken any notice?

"Because you're doing well, your godmother has sent some money and she's asked me to buy you a little something with it. So, is there anything in particular you would like?"

I could not believe what I was hearing, and despite being still in shock, I knew straight away what I wanted.

"Can I have a pair of gym shoes, please?"

All my fears had melted away and all I could think of now was that at long last, I would have a pair of gym shoes for the P.E. lessons. I was already picturing myself running, jumping, sprinting, and skipping in my brand new pair of gym shoes. Teacher would be so impressed.

"All right, Martha Bertrand, off you go now…"

I ran up the stairs two steps at a time, or was it four? In any case, I felt as if I was flying. At the top, I burst into the dormitory feeling as victorious as a soldier who has just cheated death.

I was immediately besieged.

"What did you do?"

"Did you get punished?"

"Did you get a smack?"

And as I walked the whole length of the corridor feeling so important, and oh…so superior, I smiled at the girls, trying to decide whether I should tell them or keep them guessing. It would have been fun to make the moment last, to carry my head higher still instead of seeking refuge behind someone's shadow. I wanted to pretend that I had come through some incredible ordeal, but I was so overwhelmed by the most enormous sense of relief that fabricating a tall story would actually have spoilt this glorious moment for me. So, I told them exactly what happened. Incredibly, no one believed me, and the more I insisted that, God be my witness, this was the entire truth, the more they accused me of having something to hide.

"We'll find out anyway…when you get your punishment."

By the time I got my gym shoes, everybody had forgotten about the incident.

"Why did you get a pair of gym shoes?" Chantal asked.

Feeling quite mischievous and in the mood to cause a stir, I trumpeted:

"Because I'm Sister Marie-Catherine's favourite!"

Then, with a victorious grin, I grabbed Maryse's arm and walked away. Maryse herself did not know what to make of my earth-shattering statement—'fancy my friend being Sister

Marie-Catherine's favourite!' I could almost hear her think—and avid to hear some unthinkable truth, she kept asking: "Is it true? Are you really?"

After we had scrubbed the dorms, the washroom, the toilets, and the stairs, it was time to go to catechism, in the presbytery opposite the church. We were despatched in small groups, and when I looked at ours, I saw Martine C.

"Maryse, Martine C. has been put in our group!" I protested.

It was not her lack of intellectual skills or her unattractive features, with her flapping ears, that I objected to, but rather her limp personality and wailing voice that made her sound as miserable as sin. Maryse was no shining star herself and several times, she had come very close to a public beating in the refectory, but at least she had plenty of redeeming features. For a start, she was the best teacher impersonator I had ever come across and, far more importantly, she made me laugh.

The presbytery was a crumbly old building with dark corridors and dusty rooms. The room itself was so small that all the desks had been pushed together in long lines, so as to allow extra desks to be squeezed in. *L'abbé Jean-Marie* was in charge. He made us write our names on a piece of paper, checked where we were at in our religious journey, and proceeded to examine the parables related to specific times of the year.

Here, everything was done the opposite way to that of the nuns' and the teachers' I knew. The atmosphere was relaxed and amiable, and the priest taught with a bonhomie and patience that stood in stark contrast with the rigid, disciplinarian methods to which I had become so accustomed. What's more, *l'abbé Jean-Marie* actually wanted us to speak *and* participate. It was so unexpected that, at first, tongue-tied, I could not bring myself to say anything...until the priest casually mentioned the name *Yahvé*. I turned to Maryse with a quizzical eye.

"Yahvé? Who is he?"

"I don't know," she whispered back, shrugging her shoulders.

"Now, has anybody got any questions?" *L'abbé Jean-Marie* enquired.

I sheepishly raised my hand and muttered: "Who's Yahvé?"

The priest looked quite shocked by my ignorance.

"But…Yahvé is the name of God…as first mentioned in the book of Genesis…"

I looked back at him, more confused than ever. We had never heard of the book of Genesis, because if we had, we would have known that Genesis was the first book in the Old Testament as described in the Bible. I suddenly had a flashback where I saw myself asking Sister Bénédicte if I could read the Holy Book. It was not long after I had done my first communion, but she had replied:

"You're too young to read the Bible…"

"Why? I've done my first communion, so I have all the knowledge and wisdom I need to read the Bible."

"You! Martha Bertrand…knowledge and wisdom…" She had riled, putting extra emphasis on the word *wisdom*. "Besides, you wouldn't understand it."

"But I understand all the story books…"

She had smiled but said no more. So I had to resign myself to praying to God, Jesus and Christ when, in fact, the only religious concept I could really grasp was the story of Baby Jesus. And now, according to *l'Abbé Jean-Marie*, there was Yahvé too.

"Why is he called Yahvé?" I continued, determined to fathom out the mystery.

"But…" the priest continued, shaking his head in despair, "that's His name in Hebrew."

Maryse and I looked at each other, enlightened with this new wisdom. Then, her hand shot up.

"Are we gonna have to learn Hebrew as well, then?"

L'Abbé Jean-Marie smiled.

"That won't be necessary...as long as you understand who Yahvé is. After all, Hebrew was the language of Jesus."

"So, why is everything in Latin?" another girl asked.

"It's to do with particular events, place and time, but if we start delving too deeply in the *raison d'être* of everything in God's kingdom, we'll never have time to learn what happened to St. John the Baptist's sheep."

"They jumped off the cliff!" One girl chuckled.

We all laughed.

"Wrong sheep," the priest corrected with a smile. Then turning serious again, he added: "Actually, that is quite an interesting lesson with an important message, so I'll tell you the story of Panurge's sheep."

We sat, enthralled, listening to how Panurge, in an act of revenge, had forced the sheep of his arch rival to jump off the cliff. That was supposed to be a lesson on magnanimity and tolerance, on forgiveness and how to turn the other cheek. In the eyes of God, we were all 'brothers in arms', but in our cloistered world entirely ruled by a bunch of cantankerous women, the lesson was completely lost on us. All Maryse and I could see was a flock of sheep looking at each other with stupid eyes and baying inanely as they jumped mindlessly over the edge. We giggled irresistibly, and on the blank sheet of paper *l'Abbé Jean-Marie* had so generously given us, we drew with gay abandon woolly blobs with match-stick legs flying off the page. Sheep, if not us, were well beyond redemption.

*

Thursday afternoons were spent going on endless walks, with no particular aim except to expend our surplus energy to tame the wild spirit within, and make us more amenable to a regime as rigorous as ineffectual. Occasionally, these exhausting walks would lead to yet another church where we had to kneel and pray, ask for forgiveness, and seek the redemption of our souls. Then, in the midst of our prayers, we would hear the tyres of 2CVs screech outside the tall double doors and the nuns would spill out with their habits billowing like mini *montgolfières*. It was, to all intent and purposes, a purgative Calvary to absolve the sins we had not yet committed, a time which should have been spent in normal childish pursuits, but which was instead dedicated to the contemplation of God and His almighty power. I rebelled...secretly. Any other way would have been foolhardy. I no longer wanted the love of God; in fact, I decided, I did not want anybody's love...ever. But, I could never turn my back on little Jesus, for He, just like us, was a victim, and just as with us, He was powerless against the wickedness of man. He was good...but *they* were not. He fought against evil...but *they* revelled in it. He saw the light... but all *they* saw was the dark visions of Hell.

From then on, my attitude changed. I developed a cynicism that surpassed Maryse's raw caricature of the adult world. I became more detached and aloof, and despite my diminutive size, I began to acquire a stare, eloquent and sustained, which was often read as sheer insolence, and which often landed me in trouble, but which, as a strange consequence, began to make me noticed by my peers.

CHAPTER XI

Easter was spent at Sangatte. I loved Sangatte. After school, it was my favourite place, my own sanctuary where, despite being surrounded by a landscape pockmarked with bomb craters, soldiers never came to disturb my dreams. It was calm and tranquil, with only the whooshing of the sea rasping the fine golden sand and the hushing of the wind murmuring untold secrets of the surrounding fields. But, what would it be like with Sister Marie-Catherine? I did not really want to think about it, not just yet, so I would have to block any thoughts of doom and gloom, and hope for the best.

The temperature must have been well below zero and some remnant of snow still lay on the ground. During the day, we were thrown outside to play on the frozen lawn with nothing but our imagination to entertain us. I did not want to move, and sought shelter against the wall where the wind blew less cuttingly.

"Come and play!" Roberte shouted.

"I'm too cold!" I protested.

"If you run around, you'll soon warm up…"

"I don't want to…I'm too cold."

"Oh well, please yourself."

I watched her run around with other girls while I stood in my little corner, blowing on my fingers to warm them up and wondering if, perhaps, she might be right and I should stop acting like a little wimp. I nearly went, but in the end, I crouched down to the ground, pulled my clothes as low as possible to cover as much of my body as I could, then I buried my hands in my lap and waited until we were allowed back inside the building.

There were not as many of us here, as girls were allowed to go home during the school holidays. One benefit was that the rules were slightly more relaxed. The dormitories were by far the best surprise. They had all been given names, drawn from children's books or Disney characters. The Snow White dorm was allocated to the youngest girls and had two rows of little wooden beds exactly like in the story, with red and white chequered curtains on the windows and on the beds, pyjama cases in the shape of the Seven Dwarves. Maryse and I argued as to which ones we would have.

"You can have Dopey!" I teased.

"And you can have Grumpy!" She retorted sharply.

In the end, she settled for Sneezy and I settled for Bashful. The beds, however, looked very small, even for us.

"Are they big enough?" I wondered.

Instead of a reply, Maryse went to lay on the bed closest to the door.

"Yeah!" She confirmed with glee, "they are."

I followed suit. The mattress was so soft that for a moment, I thought I was going to disappear through it.

"They are really comfi..." I declared dreamily, staring at the exposed wooden beams on the ceiling. "It's just like in Snow White!"

Then, I set off in another dream in which I saw Snow White singing by the stream or chatting to the little animals in the forest—peace and harmony. It was another of my dreams, and I wished I could transpose myself into a beautiful world bursting with colours and filled with sweet natured creatures. There was music too, and when people spoke, their words came out in a gentle rhythm like musical verses, lulling the senses with an enchanting, riveting sound. Peace and harmony—but that's all it was…just a short-lived dream.

Sister Marie-Catherine appeared at roll call in the large playroom. Her composure was most unusual. In fact, she seemed in a positively good mood. We almost gasped when her face suddenly broke into a smile.

"During the holidays," she started, "we're going to start rehearsing for a special show and we're going to perform it in front of all the Sisters and your parents, so it will have to be absolutely perfect!"

A stunned silence followed her announcement, then, little by little, as the news sank in, girls began to spread whispers of excitement.

"It will be called the 'St. Cyrian Ball', and Sister Adèle and Sister Marguerite from the linen room have kindly agreed to make up the costumes. It will be a grand occasion, the grandest of all, with costumes like you've never seen before, and you will have to show yourselves worthy to belong to this prestigious elite."

L'école de Saint Cyr was the elite school founded by Napoleon who, regardless of class or breed, wanted the very best men to lead his armies. If his armies walked on their stomach, their victories were purely won on merit. The uniforms worn by the officers sported gold braids on the epaulets, which made them look stunning and set his men apart from the bedraggled hordes of faithful foot soldiers. That was the only bit we were interested in: the officers would wear the most glamorous outfits we had ever seen and the girls would don splendid taffeta dresses puffed up to the waist. How exciting. Life was beginning to improve.

Being selected by height, I was paired off with Maryse. Sister Marie-Catherine pushed me in the position of the officer, while Maryse, with an exaggerated hand and arm movement, pirouetted in front of me. We stared at each other and giggled at the unlikely parts we were about to play. With my hair chiselled so short, I looked like a boy, therefore well suited for my designated role. The rehearsals began amidst a frisson of excitement that we were almost afraid to display. The girls danced and twirled graciously while we, the officers, marched to the tune of military music. It would have been almost possible to enjoy ourselves had it not been for the strict order of play imposed on us by Sister Marie-Catherine who, unwavering in her new mission, lost no time in beating some rhythm into us. She clearly did not like the way Maryse executed her steps, especially her curtsy.

"Do the curtsy one more time!" The nun ordered, and Maryse, with the look of fear in her eyes, drew her right leg back in a semi-circular motion.

"No! No! No! Try and be more gracious...and smile for goodness sake!"

Responding instantly to the strict orders, Maryse grinned to try and look as if she was having the time of her life, and executed another curtsy.

"Not like that! You useless girl!" The nun blurted out.

Suddenly, I felt her iron hand clasp tightly around my arm, as she shunted me into a different position.

"Martha Bertrand, you'd better do it!"

Reluctantly, Maryse and I swapped places and I found myself putting all my effort and concentration into performing a curtsy that would satisfy Sister Marie-Catherine's high expectation. It was almost what she expected, but not quite, so she grabbed my leg and nearly toppled me over as she pulled it in the right position. I'd rather be the officer, I moaned, aware that I possessed none of the airs and graces of an aristocratic lady, but all the rigidity better suited for a dashing young officer standing to attention.

At night, in the Snow White dormitory, we were able to retreat into our glittering world of dreams. I saw dashing officers rushing to my rescue, fighting for their honour and covered in glory. Unfortunately, they never visited me in my dreams, but their reassuring presence was enough to keep the relentless army of faceless soldiers away from the murderous battlefields. No one would die tonight and nobody would scream.

*

On the eve of Easter Sunday, we went to bed early so that we could go to the midnight mass.

When the supervisor came to wake us up, I could not open my eyes. At night, I was always ensconced so deeply in my dreams that it felt as if I was leading another life. I sat up, rubbed my eyes, peered at the others in the dormitory...and let my head fall back on the pillow.

"Martha! Martha! You're going to be late!"

The voice echoed somewhere in my dream. I did not know who was speaking, and as long as it was not the supervisor or Sister Marie-Catherine, I was quite happy to ignore it.

"Martha! Mlle Bernadette is coming!"

The dream bubble popped and I sat bolt upright. I got out of bed, fumbled about to find my clothes, and walked out in a daze.

We gathered outside on the main lawn. The cold fresh air finally managed to revive me completely. High above our heads, the stars shone like little diamonds and reminded me of the Seven Dwarves who worked surrounded by the sparkling beauty of precious stones.

Mlle Bernadette pointed at the sky.

"Look at that bright star over there. That's the Northern Star…and if you look there, to the right, you'll be able to see the Big Bear, and over there the Little Bear. You can even see the Chariot. Can you see it?"

I looked hard…everywhere. The girls around me marvelled at the mystical heavens, gasping with delight and murmuring in amazement:

"Yes, I see it…I see it!"

But all I saw were sparkling diamonds twinkling haphazardly in untidy clusters high up in the sky.

As the priest celebrated mass and we listened to the story of the sacrificial lamb, outside a strange sound began to invade the small church through the paned-glass windows. It came in intermittent blasts, vibrating through the glass like the mournful cries of a dying soul. Inside the church, people began to throw quizzical glances at each other. What on earth was it? The distant wailing continued as we walked back to the holiday home.

"What is it? What is it?" We all asked with a distinct note of anguish in our voices.

"We don't know," was all the reply we could get from Mlle Bernadette.

The loud lament went on all through the night, filtering through our deep sleep as if determined to disrupt the peace and quiet of that freezing night. The following morning, as we went down to breakfast, we learnt that a large fishing boat had floundered on Blériot Plage. It was rare to learn anything from the supervisors, so rare in fact that it was impossible to tell how much they knew, but in this instance, they knew as much as we did about Louis Blériot—that he was that daredevil aviator who had made the first successful flight across the Channel. There was also a bronze statue that stood not far from the *Colonie Saint Joseph des Flots*, which the supervisors had proclaimed to be that of Louis Blériot, until a girl pointed out that the name carved in the sandstone stained with verdigris was actually that of someone called Hubert Latham. Of course, none of the supervisors had ever heard of the man, and knew even less why he should be remembered with a statue of his own. They even started deliberating whether he might have been some illustrious English soldier who had distinguished himself during the last war before being slain on this very spot. In actual fact, Hubert Latham was very French indeed, of English descent perhaps, but born and bred in France, and what the supervisors should have been able to tell us was the fact that he was Louis Blériot's closest rival, as both men raced to make that first successful flight across the Channel. Monsieur Latham may have been pipped at the post by the intrepid Blériot—and as in the battle of Waterloo, the weather was to blame—but it was *his* statue, and not Blériot's, who now stood in a proud pose, with his eyes permanently scanning the ocean as if still measuring the full consequences of that failed historical leap. Every time we had passed his statue, we had raised our gaze over his elegant silhouette, in the mistaken belief that it was Blériot we were staring at, admiring, and applauding. Worse still for our victorious Blériot, his courageous deed in a flimsy plane, whose primitive engine spluttered oil and grease all over his goggles, had now been superseded by the floundering of a ship on the very beach that bore his name. Sadly for him, his fame sank with the unfortunate wreck, and from that day on, we no longer asked to go to *Blériot Plage*, but to 'the broken boat'.

"Did lots of people die?" One of the girls asked, revealing the morbid fascination with death that post-war children had inherited from their forebears.

Death around these parts was distinctly visible in the shape of the ghostly shadows of lost fathers and sons who had fallen in the bomb craters that had become our playground. As children unable to understand the difference between patriotic deeds and martyrdom, we ran totally carefree, squealing with excitement, unaware of the ultimate sacrifice made by thousands of young men who had lived only so that they could die for their country.

After the summer holiday came to an end, we returned grudgingly to *Saint Vincent* where we settled more quickly than we thought back into the strict regimented routine. From now on, most Thursday afternoons were set aside for rehearsals. The rigorous programme had not quite managed to extinguish our spirits, despite being overshadowed by Sister Marie-Catherine's impossible standards. It was that or face being thrown out of the production altogether, and once we had caught a glimpse of the glamorous costumes, we wanted to stay in, no matter what.

In June, we were ready to perform. The costumes were fitted and numbered...and I moaned and groaned that I still wanted to be an officer. It was, by the orphanage's standard, the most lavish production to date, but what none of us realised was that the show had become Sister Marie-Catherine's very own mission. Replicating Napoleon's idea when he had founded '*L'école de Saint Cyr*', she was going to put us through our paces and show everyone that she had the best disciplined and the most orderly troops in the whole orphanage. Through our perfectly timed steps, our synchronised moves, and our magnificent costumes, she was going to dazzle the public and silence her critics. In front of their very eyes, like an expert conjurer, she was going to prove that it was possible to instil order and discipline into a bunch of scruffy, snotty little girls who had come to her straight from the gutter.

The Sisters gathered in the communal playroom, closely followed by a small horde of bewildered parents who kept scouring the room and the rows of smiling faces neatly lined up in front of them, wondering what on earth to expect. As Sister Marie-Catherine had so enthusiastically declared all those months ago, back at Sangatte, nothing like this had ever happened before. A seat in the middle of the front row was left vacant for the Mother Superior. She was on her way. We stood in our pairs, we girls holding gracefully a pleat of our stiff organza dresses in our right hands, while our dashing partners proudly displayed their glittering epaulettes on their resplendent royal blue uniforms, standing to attention. And, we waited patiently, very patiently in our rigid positions.

Finally, a nun entered and announced in a rather excited voice:

"Mother Superior's coming!"

Immediately, Sister Marie-Catherine sprang into action. With a stern inspectorial look, she checked our positions, our lines, and our costumes before dashing to the small portable record player on the left-hand side of the packed room. A general hush spread around the room as the Mother Superior made her entrance and took her seat, right there in the front row.

Sister Marie-Catherine started the music and at her signal, we began to march...in line, in formation and in rows. We looped around each other marching to the gusty military tune, and with the perfect precision of a military drill. We marched up and down the communal playroom, right up close to the front row where all the Sisters were seated, before spreading out to the wings. We marched in squares, in circles, and in symmetry. At the end of the performance, we did a little twirl and curtsied or bowed to our partners; then turning to the front row, we curtsied and bowed to Mother Superior, remembering to smile.

Sister Marie-Catherine got up, her eyes sternly fixed on the military lines. She looked pleased. Everyone had managed to execute the military steps at the right time and in the right place. The audience clapped and the nuns clapped too, marking their approval with a discreet nod of the head. By now, the parents who had managed to make it to the performance were cheering more heartily, waving their arms around trying to catch the eyes of their proud daughters, but standing to one side, Sister Marie-Catherine had eyes for one person only: the Mother Superior. Had this not been a brilliant display of order and discipline? Was she pleased? Did she approve? Had she finally understood what she was trying to achieve?

The Mother Superior rose silently from her seat, smiled at us, and left. Nobody could tell what she was thinking, but the fact that she had not even bothered to look at Sister Marie-Catherine made me wonder. Is this not what she had expected? Had she not been impressed by the impeccable timing, the good order, and the perfect discipline? What about the uniforms? Were they not simply magnificent?

I had only seen Mother Superior once or twice before, and only fleetingly when she had been on her way to chapel, but her attitude of utter *froideur* towards Sister Marie-Catherine had revealed more about the two nuns than any words could have expressed. In that brief instant, I had seen and understood more than I wished to know. The burden of truth...children should not be laden with the burden of truth. What would happen now? Time would tell when the bell would toll but we, children, would never be told.

CHAPTER XII

At school, a dreadful thing was about to happen. Rumours ran wild that the chestnut tree, my beautiful tree underneath which I had sought shelter, whose multifarious branches made me feel so safe, and whose flamboyant leaves brushed languidly over the red brick building, was to be cut down. It had grown too big, practically touching the walls, and had been declared a liability. The news hit me like a blow in the stomach. For a moment, I struggled to breathe. I felt faint. The tree and I had been together ever since I had joined *Ecole Notre Dame*. We had become close companions, growing and blossoming together with each passing of the seasons. Now, I could not imagine life without it, and sitting at my desk by the window, I rushed through my work so that I could have more time to look at it while I mulled over the words of a Victor Hugo's poem the teacher had once read: *il pleut dans mon cœur comme il pleut sur la ville*...the rain could fall on my heart just like it fell on the heart of town—but it could never drown my feelings, and the melancholic glances I threw to bewail its beauty, its grandeur, and its magnificence, did nothing to diminish the immense sorrow I felt. I took several deep breaths to fill my little lungs as much as I could with its subtle smell and breathed once more to savour the musty aroma of its bark weeping in agony.

I had already lost the ivy wall, now I was about to lose this majestic tree—my tree. I was devastated.

Then one day, they came, men in overalls carrying their murderous instruments. The weather was hot, and as they prepared for the final execution, their metallic clatter resounded like a death knell through the open windows.

A few minutes later, Mlle Claire started the dictation, while the men below began their sinister task; and as the teacher tried to raise her voice above the savage drilling and sawing, dissecting each syllable with particular care, I could hear nothing but the last groans of my dying tree. The teacher must have noticed something for, as she weaved in and out of the desks enunciating each sentence clearly and pointedly, she stopped next to mine and enquired in a dry voice: "What's the matter with you?"

I looked at her, unwilling to reveal the real cause of my distress. It was a private matter between me and the tree...no one else. So, I replied wincing: "I've got a sore tummy."

Her quiet 'humph' was instantly drowned by the continuous sound of sawing and drilling outside. Then, she resumed the dictation and continued to pace around the desks, moving further and further away from the window. There was nothing she could do for me, just like there was nothing anyone could do to save my tree.

*

As the end of the summer term approached, everyone began to talk about prize giving. Outside each classroom door, there was a chart posted on the wall, recording the progress of each pupil. I hardly ever bothered to look at it, knowing that wherever I stood in the chart, nobody would take a blind bit of notice, but Michèle, a classmate blessed with the most fabulous shock of golden curls, whispered to me: "You're gonna get the 1st prize, aren't you?"

"Am I?" I said, trying to look vaguely interested.

"Well, look, your line is higher than anybody else's."

I gave a cursory glance at the board. Having been overlooked so many times in the past, I knew not to expect anything, so I shrugged my shoulders and refused to give it a further thought.

On the day of prize giving, we gathered in the main hall. It was such a small hall that only one class could fit in at any one time, especially if parents were allowed in, as they were on this day. On cue, our class lined up on the stage, and with my name starting with a B, I found myself right up there, in the front row. The sea of adult faces staring back at us made me feel nervous, awkward, and unhappy to be standing in such a prominent place, and the more adult faces I counted, the more self-aware I became of the clothes I was wearing, that orphanage uniform with emblazoned on it all the stigma and prejudices that went with belonging to such an institution. At that moment, the subdued crowd, craning their necks to raise their gaze above the rows of white bobby socks and navy blue hemlines, became a blur, a moving mass that seemed to be reeling out of control. I felt nauseous, helpless, and before I knew it, I was fleeing the stage. Mlle Claire caught me just in time and pushed me back in the front row. I could not shut my eyes, but I closed my mind to the scene below. When my name was called, I advanced towards Mother Superior, ignoring everything else around me, did a little curtsy, and took my prize, remembering to say thank you. I returned to my place with my head bowed low. When I eventually raised my head again, all the adults were staring back at me with puzzled faces, and I could almost hear the same question etched on their minds: Who the hell is she? Then someone remembered to clap, and a faint applause followed while the assembled parents continued to wonder who I was.

At long last, we returned to our places in the hall, and only then was I able to relax a little. Soon, I would be able to glance at my new book. I wondered whether it would be a dictionary or a Junior Encyclopaedia. I would rather prefer a Junior Encyclopaedia, I thought, there were lots of pictures and so many more words to read, but the book seemed somewhat too light and too small for that. Perhaps, it was an exciting storybook, and I felt a frisson of excitement as I pictured myself settling in a hidden corner and feverishly opening the first page. I settled back in my seat, brushed my skirt in a self-conscious way, and threw a surreptitious look at the cover so that I could catch a glimpse of its title. When I read it, my face froze in complete horror. I could not believe it! Snow White! They had given me Snow White!

I was mortified, worse even, I felt totally humiliated. I had just been given the first prize for academic excellence and all they could think of giving me was a baby book, a baby fairy tale, a story that I had read when I was two thumbs high. It would have been better if they had given me nothing at all, I snorted to myself. My good work would have gone unrewarded—I was used to that—but at least, I would not have felt utterly humiliated. Voltaire had it all wrong when he had declared in his usual cynical fashion, 'it is better to be hated than ignored'. The man had clearly never been humiliated in his life; how would he have liked to have had his *Lettres philosophiques*' rewarded with a set of baby books—fairy tales of all things? There they were telling me to grow up all the time, but when it came to giving me a book, all they could manage was a childish tale aimed at teeny weeny toddlers. I was fuming! My earlier melancholic mood had now been pushed aside by a kyrielle of unspoken insults churning in my head and bursting to come out—and there were more. When I go to Heaven, I am going to seek out Monsieur Voltaire and I am going to tell him that I'd rather be ignored than thoroughly humiliated. I am going to stamp my foot on Heaven's floor, hit my sides with my clenched fists, and shout at him: "*oui, monsieur*! Any day, *monsieur*!" Yes, that's the first thing I would do. I suppose his argument was that there had to be love before hatred, pride and joy before humiliation, but he had not met my teacher and he definitely had never met the likes of Sister Marie-Catherine.

Worse still! To add insult to injury, I later discovered that the girl who received the 2nd prize had been awarded a dictionary. That was it; I wished I had never been top of the class. Quite frankly, I had no idea how I got there in the first place and, to tell the truth, had it not been for the threat of a good old beating in the refectory, I would have been quite happy to languish at the bottom of the class. After all, I did nothing that could justify this extraordinary placing: I had no books to do any extra work or reading, whether I wanted to or not, no help of any kind whatsoever and, to cap it all, I had the notorious reputation of being breathtakingly lazy—so how on earth did I manage to be top of the class?

After the prize giving ceremony, we had an extended break. I stole myself to the classroom, checked that there was no one around, and closed the door. Then, I opened the book, tore out the label that had on it: *1st Prize awarded to…*, so that the book could not be traced back to me, and I lifted my arm as high as I could, so that when the book dropped in the waste paper basket, it would drag with it all the anger, fury, and contempt I held for it. Then, I decided in a huff, upon my return to *Saint Vincent*, all I would have to do was claim that I never got a prize at all—that way, no one would ever be able to remind me of the most humiliating moment of my life.

Since there was no one else from the orphanage in my class to witness my utmost humiliation, no one would be any the wiser—or so I thought.

After school, I was walking resolutely silent beside Maryse.

"Didn't you get any prize today?" She asked somewhat surprised.

"No," I replied with such vehemence that I hoped it would draw a line on the matter.

"Didn't you?" She said rather surprised. "I don't believe you...you must have had a prize. I know you've got the best results...I've seen your line on the chart."

"Well, I didn't get any...I didn't get any at *Sainte Germaine* and I certainly won't get any here."

"You're lying, aren't you...? I know you got a prize."

I looked at her face and studied her expression carefully to see if she really knew or whether she was bluffing. She nudged me again.

"Go on, tell me. You did get a prize, didn't you? What was it? What did you get?"

I looked at her again and could tell that she was not going to relent. And really, I could not be bothered to lie anymore. So, I told her.

"Promise you won't tell anybody!"

"No, I won't," she vouched, crossing her heart three times.

"I got Snow White," I mumbled discreetly from the corner of my mouth.

Just as I expected, Maryse burst out laughing.

"Snow White!" She chortled in a loud voice.

"Shush! You promised you wouldn't tell."

But my words were drowned in her fit of giggles.

"What did you say?" The girl in front asked, hoping to join in the fun.

"Nothing!" I replied curtly. "We're just having a joke."

But the girl's curiosity was far from satisfied.

"Maryse, why are you laughing?"

I grabbed Maryse's arm and warned through my gritted teeth:

"Don't you tell her...I'll never forgive you if you do."

Maryse straightened herself up and in between two laughs managed to spurt out:

"It's none of your business. Go and blow your own nose!"

Then, she turned to me again.

"Come on, show it to me...where is it?"

"I haven't got it. I threw it in the bin."

"Did you? Oh! You shouldn't have. You could have given it to me, I would have read it."

"Well, if you really want it, it's in the bin in my classroom," I replied, somewhat surprised that she should want to read such a book, but I was forgetting that Maryse was behind me in her studies. In fact, she was a whole year behind—a fact I found difficult to remember, simply because I never felt superior to her, and for a very good reason. She was the one who usually came up with all those entertaining ideas about witches and all, and her repartees, always delivered with cheeky effrontery, were invariably funnier, sharper, and wittier than mine. She was very clever in that way, and in my view, this was a far better attribute than merely being top of the class.

CHAPTER XIII

Every now and again, we were offered short glimpses of the real world that existed outside of *Saint Vincent*, mostly through trips to the cinema.

The most exciting part about these outings, as far as we, girls, were concerned was that on the way, we often passed small groups of trendy youths nicknamed '*les blousons noirs*' or '*les yé-yé*', simply because they wore blue jeans, white T-shirts, and black leather jackets '*à la* James Dean' or hummed hits from the Hit Parade that contained lots of 'yeah yeah'. What's more, in order to perfect their really cool look, these youths grew elaborate quiffs over their large forehead which they held in place with a generous dose of brilliantine. Most of them sported dark glasses whatever the weather, and chewed American bubble gum while leaning nonchalantly against a brick wall or a doorway. Some posed with their hands manly squared on their hips and sometimes, with a candy cigarette hanging from their luscious lips to complete the tableau, not having entirely made up their minds whether they wanted to portray the look of a cowboy or a hell-raising rocker. Forgetting our short hair and dowdy uniforms, these exciting sights usually resulted in a mad scramble among our ranks. We jostled, pushed, and shoved our way to the front of the crocodile file to pick discarded chewing gum from the filthy, dirty pavement, and as we chewed noisily with our mouths open wide, we sang in cool defiance the words of that song that the nun had forbidden us to sing, because it was simply too 'vulgar': '*it was an itsy bitsy teeny weeny yellow polka-dot bikini...*' while swinging our hips *à la* Brigitte Bardot.

The newsreels always seemed to unravel stories and events that were all the more moving, profound, and sometimes shocking than they were always delivered in black and white to create a sombre, almost lugubrious atmosphere, and accompanied by blasts of the most dramatic music for maximum effect. The deep resonant voice of the announcer never failed to add to the poignancy of some tragic event being played out somewhere by strangers in a strange land.

It had been decided on our behalf that we were too grown up to enjoy light-hearted entertainment such as Disney films, so we now had to sit through conscience beating epics such as *Benhur* and *Spartacus*, during which I watched most of the actions covering my face with my hands and peering at the big screen through gaps between my fingers. With their gory scenes of the worse cruelty I had ever witnessed, these biblical epics were nothing more than short visitations to hell, and terrified me. For two hours or more, we were forced to watch Roman soldiers systematically torturing and slaughtering Christians—people like us—in a ruthless attempt to make them renounce their faith in Jesus and their belief in God. I was caught in a religious dilemma, knowing that I would never have the courage or the bravery to affirm or deny my beliefs, and if a Roman centurion had confronted me about my faith, I felt sure that I would have feigned complete ignorance to save myself, if not my soul. Neither a saint nor a martyr be...

Right here, however, on the huge panavision screen glaring in front of me, *Benhur* and *Spartacus* battled the Romans, unafraid to declare themselves as the Roman Emperor's nemesis. They became mine too. It was not their fault, and

I was not siding with the Romans—no, not me, the good Catholic that I was—but I wanted my allegiance to God to be loving and peaceful, not brutal and gruesome. The only love I was prepared to acknowledge was one that existed in peace and harmony, not one that brought images of blood and war, and while the Romans massacred the Christians up there on the big screen, all I wanted, as I crouched even deeper into my seat, was to escape…I wanted to flee to a world where I would be able to live in peace and harmony surrounded by books and wrapped up in my dreams.

If the cowboys and Indians did not seem real—they lived too far away, in a foreign land called America—the Romans, and their betrayal of God and Jesus, were all too real to me and, as we made our way back to *Saint Vincent*, in a subdued silence, dazed and traumatised by the scenes we had just witnessed, I half expected Roman soldiers armed with their long murderous spears or treacherous swords to appear at any moment, on horseback or on foot, and herd us all into arenas full of lions, or into fields full of crosses. *Mon Dieu*, how excruciatingly painful it was to be a Christian!

Films about the Second World War came almost as a relief, despite the bloody battles and the systematic gunning down of soldiers who were on our side. At least, these films had the knack of erasing effortlessly, and in one stroke, the horrendous scenes of war with their nice catchy tune, and by the time we reached *Saint Vincent*, we could whistle the theme tune or sing all the words of memorable hits like *The Inn of the Sixth Happiness, The Bridge over the River Kwai*, or *The Longest Day*. With time, this last tune became our anthem, our way to rile behind her back the brutal beatings and the oppressive regime of Sister Marie-Catherine.

*

That summer, when we returned to Sangatte, I was delighted to discover that I was still small enough to fit into the little beds in the Snow White dorm. Maryse had the bed next to me. That was the good news. The bad news was that Mlle Pierrette was back. I had never set eyes on her before, but from all accounts, if anybody was capable of matching Sister Marie-Catherine's brutality, it was undoubtedly this buxom woman from the Moselle region who spoke with a harsh guttural accent that made her words rack deep in her throat or whistle through her tight lips. Her long grey hair was invariably pulled back in a tight bun, leaving her dry eroded features free to angle her victims and pin them to the ground from just a few paces. I did not know what to believe at first. Girls were prone to exaggerate; after all, who had not told a story with a few details added to revile or beguile? But as I was relishing the beginning of the holidays, I was about to discover the exact measure of her ruthless streak.

It was on a warm summer evening, after we had watched the flamboyant sunset disappear into the calm sea; its suffused rays painted the darkening sky with bold splashes of pastel orange and glowing red. We tossed and turned in bed, unable to go to sleep. Our little gang, Martine C., Annie B., Maryse, and I were all tucked into bed in the same half of the dormitory. Rather than going to sleep, we sat up and launched into a rendition of *The Longest Day*. This was our song, the tune we used to smooth out the harshness of a system we thoroughly despised. We sang the refrain with gusto, pledging to blast our way to victory through the power of cannons and the blood of our companions. The more we sang, the more we felt strong, brave, and emboldened. The other girls on the other side of the dormitory listened rather bemused, but did not join in. They knew better. Then hearing some hurried footsteps, Chantal, whose bed was closest to the door, shouted in a loud whisper: "Someone's coming!"

Immediately, we dived under our blankets and pretended to be asleep. Soon after, an angry voice pierced through the thickness of the blankets and rasped:

"Who was singing?"

At first, nobody moved.

"I know *who* was singing..." The voice continued. "I could hear you from the far end of the corridor! If you don't own up now, the punishment will be doubled."

The threat sounded awesome, so one by one, we pulled off our blankets and sheepishly put our hands up. Mlle Pierrette was standing in the doorway rigid, her lips pressed hard against her teeth and her fists clenched tightly as if she was restraining herself from lashing out at us. Then the retributions began.

"Maryse G., come here!" She blasted.

Maryse got out of bed and went to stand in front of the supervisor. Without saying a word, Mlle Pierrette grabbed her by the hair, lifted her off the ground, and shook her with all her might. After a good few seconds, she put Maryse back down again. Now it was my turn. As I got out of bed, I glanced at my friend and saw a pained expression on her face but no tears. I then looked at Mlle Pierrette: she was built like an Alsatian cow and set with arms the size of a wrestler's. She was brutal, but shrewd, and knew exactly how to inflict the maximum pain without leaving any marks. I felt her iron grip pull my hair really hard, as she lifted me off the ground. She shook me so violently that I felt dizzier and dizzier. Then, sooner than I expected, she put me back down again. Had she run out of strength or was she sparing her energy for the others? Either way, I counted my blessings and ran back to my bed. I did not cry...I could not cry.

After all the culprits had been appropriately dealt with, she turned her heels and, with our heads still buried under the blankets, we listened to her heavy footsteps echo all the way down the corridor. Then, a door swung shut and the silence returned. I emerged from under the blanket and looked at Maryse. She was lying on her back with her arms tucked under her head looking at the ceiling. Then she turned to me and whispered:

"She's not just as ugly as sin, she's as revolting as a farting canon...!"

"God, Maryse, don't make me laugh now...we're gonna be in trouble again!" I whispered back. Then, I tossed over and went to sleep.

The rest of the summer passed with no further incidents. Mornings were spent hanging around the front lawn, sitting in clusters while cursing the Alsatian cow, running around, or simply gazing dreamily at the distant horizon, trying to imagine living in the promised land over there in America, as mistresses of a castle or a palace, being served lots of food and lemonade on silver trays expertly carried by a large retinue of coloured domestics, who always looked so happy and extremely friendly, and who stared at you with their great big white eyes and smiled with their dazzling white teeth, just like we had seen in American films.

When we were not playing mistresses of the castle, we fantasised about marrying an American, because our preconception was that all Americans were rich and lived in grand houses in the land of plenty, where chewing gum came from and where every family lived happily ever after, singing and dancing around the furniture.

After lunch, we had to go to bed for our afternoon nap. This was by far the most boring time of all. After the afternoon nap, we went for long walks, and I vouched then that when I grew up, I would never go for a walk...ever again. Our favourite destinations, however, were to 'the broken boat' so that we could stand in awe in front of the enormous rusting wreck, or play in the bomb craters that lay like large dimples everywhere in the fields. We happily ran in and out of the holes, oblivious to the historical significance of the craters that scarred the landscape, until one day, a member of the public found an unexploded bomb. The municipality acted quickly. They removed the bomb and warned the Sisters to keep us away from the wire fence which surrounded the holiday home, as they were going to detonate it in the sea, right in front of the *colonie* at three o'clock in the afternoon.

At half past two, all of us gathered in the little ones' play area situated behind the main lawn and we waited... nervously.

"What's going to happen?" I asked the supervisor.

A girl butted in.

"There's going to be a huge bang!"

"Like fireworks?"

"Bigger than that! And it's going to be so big that the ground will shake!"

"And thousands of little bits are going to fly in the air..."

"Oh my God!" I gasped panicking. "What are we going to do?"

"Let's get into the sandpit and hold together; that way we'll protect each other."

The sandpit was built against the wall at a right angle from the beach, so we would be safe there. Wasting no time, we locked our heads together and leaned against the wall, giggling the whole time. After a few minutes, still nothing had happened, so we broke up the human ball and went to investigate.

"*Mademoiselle?* Is it three o'clock yet?"

"It's gone three."

"They're late!" A girl pointed out dejectedly.

Half an hour later, we gathered at the gate of the baby area, disappointed that so far nothing had exploded.

"Are they going to do it then?" Another girl asked impatiently.

"They have to wait until high tide," replied Mademoiselle. Then she added: "Perhaps they've changed their minds... perhaps, they've decided to do it another day..."

We looked at her trying to decide whether she was teasing or suddenly enlightened by a prudent thought.

"They could have told us!" A girl riposted sulkily.

Suddenly, the air was shaken by a muffled noise which sent a huge spray of water shooting several feet up in the air, and fell back down again with a loud whooshing sound. Then, very quickly the calm returned.

"Is that it?"

"There was no earthquake," I remarked, disappointed.

"Well, there we are, I think it's safe for you to return to your play area," the supervisor stated, unlocking the gate.

After the explosion, we all pressed Mlle Bernadette — rather than the Alsatian cow, for we knew she would say no— to let us go to the beach, but the area had not been declared safe yet, so we would have to wait another day.

Surprisingly, despite the holiday home being situated right on the seafront, we rarely went to the beach, except to go on endless, exhausting walks, but on this occasion, we went, because the supervisors were as curious as we were to examine from up close the scars left by the wartime bomb. At low tide, we hurried down the beach, eager to be the first to find the big hole that the bomb would surely have left, but after several tides sweeping the beach high and low, the waves had smoothed out the area completely and erased the last remnants of a war zone that had become our playground. With no crater to explore, we moved on to look for bits of shrapnel and rummaged through pebbles, stones, and empty seashells, but found none. Behind us, the dunes stood still, buffeting the long sigh that had long died, and burying in its fine golden sand the ghostly spectre of the last war cry.

At the end of August, all the preparations began for our return to *Saint Vincent*. The presence of Sister Marie-Catherine became more prominent, the supervisors fretted more feverishly, and a whole sense of foreboding stifled the atmosphere and stilled our desires for more adventures and exhilarating escapes.

Wondering aimlessly on the lawn, on that last day, we waited nervously for the coaches. Despite the warm sunshine, it felt cold. The noisy arrival of two coaches spluttering puffs of black smoke provided the last excited cries that would die down instantly as the holiday drew to a close. And, when the time came to board the coach, we rushed *en masse* to climb the high steps, fighting for window seats; but once we were settled, a subdued silence superseded the light holiday mood. We sat stiffly in our seats unwilling to express the high anxiety that threatened to erase the happy memories of the long summer holidays. It seemed that we were all busy blocking from our minds any thoughts that would bring us prematurely back to *Saint Vincent*, because we knew that, upon our return, we would don the dark uniforms with their stiff cardboard collars, we would sit in eternal silence while listening to endless castigating sermons…and we would march…in the snow, in the wind, and in the rain…and we would go on marching to the slow rhythm of each day.

CHAPTER XIV

The new term began. Standing to attention in the refectory and fidgeting nervously with my fingers tucked behind my back, I observed the new girls, and my heart went out to those who stood proudly with their heads held up high, oblivious to what lay ahead. Soon, they would be moulded like us, turned into toy soldiers whose hair would be savagely cut with a blunt razor blade, and who would have to learn very quickly to weather the wild moods of the nun in charge, and to bathe in the tiniest ray of sunshine. We would teach the new girls how to rise above the ignominy of it all. We would stand by them, comfort them, and dry their tears when a ruthless hand would hit once too often. And, we would tell them that it was all right to cry, even though very few of us did, because we had our dignity and our pride, and Mlle Alice had said: "Little angels don't cry".

One of the new girls was Nadine. There was nothing special about Nadine: she was very bright, very clever in fact, and not particularly mischievous. Her blond hair and big blue eyes were the only unusual features for someone born in Indochina, but what set her apart from the rest of us was the fact that she had a pronounced limp as a result of contracting polio at an early age. To most of us, this was not a physical oddity that made people stop and look twice, not like with Mlle Alice and her missing thumbs—and the 'thing' she had on her back. In fact, having grown up with Nadine, we barely noticed that she did not walk like the rest of us. Many times, I had seen the sheer determination on her face to conceal her handicap and observed how she used her hand to swing her atrophied leg forward so that she could keep up with the rest of us. Besides, I, better than anyone else, knew that she had a strong resolve, that she could hold her own, and that she was a redoubtable competitor bestowed with an extremely agile mind.

On that first morning, as we stood silently in the refectory to recite our prayers, I could sense that everyone had the same thought in mind. What would Sister Marie-Catherine make of Nadine? Would she subject her to the same treatment? Would she force her to march in the ranks or go on those endless walks? In the stifled silence, we feared for her, and we feared for the new girls.

Sister Marie-Catherine threw a cold glance around the room. The supervisors bristled on their seats until the nun gave the signal for the start-of-term ritual to begin. The roll call reeled out the lists of familiar names with detached indifference, but when Nadine's name was read out, everybody held their breath. I looked up. Not a twinge from Sister Marie-Catherine. Afterwards, we lined up in the central alley in order of height. If we had grown, we would be given a bigger uniform, with the compulsory headband, stiff collar, and a new number. And when all was done, we would be reminded of the rules, of the crosses, and of the consequences of an unguarded word, a careless gesture, or a little mischief. And while we waited for the next command, everything stood still; nothing could be heard...except for the occasional sigh, a barely perceptible anonymous sigh that died away in the cold atmosphere.

Things rarely work out the way we expect them to, and Sister Marie-Catherine confounded us all by taking Nadine under her wing. Could it be that, through Nadine, she saw the way to her own redemption? Did she see it as a supreme act of salvation with which to absolve all her sins? We did not know, but what we knew for sure was that, whatever caused her to behave the way she did, Sister Marie-Catherine had a conscience. Here, among the sinners of the Junior Section, she began the process of self-purification through acts of contrition, penitence, and through Nadine. She would blind God with her fervent devotion and show the rest of us—and Mother Superior—that she really was a better person than we gave her credit for. From then on, Nadine became her mission and she fought mightily hard so that doctors would hear her pleas and do anything they could, free of charge, to improve Nadine's condition.

Unwittingly, by dragging her from hospital to hospital and shunting her between doctors, consultants, and surgeons, Sister Marie-Catherine had created Nadine's own Calvary. With her sharp and astute mind, Nadine had perceived the personal—though not entirely selfless— motive in the nun's actions, and her insides seethed with anger at what she saw as a pitiful display of cheap charity. She found the whole process deeply demeaning—one which profoundly wounded her pride. She would have loved to resist and reject all the unwelcome attention, but she knew that no one could cross Sister Marie-Catherine's path, especially if you happened to be on it at the same time, driven by the same blind determination. The end result of all the examinations, prognostics, and discussions was that Nadine, to her horror and dismay, was fitted with an iron frame. She hated the thing with a vengeance and always referred to it as '*un tas de féraille*', a heap of metal that she grew to despise more than the devil himself.

The first time she had to go to school, pounding the

pavement with the cumbersome contraption, she was spitting fire at the sheer frustration of being used by adults as a billboard screaming to all and sundry a love and dedication that was never there. On that first day, unable to face alone the ignominy and the glare of children who did not know how to respond, she pleaded for us to form a protective shield around her so that nobody would be allowed to ogle and stare at her ugly iron frame.

Gradually, the hot flushes of Nadine's traumatic first days began to cool down and life resumed its ordinariness, though never tranquil, never gay. Nadine got used to her iron frame, although she never ceased to loathe it with all her might, and we got used to seeing her walk, run, and even skip with it. She continued to taunt me about my academic progress and started the race as to which one of us would finish our homework first. She often won, but I usually followed closely behind. In so doing, she resurfaced an unwanted competitive streak in me that had almost disappeared. Now that Nadine was back in the fray, I would have to remain at the top of the class, whether I wanted it or not. Fortunately, here in the Junior Section, there were very few opportunities to interact, which kept her at a safe distance from me. What's more, she soon found her little niche among Sister Marie-Catherine's favourites where the special attention she received made her soon forget about me.

*

Life would have been almost bearable if the supervisors had not felt obliged to treat us with the same brutality and ruthlessness as the nun in charge. Gradually, their brutal approach permeated through our games. Frustrated by the supervisors' over-zealousness in dishing out punishments—most of them given for the most benign reasons—we wanted to rebel, but the only way we could do this without fear of retribution was through our games. On the rare occasions that we were allowed to watch television, we cringed and cowered at war films and westerns, but cheered jubilantly at Rin Tin Tin and Zorro. Once the episode was over, we carried their heroic deeds into the playground where, for lack of any other more suitable games for girls, we re-enacted the war or battle scenes.

Amongst the mock battles and the howling cries of Indians storming an invisible wagon trail, a new girl arrived. Her name was Annick. She looked brash and confident, and had already distinguished herself by flaunting her relatively long hair.

"Why are you allowed to have long hair?" Roberte asked.

Annick flicked her hair back in a defiant gesture and replied:

"Because my dad told Sister Marie-Catherine that he would punch her if she dared touch my hair."

We stared at her tresses with envy and secretly wished someone would stand up for us the way Annick's dad stood up for her.

Her air of quiet confidence and natural aplomb stood in complete contrast with the sheepish submissive way in which we had been conditioned to behave. Hence, she found no resistance when she elected herself as our leader and started to organise our games, mainly battles between cowboys and Indians. What's more, she was a real asset to have in one's camp, as she knew how to make bows and arrows. Her brothers had taught her, she boasted. Soon, the lower branches of the poplar trees were decimated, despite the repeated cries of nuns passing by, "Leave the trees alone!"

To add to our ammunitions, the long walks had now become hunting parties during which we scoured every bit of vegetation in search of pieces of wood that could easily be shaped into a useful weapon to fight as a cowboy or an Indian. Then, back at *Saint Vincent*, Annick announced that there would be a 'big battle', and, setting our hearts on this new exciting craze, we enthusiastically prepared for the final showdown. Annick rounded up her 'men' and proceeded to check all the makeshift weapons; anything unsuitable was thrown over the side, or with her dexterous skills, transformed into a flexible bow or a double-barrel revolver. Then, the 'big chief' (herself) and the 'head of the cavalry' (the biggest girl in the Junior Section) met to discuss the time and place of the big fight. The only free time we had was on Thursday afternoons, after the long walk, so all the participants were warned to take sides and be ready, armed with whatever they could lay their hands on. Before I could object, I had been pulled on the cowboys' side and only agreed to stay after I had been assured that *this* was the stronger side. However, preparing to fight opposite Annick's camp made me wonder whether it might not be better to lay down arms right away. She looked too good and, with her long tresses and her headband pulled over her forehead, she really looked the part of the all-powerful 'Grand Manitou'.

On the designated day, the obligatory walk took us along the canal. Annick walked up and down the crocodile file in order to dispatch her last orders down the line. We scavenged through the vegetation more thoroughly than ever before in the hope of finding sticks better than the ones we already had.

Upon our return, the two camps gathered in their separate corners and the leaders plotted the moves, speculated on the other side's strength, and assured their teams of a quick and easy victory. Annick's camp put their headbands over their foreheads and yodelled the Indians' war cry to indicate that they were ready.

At the Indian Chief's signal, both camps faced each other, in two long lines.

Annick wielded her makeshift tomahawk and sent her team into a yodelling frenzy.

"*En avant!*" She yelled as she launched the assault.

We clashed noisily amid the clacking of wooden sticks and war cries, and while we bashed and hit each other—but not too hard, please! I don't want to get hurt—, over there, well removed from the warring factions, Annie Brenn was sitting on the low wall, shaking her head and muttering words of disbelief. Not for her to get involved.

"Why can't you find some more gentle game to play?" She yelled at the fighting hordes.

But of course, as always, her pleas were ignored, deafened by our war cries, as we continued to bash and hit each other with sticks in the shape of rifles, daggers, or bows. It was all right, we riled, as long as we did not tear our clothes. Suddenly, someone heard a piece of material tear loudly through the air.

"*Mince alors!*" Annie B. wailed, looking at her torn pocket. "I'm in real trouble now!"

Instantly, the fighting hordes stopped. Annick sounded the victory cry.

"Ok, guys, we won! Take away the prisoners!"

Victorious cheers rose all around as the defeated cowboys scampered away.

"Don't take me!" Martine C. wailed. "I was an Indian!"

The Indian turned to Annick.

"Chief!" She called out. "Was Martine C. on our side?"

"No, not her..." She replied, with a distinct note of disdain in her voice. She nearly added something else, but abstained.

Most cowboys had disappeared by now, probably into the toilet block, to escape capture, but as a brave soldier, or simply because I was too slow to react, I suddenly found myself left with only a handful of others to save the honour of the defeated side.

"Ok, guys, give them the Indian torture." Annick ordered, after her side had gathered enough prisoners.

"What's that?" Her faithful sidekick asked.

"I'll show you…you take their wrists like that and twist the skin in opposite direction until it hurts…that's called the Indian burn."

When Annick saw me, she gave me the once over, just like an army general inspects a dodgy character, and asked:

"Were you a cowboy?"

Suddenly, all my thoughts of honour, courage, and bravery deserted me, and while I fumbled awkwardly with my headband in my hands, I sheepishly replied:

"Er…I'm not sure…"

"She was a cowboy, Chief!" Someone decreed.

"No, she was an Indian," another girl avowed.

Annick looked me straight in the eyes, put her firm hand on my shoulder, and declared:

"Well, from now on, you'll be an Indian."

I gave her a quirky smile in return, grateful to have been spared, although what I really wanted to do was to tell her that I did not really want to be either; I would rather stay out of it all and not get hurt. I was a dreamer, really, not a fighter.

Despite being relatively new, Annick had quickly discerned the group of Sister Marie-Catherine's favourites and immediately sided with them. As to be expected, Martine and Beatrice, known to us as the rich sisters—whose pristine white underwear were the envy of the whole dormitory—were among them, along with the better looking, more feminine girls. She quickly emerged as a natural leader, and despite her medium length plaits, she was more of a tomboy than those of us who had had our hair shorn to the scalp.

With the arrival of Annick, our attitude towards the almighty authorities began to change. She knew more than the rest of us about what was going on in the outside world and, emboldened by her dad's staunch support, she was not afraid to stand up to the ridicule of the strict military regime. As usual, I observed the unravelling of events from a safe distance, never getting involved, but savouring all the same the delectable satisfaction of seeing one of us courageously stand up against the oppressive regime. Often, the supervisors did not know how to react, so shocked were they to come up against a girl who had the effrontery and the sheer insolence to answer back. It may have looked like defiance to them, but to us, it was a silent victory where the adults' ridicule had succumbed to the arrogance of youth. It was the beginning of a new dawn, when both cowboys and Indians would readily fight against one common enemy.

Gradually, I detected a tangible shift in the atmosphere. Sometimes even, when Sister Marie-Catherine was absent and the supervisors were left solely in charge, some rebellious streaks began to appear. We continued to march, but every now and again, someone would make a few quick steps or heckle in the ranks and we would all collapse in laughter. On these occasions, our feet did not pound the tarmac so hard, and our arms swung rather limply on our sides. Then a girl would whistle the first few notes of *The Bridge over the River Kwai*, and emboldened by her example, several others would follow. And we laughed even more as we watched the supervisor jiggle on the spot like a Jack in the Box trying to catch the culprits. Then, taking large strides, the supervisor would scour the ranks and yell: "Silence! Be quiet! Silence or everyone gets five crosses!"

Then, rightly or wrongly, girls would be singled out and crosses would fall. It was a comical display of usurped authority which never had the same hold as Sister Marie-Catherine's rigorous ways.

If any mischief happened in the dormitory, we were thrown without a further thought into the attic and left to cool down for a few hours. Sometimes, the supervisor would forget and the girl had to stay there for the whole night.

Having, up until now, behaved like a silent, resilient victim, accepting of my fate, I was slowly raising my head over the parapet. One evening, after I had been brave or foolish enough to give Annie Brenn a piece of my mind—but only because I knew Sister Marie-Catherine was absent, away on a regular retreat—I was thrown into the attic. To my surprise, Nadine was already there, sitting in the little square at the bottom of the stairs that led to the main area of the attic.

"What did you do?" I whispered.

"Same as you," she replied rather curtly.

"What? You answered back?"

"So..." She retorted, proud.

Thrown together in a small draughty place, I could feel her animosity gradually melt away and we began to chat. We talked about the rich sisters, gloated over their beautiful neat clothes, the splendid house where they lived that only one other girl had seen. Apparently, it even had a swimming pool in the garden. I was in awe.

"Are they millionaires then?" I asked, picturing in my head children with beautiful long hair and rich clothes that I had seen in opulent American films.

"Yep..." Nadine replied, glad to show that she still knew more than I did.

"So, why are the girls here?"

"Their parents are getting divorced..."

"Divorced? What does that mean?"

"They're separating and it's getting very nasty...Beatrice told me."

Very little of this conversation made any sense to me; the word 'parents' was a blanket term that I was not sure how to interpret. I had heard the word 'father' many times before, as the priests were often called Father, and since the girls referred to the men they knew as 'father', I had always assumed that it was simply another word for man. As for 'mother', that word left me even more confused. Apart from the Mother Superior, the only time I had come across this word was in reference to the women who waited every day at the school gate. I had therefore concluded that mothers must be doorwomen whose job it was to collect children from school. Hence, when Nadine mentioned the word 'divorce', I really did not know what to make of it, but far be it from me to admit my ignorance, especially to her. I would simply have to change the subject. I looked up the narrow steep staircase and asked:

"Have you ever been upstairs?"

"No," Nadine replied on a tone that hinted loudly, *'and I'm not going up there either...'*

"If you go," I said, trying to sound brave, "I'll go after you."

"No, you go first..."

We both looked up and stared silently at the ominous black hole that hovered at the top of the stairs, unwilling to betray our overwhelming fears to one another.

With words of damnation and hell that had been constantly crammed into my young head, the still silence of the dark hole conjured up tenebrous pictures haunted by the devil. Was he lurking up there, waiting for the perfect moment to steal our souls? Right now, abandoned to our fate, we felt weak and vulnerable, powerless against the ignominy of religious figures—too quick to blame us and forsake us— and defenceless against the irresistible lure of the devil. In this dark hour, who would come to our rescue and save us from the satanic monster? The pictures in my head became increasingly vivid; I even thought I saw a nebulous shadow gesticulating at the top of the stairs. I gripped my nightie tightly around me and rested my head on my knees. I could no longer bear to look.

"Where's the light switch?" I eventually asked.

"It's up there...at the top of the stairs...on the wall."

Trying to muster as much courage as I could, I forced myself to imagine a less daunting picture of the ghostly attic.

"Let's go up together!" I suggested.

"All right, but you go first," Nadine agreed.

"No, you go first."

"No, you go first."

"You're scared, aren't you?" Nadine riled, nudging me in the ribs.

"Of course I am. It's all dark and there're probably ghosts up there," I said, preferring to mention ghosts rather than the devil.

"No, there aren't...ghosts don't exist anyway," she declared in a matter-of-fact way.

Typical. Nadine had always had the knack of making me feel like an idiotic airhead and I felt rather stupid just having mentioned them. Besides, if truth be known, I was far more frightened of the devil than of the odd mythical ghost, whose existence had averred too elusive to prove.

The devil...*Mon Dieu!* God knew how I feared the devil, so much so that in the past, I had wondered whether it was *he* who was invading my dreams and playing tricks on me. Was it *he* who was hiding behind the clowns' faces, or leading the unfortunate soldiers to their agonising deaths? In the dark atmosphere of the sinister attic, I could not bring myself to even utter his name, in case he was listening and thought that I might be calling out to him. If I had been smart, I would have called on my guardian angel to protect me, but all I could see in my mind clouded with a thick mist of fear was the devilish grin of an old man, all dressed in red and carrying a flaming trident, beckoning me with a long crooked finger to come closer and closer to him.

I shook my head to dispel the frightening images. Then, I took a deep breath and began to climb the stairs ever so slowly. Then, halfway up, I stopped abruptly and shot straight back down again.

"I can't do it! I'm too scared! You go!" I whispered in a panic.

"Did you see anything?"

"No. I didn't want to look...it's too scary!"

Nadine got up and began a slow shuffle up the stairs. At about the same height, she turned around, looked at me, sat down on a step, and slid all the way down on her bottom which, for her, was faster than trying to scamper off on two unbalanced feet.

"I'm scared! I'm scared!" She whispered, huddling herself against me.

We held each other tight, seeking reassurance from one another's presence. Then, in a desperate attempt to divert our attention away from dark holes and ghosts, we racked our brains for something else to talk about. The only topic of conversation we could think of was the adults in charge of us, but even in the seclusion of the dark attic, we were too scared to mention Sister Marie-Catherine. So, we limited our sneers to the supervisors whose facial discrepancies were one-by-one dissected with glee. We sniggered at Mlle Bernadette's protruding lips and chin shaped like a clog. We decided that Mlle Roseline looked reasonably normal, although her nose was as long as that of Pinocchio's when the wooden puppet was lying. Then, we swiftly moved on to our favourite taunt: Annie Brenn. The mere mention of her name was enough to set us off, and we muffled our irrepressible giggles in the many folds of our white nighties for fear of getting into even more trouble. Suddenly, we heard her heavy footsteps creak on the wooden floor. We looked at each other, and despite the near complete obscurity, I could tell Nadine was thinking the same thing as me: *Oh God, we're in trouble now.*

Annie Brenn opened the door and whispered:

"Off you go...back to bed now...And I don't want to hear you again!"

We were confounded. Perhaps she had a heart after all...or was it out of pity for Nadine?

CHAPTER XV

During term time, the perpetual motion of our strict routine was interrupted only by the changeover of the team of supervisors. Mlle Pierrette, the Alsatian cow, returned, and with her, a new one appeared. Her name was Brigitte Duval. She was rather petite with short dark hair bobbed around her stiff features. On that first day, she began to pace the central alley slowly, scrutinising our anxious faces while wringing her hands. Through her viper's eyes, she wanted to establish an instant eye contact that would tell us all from the outset that being new did not mean being soft, naïve, and easily fooled. Her pursed lips indicated quite clearly that she meant business, that her bark would bite, and that her diligence to impose discipline would only be surpassed by Sister Marie-Catherine's own ruthlessness. Quickly, she sided with Mlle Pierrette in whom she found a ready ally as cruel in her intentions as she was in her actions. Annie Brenn, whom she found too soft and too stupid, was summarily relegated to the role of subordinate to *them,* as well as to Sister Marie-Catherine. Straight away, we knew she would be a force to be reckoned with and we waited in a stiff silence to see who her first victim would be.

We watched her walk back to the top of the refectory, but halfway there she stopped, did an about turn, and smiled...a mocking, sardonic, sneering smile. Sister Marie-Catherine had found her match, and the new supervisor wasted no time in putting her newly-acquired authority to the test. She yelled insults and watched for our reaction. When she failed to get any, she picked on someone, anyone, and started to ridicule her hapless victim with a string of personal insults that started with the girl's physical appearance and extended to deride her family's social circumstances. And once she was in full flow, there was no stopping her. Her hurtful words and callous remarks slipped through her lips as sleekly and smoothly as a lancet cut into a wound. It was painful for us and it was painful for the girl who would eventually burst into tears. At that point, Brigitte Duval would swing her shoulders triumphantly and resume her search for her next victim.

As she got to know us better, she gradually built up a cluster of favourite victims, and we, in turn, could now tell when she was about to spit, for her eyebrows would lift, her eyes open wide, and her lips purse in stiff lines like stitches on a tight wound. To complete her threatening stance, she would hit herself in the sides with her clenched fists and stamp her foot violently on the tiled floor; and as soon as she detected a mere quiver or the look of fear in someone's face, she was ready to pounce. Like a starved hound, she wanted blood and she sniffed, growled, and snarled in her search for it. Her sermons at prayer time in the refectory had become parodies of public degradation and humiliation. Then she would set about to single out her victim, and as I forced myself to avoid her murderous gaze, I felt like one of those Christians thrown into the middle of the bloody arena, left to die at the mercy of a wild lioness. It was scary. Unfortunately, it was all too easy to become the 'pick of the day'. A sneeze produced at the wrong time, a slight cough or a suppressed yawn, or something as banal as a bored look, all qualified to make you 'pick of the day'; and when her eyes had set on her victims, she would pounce on them, throw them brutally out of their ranks, and lash out a renewed kyrielle of fresh insults.

"You don't deserve to be here. You're the scum of the earth and the only right place for you all is the gutter! That's where you belong! This place is too nice for you, you bunch of ungrateful, good-for-nothing, filthy wenches."

She frequently exploded in these unprovoked attacks, displaying a pathological obsession for insults which she churned over and over again like a barrel of soured milk that had gone off in the heat, spreading around the pestilence of rotten words covered in contaminated spit that tumbled shockingly out of her foul mouth.

In her unremitting quest to gain complete authority and enjoy absolute power, she had surpassed Sister Marie-Catherine and Mlle Pierrette in the amount of cruelty she could inflict. As a result, we detested and loathed her with every ounce of our little bodies but...for some inexplicable reason, we did not fear her in the same way as we feared Sister Marie-Catherine. Although unaware of it at the time, we had, subconsciously, worked out that the nun's somewhat erratic behaviour had a neurotic origin—spurned on by pathological impulses, over which she had no control—which meant that, as far as we understood it, Sister Marie-Catherine could not help herself and we had learnt to duck and keep our heads below the parapet.

Brigitte Duval, on the other hand, was quite a different evil altogether. She was cold, ruthless, calculating, and so manipulative—even with her own colleagues—that she had become predictable in her demonic ways. In our eyes, she was cruel with intent and, to us, that was unforgivable. From then on, as soon as I detected that Brigitte Duval was about to launch herself into yet another tirade of stinging insults, I would switch off automatically and transport my thoughts into a far away world where I could evolve happily in peace and harmony. On one such occasion, I must have looked too serene, too content—or was I sneering—for suddenly, I heard my name screech down the main alley of the refectory.

"Martha Bertrand!" I heard the woman scream. "You little pagan! Stand in the alley! I want everybody to see what a pagan looks like!"

She paused to allow the full force of her words to stir every conscience that stood bare in the room. Her head jerked spasmodically from side to side, looking for an approbating glance that would have approved the choice of her victim, but everywhere around the room, the girls' gaze remained resolutely fixed on the ground, on their feet, or on the table in front of them. I shuffled grudgingly towards the central alley as the supervisor's voice thundered once more.

"Look at her, there isn't an ounce of contrition in that face. You're an arrogant, insolent wench and the only place fit for you is hell! That's five crosses for you...that should take that grin off your face! Repent, filthy wench, repent!"

I would have liked to defend myself and explain that I was not grinning, I was only daydreaming, but the insult stabbed me so hard in the heart that I felt my little unblemished soul crushed to the core. Being called a 'pagan' was the worst insult anyone could have thrown at me, and I was hurt, deeply hurt, and humiliated, but I clenched my jaws, tucked my hands behind my back, and stared at my feet, determined not to show how upset I was. In my time here, I had worked out that my best defence against all adults was not to show any feeling or emotion, because I instinctively knew that this was the door through which they could detect our vulnerability—and the more vulnerable we looked, the easier it was for them to hit us and hit us hard. I stood in the alley, forcing myself to look strong, but Brigitte Duval interpreted my stoic look as supreme insolence and proceeded to empty her whole repertoire of the most hurtful insults she could think of in order to make my humiliation complete.

Alas, I had become one of her favourite targets, a fate rendered worse by the fact that she knew I had no one to protect me, and nowhere to run for cover, and by the look of evil in her eyes, I could tell that she revelled in my misfortune. With her repeated assaults, I soon gained the sobriquet of *'souffre-douleur'*. We all knew what it meant, for we had learnt in History that no royal child could be beaten, punished, or chastised, so the Royal Court used to employ peasant boys to take the punishments instead, which is how the term came to be. The *'souffre-douleur'*, the pain bearer, the pagan, the wench from the gutter—how awful it was for me to be known by those terrible words. I was now the peasant girl picked to take all sorts of punishments on behalf of a crazed woman who did not have the intellectual insight or the cerebral powers to work out that, if the blows made her feel a winner every time, in the eyes of Almighty God, she would forever be a loser.

From that day onward, she would never let go or relent, almost to the exclusion of everyone else. I could feel her eyes preying on me and following my every move, as if in a hypnotic trance; and on her bench, she always positioned herself in a half-sitting pose nearest to the alley, so that she could spring out more easily and pounce in a flash on her familiar prey.

One evening, it was the turn of my team to clear the refectory. After everyone had filed out to make their way silently to the dormitory, I began my chores by cleaning the floor. I scrubbed the tiles vigorously and tried to move swiftly so that I would not be the last to finish my duty. In my industrious diligence, and lost in my own thoughts as usual, I had forgotten that I had displaced the bucket of water and put it right behind me. As I worked my way energetically down the main alley, the inevitable happened. I bumped into the metal pail and knocked it over. The murky water spewed out all over the red tiles in an unstoppable flow which moved like a tidal wave towards the supervisors' feet. Brigitte Duval sprang out of her seat and shouted to Mlle Pierrette: "Grab her!"

I did not even have time to catch my breath for, almost instantly, their steely hands manacled me and dragged me all the way to the top floor, through the dormitory, straight to the washroom, and threw me in the shower. Up until then, I had made no attempt to resist—there was no point—two adults against me, I did not stand a chance.

"A cold shower, you filthy pagan, that's what you deserve!" Brigitte Duval yelled.

As she threw her threat, both women started to pull my clothes off, and it was only when I was left standing with just my vest and pants on that I decided to fight back. And I fought like a little tigress. They could do whatever they liked to me, but the one thing I would never ever allow anyone to do was to steal my soul or my dignity. I started to kick and punch as hard as I could, and the more I lashed out at them, the stronger I felt, and the more I kicked and fought, but they would not let go. So, as a last resort, I dug my teeth hard in their hands and arms and anything I could reach, and like a baby shark, I refused to let go. The Alsatian cow howled in pain and retrieved her hand.

"All right, you stupid little wench! You'll just have to go under the shower like that."

Their hands pushed me firmly under the shower and the Alsatian cow held me there while Brigitte Duval switched the shower full on. The rage that was boiling inside me was so intense that I did not feel the cold jets hit my little body. In fact, through some mysterious alchemic process, the rage and anger that I felt gnawing inside me suddenly turned into a strange sense of victory. All I could think of now was that they had not managed to undress me and now they would have to find some dry clothes from somewhere, since I did not have any spare. How were they going to explain that to Sister Marie-Catherine? I riled silently, because, it had to be said, although I feared her as much as anybody else, Sister Marie-Catherine had never picked on me. With all her faults and psychotic behaviour, she had always behaved with circumspect towards me, and even treated me with a certain reserve, almost in awe, as if wary of how much I could understand of what was going on. Brigitte Duval and the Alsatian cow clearly did not know this and the prospect of them getting into trouble because of their reckless behaviour pleased me no end.

"All right, that's enough now," The Alsatian cow decided, turning the shower off.

As I stood in the shower dripping wet and shivering, I felt more confident and stronger than ever before. What were they going to do now?

Brigitte Duval disappeared off. The Alsatian turned her heels and said:

"I'll go and fetch her a towel."

I stood in the cubicle, shivering uncontrollably, my teeth shattering and my lips turning blue with cold, but I did not care. A short while later, the supervisor returned with a towel and threw it at me. It was not mine.

"Take your wet clothes off and go to your bed while I go and fetch you a dry vest and pants." Then she closed the shower curtain with a sharp tug. At that point, I knew I had won, and instantly, I felt a warm glow wrap around my shivering limbs.

Back in my dorm, Roberte threw a puzzled glance at me. "Why are you all wet?"

"I've just had a cold shower…"

"Why?" She exclaimed.

"Because I spilled the bucket of water in the refectory… now they've got to find me some dry clothes. They're going to be in trouble…" I sneered while Roberte continued to stare at me, rather bewildered and totally confused by my reaction.

*

Life continued with Sister Marie-Catherine behaving like a demented shrew, the supervisors hitting harder than ever, and us re-enacting war games in the playground. Any outsider would have undoubtedly found it most odd that we should be allowed to hit and bash each other freely whilst being strictly forbidden to show any kind of affection towards one another, no matter how small. This prevailing violence made me keener than ever to distance myself from everybody. I did not want it and I certainly did not want to be part of it.

Thank goodness, I had Maryse to stand by me. She may not have been the brightest intellectual spark around, but she had an irresistible sense of fun and a sense of humour that never failed to lift my spirit. The strict Catholic regime had taught me to see everything in black and white. There were goodies and baddies, good deeds and bad deeds, saints and sinners; if anyone was caught dithering, or dared stray in a grey area, they were called doubters, and that in itself was a sin, because no one was allowed to question or doubt the word of God. However, through humour, Maryse had spotted the grey areas where the ridicule, highlighted by the excesses of human behaviour, was laid bare, and always provoked a cheap and ready laugh, a trick that Molière had liberally used in his plays to amuse his public and get back at the bourgeoisie. Maryse, who, just like me, had not yet heard of Molière, was using the very same trick to get her own back on the supervisors, and together, we laughed heartily at the cheap caricatures they portrayed of themselves, unwittingly awakening a bond sealed with our names and our own brand of childish humour. Through her witty remarks, riled under her breath so as not to get into trouble, Maryse was teaching me to re-evaluate my beliefs, and I was quite happy to follow her lead, because if the grown ups' actions were guided—or even, as they insisted, dictated by God—then He was decidedly a rather different God from mine.

Keeping well away from the battlefields, we found a new game to play. We liked to pretend that we were at school together and our chosen roles never differed: Maryse was the teacher and I was the model pupil. If we could, we would sit ourselves at a table in the vast, empty refectory, where, with a look of importance etched on her face, Maryse would pace the central alley in the same fashion as she had seen her own teacher do, and start the lesson, her chin held up high, her hands tucked behind her back, her shoulders thrown well back, and her face donning an air of superior authority. Every time she passed me, she would throw a condescending stare at her one and only pupil, looking down her nose and tut-tutting at my imaginary misconduct. As for me, I was always happy to respond in kind.

"What did I do, miss? I didn't do anything...you haven't marked my homework, miss...there's more on the next page... you missed a paragraph, miss..."

After fulfilling all her tasks, Maryse would declare haughtily: "Now, we're going to start the dictation."

As far as she was concerned, this was the best bit about being a teacher. Through silly sentences, she could at will and at leisure poke fun at the adults, and no matter how outrageous the sentences were, I had to copy them down scrupulously while she mimicked all the teacher's favourite taunts: "In your best handwriting...concentrate...think of the verb endings... don't forget the adjectives' agreements...is this your best handwriting?"

And I would laugh heartily at her perfected grown-up tone of voice.

"To-day," she began to dictate, detaching every syllable to give me time to write them down, "Annie Brenn is going to trip and fall flat on her face...have you got that?"

"Yeah...but don't make me laugh too much, otherwise I can't write properly."

"Po-ta-toes have dimples like an old granny's bot-tom."

More laughter.

"Shush! Quiet in class!"

After a short pause, she continued.

"Ma-de-moi-selle Agnès is a witch with hairs on her chin..."

She let out a little giggle.

"You're not supposed to laugh!" I chortled. "You're the teacher."

Maryse ignored my remark and resumed: "Brigitte Duval is uglier than the Alsatian cow..."

At that point, we both burst out laughing.

"I can't write that!" I protested, my ribs hurting with laughter. "If they ever find this piece of paper, I'm going to be in so much trouble!"

"Don't worry, they won't find it," she declared with her usual confidence, tucking her hands behind her back and pacing around me with her nose right up in the air just like Teacher did.

"Anyway, you're not supposed to interrupt, I am the teacher!"

"All right, I'll write it down..."

After a full page of carefully phrased sentences, she gave a cursory glance at my work, wrote ten out of ten at the bottom, and handed the sheet of paper back to me.

"But you haven't check the spelling properly," I protested.

"It doesn't matter, the writing is neat," she replied, covering for the fact that she probably did not know how to spell half of the words she had had so much fun dictating.

*

At the end of the school year, the word went round that there would no longer be a prize giving ceremony. At first, I was absolutely delighted—no more public humiliation for me—but the more I thought about it, the more I became disappointed. After all, if I did get the first prize, surely they would not give me another baby fairytale. A whole year on, I stood more chance of getting a proper book this time.

The Mother Superior came around the classrooms to give out the prizes. She called my name and handed me the book: *Le club des cinq et les saltimbanques*, by Enid Blyton. I was so thrilled that I did not even listen to what prize it was. I was not really interested because, for the first time ever, I had a proper storybook to read and it was about five children, their dog, and some gypsies. From the moment I started reading the book, I was able to escape the dreadful, morbid atmosphere of the Junior Section.

*

Time was moving on and with it, my perception of life

began to change. As I watched the other girls play in the familiar playground, I wanted to detach myself from this homogeneous group. I wanted to be left alone to delve into my own thoughts. Making a conscious effort to distance myself from the crowds, I could see the perspective of things more clearly and I could begin to make sense of the situation in which I had been thrown, although I did not know why. As I stood, leaning against the redbrick wall, I felt totally detached from the scene unravelling in front of me. It suddenly occurred to me that I did not seem to fit in, and what's more I did not want to fit in—the stark realisation was that: I did not belong.

My only escape was through the one and only book I possessed which I had read from cover to cover, over and over and over again; there was not one word in that book that I had not poured over several times. And, when I finished it, I tossed and turned the book to read whatever else there was to read, the covers, the binding, the small and large prints, before starting to read the book all over again. In this way, I learnt which edition it was, in which year it had been printed and published, by whom, and all the other small prints inside and outside the covers. It was my first literary journey and it left me hungry for more, much more.

CHAPTER XVI

The summer term was slowly coming to an end. The reports had been completed and stacked on the teacher's desk, the textbooks stripped of their temporary covers and put back on the shelves around the classroom, awaiting the next set of aspiring pupils who would learn to assimilate, recite, and regurgitate their learned content without ever having to show that they had actually understood the words they would chant in parrot fashion. The drawings and written work of meritorious pupils, which had brightened up the walls, lay now on the desks of their rightful owners, and on that last Friday, at three o'clock, we sat down at our desks, eagerly waiting for the last music lesson of the year to begin. The teacher switched on the radio and the announcer's voice boomed a cheerful greeting, played a cheerful piece of music that resounded along the corridors and in the playground through the open windows. At the end, the man's voice wished us a long happy summer holiday, his departing words booming, *"Au revoir!* See you *à la rentrée!"*

I did not want to be already thinking about the beginning of next term, for all I cared about right now was our next escapade to the holiday home in Sangatte. Sitting at my desk by the window at the back of the class, my mind had already wandered off to a place of respite. My view no longer hindered by the beautiful sight of my cherished tree, I could now picture the vast open spaces of the countryside and the sea; I could even smell the crisp iodine air stirred in relentless whirls by the cool northern wind over a landscape chequered with fields and bordered with vertiginous cliffs. No sooty buildings there to block the view, no grey skies to dull the atmosphere, and no Brigitte Duval to make our lives complete and utter misery.

Outside the school, the air was hot, the pavement dry, and the cobblestones greasy from smoky exhausts constantly spewing trails of black grime. The streets smelt of dried soot interspersed with delicious culinary smells, as we passed the baker's or the chip van. In the summer, these smells left me quite indifferent, but in the winter, knowing that we were walking back to a plate of cold soup, lumps of grey meat, and burnt milky pudding, I would have given my one and only book for a hot *croissant,* a *pain au chocolat*, or a bag full of fat chips smothered in piccalilli. Unknowingly, we suffered the same *supplice de Tantale*, the mythical king who, having offended the gods, was condemned to seeing and smelling mouth-watering feasts without ever being able to touch them or eat them. It was pure mental torture but, as with everything else, we had learnt to suppress our urges and impulses, and fool our cravings by re-directing our thoughts towards something even more alluring and far more exciting—and for me, that meant Sangatte: the little marginal kingdom ruled by queen bees and guarded by little soldiers in skirts.

We had grown only a little since the previous summer, but these few extra centimetres meant that we were not able to reclaim our places in the Snow White dormitory. It did not matter anyway: Maryse was not there. She had gone home for the summer holidays. My new dormitory felt cold and bare without her cheerful presence, but at least it had a view over the sea. As I wandered from dormitory to dormitory to check who was where, I lingered at the door of the Snow

White dormitory, with its little wooden beds and the same red chequered curtains framing its small windows, and in that fleeting moment, I stole myself away and saw myself back in the little bed, curled up snugly with Bashful or Sneezy in my arms. It had not always been a dream world, and its small white walls still reverberated of that war tune that had got us in so much trouble, but if you cared to remove all the adults, it was possible to glimpse a world full of colourful, glittering sparks. I sighed with a heavy heart and a whole wave of unfamiliar emotions flooded over to fill the void that Maryse's temporary departure had created. I did not know how to interpret my sudden reaction; all I knew was that without Maryse around, nothing could ever be as much fun.

*

"Hey!" A voice suddenly hailed. "You're in the same rank as me!"

I turned around to see who was talking to me. It was Annick.

"How do you know?" I enquired, not altogether sure whether I was interested.

"Mlle Bernadette showed me the list."

"She would never do that!" I refuted categorically.

"I'm one of her favourites, remember?" Annick retorted. "Anyway, from now on, you're on my side. You'll be an Indian and you'll be the second in command," she declared, wrapping her arm around my shoulders and dragging me across the lawn.

I was a little mystified by her sudden show of interest and did not know what to make of it at first.

"You've got to prove yourself, though…"

"How?" I asked, hoping that she would not ask me to do anything too painful or too daring.

"I need a pee…let's go and pee behind the blockhaus…"

"I can't do that!" I exclaimed feeling rather prudish all of a sudden.

"If you want to be an Indian, you have to show that you're capable of courage and bravery."

That was definitely not me, I conceded to myself, remembering that I had vouched never to become a martyr simply because I could not bear the thought of physical pain.

"No, I couldn't do that…I couldn't pee in public. What if we get caught?"

"We won't…the blockaus is too far from the main building…nobody will see us."

As I checked the grounds, Annie B. and another girl turned up. Annick was straight on to them.

"You two, I dare you to pee behind the blockaus," Annick challenged them.

"We've done it before!"

"There you see," Annick said, turning back towards me. "Come on, let's go quickly."

Before I knew it, I was running with them ready to do my first dare. As we contemplated the four wet patches on the ground, someone called: *"Rassemblement!"*

"Strange," Annick remarked. "We don't normally have roll call at this time."

For fear of being punished, we all ran towards the main building where we were told to go inside the playroom. Stranger still, the playroom was only used on rainy days and it was a beautiful day outside, admittedly with a cool breeze blowing but sunny all the same.

"In your ranks!" The supervisor shouted.

We shuffled around looking for our places, puzzled as to why we had been told to come in, in the middle of the afternoon. We whispered to each other hoping to find someone who would know the answer.

"Silence in the ranks!" The supervisor blasted.

The silence returned. We stood to attention, our arms rigid along our sides and our heads held up high, all the while wondering why. Someone must have done something really bad, and they were going to be asked to own up or everyone would be punished. Immediately, I visualised our four wet patches. Oh no, surely they had not seen them.

After several minutes, the double doors swung open and Sister Marie-Catherine entered, ashen face, sombre, and pensive. Instantly, we sensed something ominous, something grave, and in a reflex motion, we steeled ourselves and prepared for the oncoming onslaught. All tense and nervous, we waited for the nun to speak. Suddenly, it occurred to me that the only time I had seen her looking so sullen was when she had announced the death of Sister Marguerite from the linen room. What would it be this time?

After a long silence, Sister Marie-Catherine crunched her hands together, raised her cornet and prepared to break the news.

"I shall be leaving soon."

Her words crashed over our heads, hit us like a thunderbolt, and almost made us topple over. Had we heard properly? Had we? Totally aghast, we stood even straighter than before, keeping our shoulders well back and our heads really high, but there was one thing we could not do: we could not look Sister Marie-Catherine straight in the eyes. What if we were all at fault, what if in some way or other, we were responsible for her sudden departure?

While we stood even more rigidly in our ranks, transfixed by the news, still too afraid to show any kind of reaction, Sister

Marie-Catherine scanned our faces for a sign, a quiver, a hint of emotion which would reassure her that, despite everything, we were upset to see her go. Her pleading eyes were begging for our support, our solidarity, our sympathy, but after years of ill-treatment, she had managed to hijack and almost obliterate the basic human emotions that should have been slowly rising and blossoming. And for once, the roles were reversed: she looked lost and fragile, with no one to turn to and not a single girl daring to show the slightest hint of support. She was on her own and she looked so vulnerable.

My head swirled with contradictory messages. She had never picked on me and I had never been subjected to any of her brutal beatings. In fact—and that was something I had kept secret from everyone else, in case I lost my popularity—she actually liked me, and she had done me favours for which I was forever making excuses to prove to my little gang that I was definitely *not* one of her favourites. But...she had been so beastly towards other girls, the weak ones, those who could not help but look a mess, those who could not march in time or sing in tune, those who wet their beds, and those who had brought shame to the fold by daring to return from school with appalling reports.

The clashing of my thoughts was becoming too painful and I could no longer bear to look at the nun, so I lowered my gaze towards the tiled floor in an attempt to block out any thought or emotion that would betray the slightest feeling in her favour.

After a long heavy pause, Sister Marie-Catherine added:
"I shall be leaving at the end of the week."

At that point, the two rich sisters who were standing right at the front of their ranks began to sob quietly. Other girls also standing near the front, therefore in a vulnerable spot, followed suit. Perhaps, they felt compelled to shed a few tears to absolve themselves of any guilt that would have pointed an accusatory finger at them and said, 'it's because of you that I'm leaving', and while the tears, genuine or not, ran more freely now, the rest of us remained standing extremely still, too shocked to know how to react, or reluctant to show the huge relief the news had brought with it.

Sister Marie-Catherine gave a quick look at the girls who were crying, but unable to deal with this sudden show of emotion, she bit her lips and dismissed us. As we rushed towards the door and spilled out onto the main lawn, whose glowing mantel under the afternoon sunshine momentarily blinded us, none of us knew at that point that this was the very last time we were ever to see her again.

Once outside, we regrouped in our familiar little clusters keen to exchange our reactions but, even though we now knew that she was leaving for good, we were still too scared to reveal our true feelings...until one girl plucked up the courage and said:

"I'm glad she's leaving!"

"So am I!" Another one agreed.

Then someone uttered the unthinkable.

"She's been sacked!"

We all gasped at the thought. Surely not. Nuns cannot be sacked. Looking after us was not a job, it was their vocation.

Now that the flow had started, everyone spoke all at once, desperate to give their verdict.

"She deserves it!" One girl spluttered.

"Yeah...she was so cruel."

And as the girls proceeded to cite the many more reasons why she wholly deserved her fate and how we would be better off without her, I felt a sudden pang hit me deep inside. Instead of feeling vengeful and spiteful like everyone else, I was full of pity for the nun. In this desperate moment, I could not help but visualise her contrite face, the way her eyes had scanned our faces in a silent plea for our support, the way she had bowed her head, bit her lips, and dismissed us without another word. I wanted to run to her, grab her dangling sleeve and say: 'I don't want you to go…we forgive you…*I* forgive you…please stay,' when suddenly I heard a voice ask:

"What about you, Martha, are you glad to see her go?"

I was so deeply lost in my own thoughts that I had no idea where the question came from. I looked at the expectant faces staring back at me, and all my courageous thoughts melted away.

"Of course, I am," I muttered almost in a whisper, seized by a pang of guilt caused by what I felt was a blatant betrayal of Sister Marie-Catherine.

Give a little ray of sunshine to children and they will instantly forget the dark, tenebrous tunnel they have just been through.

The announcement that a new nun would come to replace her erased at a stroke the ghost of Sister Marie-Catherine. She was no longer there…she no longer existed. Our minds were now wholly focused on the promise of a new arrival.

"When is she coming?"

"What is she like?"

"What's her name?"

"What does she look like?"

Mlle Roseline and Mlle Bernadette stood in front of us, for once looking relaxed and rather amused by our impatient questioning.

"All will be revealed in good time…" was all they were prepared to say.

That Sunday, *rassemblement* before lunch was called earlier than usual and we guessed straight away that we were about to meet the new nun. We were so excited that we could not keep quiet in the ranks.

"Silence!" Mlle Bernadette shouted. "Sister will not come out until you are completely silent."

Our impatient curiosity got the better of us and we obeyed instantly. Finally, a short silhouette, much shorter than Sister Marie-Catherine, emerged from the main building. The nun descended, with precision, the few steps leading to the lawn, but stopped on the very last one in order to take a good look at us. Her brown eyes sparkled underneath her cornet and her head was slightly tilted over her right shoulder in a soft friendly manner. She was smiling. It must have been somewhat unnerving to have so many faces staring back at her, but the only sign of nervousness she showed was in the way she kept wringing her hands together. Suddenly, she spoke.

"*Bonjour*, my name is Sister Catherine."

The sudden shock of hearing that dreaded name again filled us with horror and instantly paralysed our little bodies. It was not quite *Sister Marie-Catherine,* but the name sounded too similar for us to accept it and welcome it unconditionally. Sensing an instant rejection, and perhaps a mixture of fear, Sister Catherine moved swiftly to put us at our ease by announcing a few changes.

"The first thing I want to do is to get rid of that ugly word 'ranks'. From now on, they will be known as 'teams' and each team will have a name."

She paused to let us absorb the full effect of her words. We looked at one another and smiled. Then, she continued.

"Each team will have a captain and with her help, *you* will choose the name of your own team."

Still unsure whether we were allowed to cheer, we prodded, pinched, and threw excited glances at one another.

"Then, instead of saying grace before each meal…"

Sudden gasps of dismay. Surely, it must be a cardinal sin to choose to ignore God.

"…We are going to *sing* to the Lord!"

More gasps…of astonishment this time, and perhaps…of excitement. The next thing she is going to say is that we do not have to go to mass anymore. No, that was a silly thought…. that would never happen.

"And why not start straight away. Since it is lunchtime, I know the perfect song for this…" And the minute she said this, she began to sing, uninhibited by the strange looks ogling at her:

Oh la la, j'ai faim, Chef, oh la la, j'ai faim
Oh la la, j'ai faim, Chef, oh la la, j'ai faim
L'heure a sonné, Chef, du déjeuner
Bon Appétit, Chef, Bon Appétit
Bon A…Bon A…Bon Appétit
Merci, merci à vous aussi…

We had never seen a nun behave so casually, so informally before, and we giggled timidly as we watched her wide cornet swing from side to side with the tempo. At first, the new nun could not get us to sing. Having been held in such a terrorised silence for so long, we could not all of a sudden nod our heads in rhythm and sing. However, thanks to the nun's cheerful encouragements, very gradually we began to relax and sing in a rather self-conscious way, in a low voice, hardly audible. After constant threats of crosses, punishments and deprivation, how could we be expected to loosen up and do something we had never done before unless it had been an order or a necessity even, like singing hymns in church?

Sister Catherine had come here with a specific goal. It would appear that she wanted to make our lives more bearable, and…dare I say it…more fun.

A new creative activity was introduced as Sister Catherine insisted on having the daily menu posted on the refectory door, and each team took it in turn to write, decorate, and colour it. This somewhat insignificant task became a source of pride as everyone compared the elaborate work that had gone into designing each menu. Our culinary vocabulary increased daily as the nun revelled in using fancy words to turn the most boring of dishes into a more palatable course—so she would offer the word *potage* instead of *soupe*, *pommes de terre en robe de chambre* instead of the more mundane plain boiled potatoes still in their skin as usual, so as to save Sister Agatha in the kitchen the trouble of pealing hundreds of potatoes. Sometimes, we had no idea what was on offer, as we did not understand all the culinary terms, but this provided a further source of fun as we speculated wildly over what it could possibly be. And there was no point in asking, for Sister Catherine would shake her head with a knowing smile and state in her unwavering way: "You'll just have to wait and see."

On special occasions, like the 14th July—Bastille Day, or the 15th August—the Ascension of the Virgin Mary, Sister Catherine would distribute meal tokens that we could exchange for a particular course. It would be like being in a restaurant, she had explained, and taking our new parts to heart, we walked around the tables in an affected manner, pretending to be posh *mademoiselles* posing for effect in a posh restaurant that we had never seen and did not know existed.

If only Maryse had been there, it would have been so much fun. I could easily picture her scratching the tip of her nose and shaking her head in an affected manner, as she pondered over which dish to plum for. Then, having made up her mind, I imagined her pointing at her choice with her lips pursed and her little auricular finger appropriately raised for the occasion, and using a grand tone of voice and a turn of phrase normally used by posh *mademoiselles*, she would say, 'I shall have this one'. I really could not wait to tell her.

Save for the rare occasions when the weather had dictated otherwise, our daily routine remained largely unchanged. We still had to go for our afternoon nap during which we could whisper or we could read. It was then that I spotted Claire engrossed in a book, which did somewhat surprise me. Claire was not a natural reader; in fact, as far as she was concerned, reading was a downright painful chore totally devoid of any pleasure. Why should we have to trudge our way through words and sentences that revealed useless facts and parted useless pieces of information? Who cared about Vercingetorix uniting the Old Gaulle only to be defeated and killed by Ceasar? Or about Clovis, the first proper King of the whole of France? As for Emperor Charlemagne…she had a bone to pick with Charlemagne. In fact, many children had, for he was the one who decreed that all children should be able to read and write, therefore they should all go to school. Despite his glorious victories that had helped broaden the frontiers of the French territory, making France a powerful force to be reckoned with, he was hugely unpopular with the majority of pupils all over France. And while I churned all the reasons why Claire detested reading, I watched her perplexed, slowly leafing the pages of her book, lingering on certain words, and chortling quietly away in her little corner. I simply could not resist, I had to find out.

"What's that you're reading?" I asked with trepidation.

"*Le Roi des Microbes*," she said with glee.

"The King of Germs? That's a weird title. What is it about?" I sneered, ready to be gripped in a fit of giggles.

"It's about this colony of germs which lives inside this old man's nostrils...his nose: that's their kingdom."

I tried to muffle my sudden laughter.

"You're kidding me! This book is about germs that live in a kingdom up an old man's nostrils? You're making it up!" I chortled.

"No, it's true! It's right here in the book. Their leader is called Michael...and you know what? Their greatest peril is when the old man sneezes. So, Michael and his pals have to predict when it's going to happen by looking for signs up the nostrils so that they can each grip a hair just in time to make sure they don't get expelled with the snort and the spray and everything."

As Claire spoke, I was visualising the scene and I was laughing so much that my ribs really hurt.

"I don't believe you," I managed to splutter in between two bouts of laughter. "No one would ever write a book about germs...and anyway it's disgusting!"

"You think it's disgusting! Well, you should see what happens when the old man catches a cold!"

Despite laughing too much, I managed to ask:

"Can I borrow your book when you've finished with it?"

"Yeah...but I want to finish it first."

I looked at how much she had read and roughly estimated that in a day or two, it would be my turn to laugh at the adventures of Michael and his pals stuck in this old man's nostrils. Burning with impatience, every day, I greeted Claire with the same question: "Have you finished it yet?"

And every day, she gave me the same reply, "No, not yet."

"Haven't you? Why? The book is not that big. How come you haven't finished it yet?"

Two whole weeks passed and she still had not finished it. I was beginning to lose interest. I would have to find something else. At naptime and at bed time, I peered under vacated beds from dormitory to dormitory, hoping to find another book to borrow. Then one day, as usual after lunch, we played outside, running in the grass or around the *blockhaus* and playing 'tag'. In the distance, we heard someone call *'rassemblement!'* We quickly rushed to get into our newly formed teams, playfully pushing and shoving each other out of line. I was about to push Claire when she handed me the long-awaited book. Knowing what it was, I immediately snatched it from her, practically in a state of euphoria.

Lined up in our teams, we still had to stand very straight, shoulders back and chins up, which is not easy if one is attempting to read a book at the same time. So, I made myself as small as possible and hid behind the girl standing in front of me. Then, all hunched up, I feverishly opened the first page. I smiled and Claire began to giggle. Suddenly, her face went all serious.

"Watch out! The supervisor's coming!" She said in a loud whisper.

The effect was instant. I straightened up, bit my cheeks, tried to look serious…and burst out in an uncontrollable laughter. Fortunately, the supervisor did not have time to chastise me, for at this moment, the new nun with the reviled name appeared.

In her soft, gentle manner, she announced that on our next walk, we would have a specific task to fulfil. Sighs of disappointment. As if we did not have enough chores already… I scowled heavily and grumbled to myself in a rather petulant mood: whatever she asks for, I'm not doing it! And I don't care if I get punished! As I vouched to rebel, a dark cloud rumbled over my head, but through the thundering noise of my recalcitrant thoughts, I heard the nun say: "When you go for your walk this afternoon, I want you to find a name for your respective teams..."

Instantly, the dark cloud that had scrambled over my head popped and an audible sigh of relief rose to punctuate her last sentence.

"However," she continued, "you must keep the names secret for they will all be revealed at supper time tonight."

We looked at each other, thrilled to be involved in a mystery. Now, that was exciting. That afternoon, after our nap, we filed excitedly outside the *colonie*, walked up the deserted country road to Peuplingue, sandwiched between fields of barley and fields of hay, breathing with relish the country smells and the sea breeze, and with our keen eyes, we scoured the whole of nature like we had never done before, in search of a name that would be inspiring, imaginative, exciting and...easy to spell. We watched flocks of small birds fly...with no name. We picked and selected whole bouquets of wild flowers...with no name, for the supervisors themselves could not tell us what they were either. We studied with intent the old farmer on his tractor, the wooden barn full of hay, the concrete water tower standing ever so tall on the brow of the hill, and still, we could not find any word that would appeal to our imaginations and make us proud of our team.

Having ploughed the whole of the countryside in search of a suitable name, we turned our attention towards the sea. There, at last, we found something, although I was not entirely sure I liked it. Nevertheless, we settled ourselves on a dry patch of grass while Annick, the captain of our team, duly wrote the name down on a piece of paper, folded it, and handed it over to Mlle Bernadette who immediately opened it and nodded her head with a neutral expression on her face. Having fulfilled her task, Annick came to sit next to me.

"I'm glad you're in my team," she declared totally out of the blue.

"Oh yeah?" I replied trying to look suitably flattered, although I did not understand why she had said it.

I had not done anything yet; I had not even come up with any good names for the team. However, one thing led to another, and before I knew it, in everyone's mind except mine, my name became intrinsically linked with that of Annick, which did baffle me somewhat, as I had never wanted to be associated with anybody, except with Maryse with whom I shared a mischievous streak that had become our common bond—both of us having been caught in the turbulent whirls of an auspicious wind which had thrust us together at the same time and in the same place. Our relationship was more circumstantial than anything else, an accidental quirk of fate for which I was perpetually grateful. But Annick? In my mind, she was still the new girl who usually hung about with the favourites, the older girls and the rich sisters, whereas my gang was made up of the little ones, the weaker ones, the grubbier ones, sorted by size rather than by preference.

By contrast, Annick was the big Indian Chief, the leader that everybody wanted to follow, the adjudicator who would stand up for you, unafraid to answer back on your behalf, the organiser, the supporter of one and all, and now, apparently, my new friend. I did not know what to say.

*

"*Rassemblement!*"

God Almighty, how we came to loath that word. The minute we started to enjoy ourselves, we had to drop everything and scurry like little bunnies from every corner of the main lawn to line up in our teams. It was such a joy-killer, so tedious, and so boring.

Sister Catherine, perhaps because of her petite size, had taken the habit of standing on the steps in front of the main door, and from there, she proceeded to unfold the pieces of paper very slowly while we waited with bated breath to hear the new teams' names. Having opened all the papers, she scoured our faces lengthily, in a blatant ploy to test our patience further, and deliberately prolonged the moment when all would be revealed, because, in her mind, the suspense was part of the fun.

Eventually, she read out the first name.

"*Les grenouilles!*"

The word caused an instant roar of laughter. Who on earth came up with that name? 'The frogs?' Some girls actually wanted to be called 'the frogs?'

"That's us! That's us!"

More laughter. That was Martine C.'s team. I did not know who their captain was, but they certainly showed their spirit.

Sister Catherine raised her arms to appease the excited crowd.

"*Les libellules!*"

Now, that was a good name, rather intellectual I thought, as this was not a commonly known word among us, but this was hardly surprising coming from Marie's team. After all, Marie, who, I had deduced, must be a year older than me, since she was in the year above me, was considered the cleverest girl of the Junior Section, the top pupil of her year, who always returned from school festooned with all the top prizes. 'Dragonflies' may not sound *très recherché* in English, but to a bunch of primary school girls with a scant knowledge of natural history, it certainly did.

"*Les hirondelles!*"

I really liked that name and wished I had come up with it myself. 'The swallows' sounded like everything I aspired for: freedom to fly anywhere towards exotic climates in search of new adventures and new discoveries. I wished I was in their team.

Then, the name of our team was finally revealed.

"*Les coquilles!*"

More laughter. I know, the name did not sound very inspiring and I even cringed when I heard it, but we were by the sea and the beaches were covered in seashells!

The main difference for us girls was that we were no longer merely identified by a rank or the number on our uniforms. We were now able to identify with a homogeneous group that was our team, and we wanted to strive and excel towards a common goal: to uphold the good name of our newly formed group and gain a lot of pride from it. It was not much, but far better than being called 'little wenches only fit for the gutter'.

To increase our interest and sustain our attention, Sister Catherine took the habit of pitching the teams against each other by setting little challenges, and as we became a little more relaxed about the nun's radically different approach, her novel strategies gradually met with our full approval.

Suddenly, we worried that Sister Catherine was not here to stay.

"Are you coming back with us to *Saint Vincent?*" Annick asked.

"Would you rather I did not?" She teased, unwilling to reveal her plans.

"Are you?" Claire repeated insistently.

Sister Catherine smiled and gave us a cryptic answer, which was to become one of her trade marks.

"You'll just have to wait and see."

Her refusal to give a straight answer was beginning to irritate me and there was only one way to deal with it: by not asking any questions, which was probably what she was aiming for. Again, the way she had us weaving around her little finger, always gaining the upper hand, was greatly annoying too, but the reason why she excelled with so much ease at leading us by the nose—as the French expression goes—was because, unbeknown to us, Sister Catherine had a keen interest in child psychology—which is probably why she had been chosen to replace the formidable Sister Marie-Catherine—and we became a ready source of clinical subjects on whom she could experiment at leisure.

It took me a while to realise that I had become her favourite source of study, because, as far as she could make out, I had confounded all known theories by being the one child in the Junior Section with no known background, no emotional or affective ties, and no environmental advantages, which would have stimulated or satisfied my insatiable intellectual curiosity. What's more, I had experienced the most oppressive of regimes, which, according to all the learned psychologists, should have thwarted my burgeoning personality and destroyed my youthful spirit, and yet...I was thriving. She was flummoxed. *Give a little ray of sunshine to a child and she will soon forget the dark tenebrous tunnel she has just been through.*

The next assignment we were given, as we prepared to depart for yet another of those compulsory walks, was to come

223

up with new words to a familiar tune, which we would all sing at our next gathering. Our team, *Les Coquilles*, immediately agreed that it should be written around Sister Catherine because, so far, she had done such a good job at making our lives more tolerable that it would be a fitting way to show our heartfelt gratitude. The team chose a nice piece of dried grass and sat down. I chose my own little patch slightly apart from the others, and quickly settled on the ground.

"No, no, Martha," Annick said with pencil and paper at the ready. "You come and sit right next to me. I need you here because you're good with words."

And, while the rest of the team came up with the ideas, I came up with the rhymes. After we had written half of the song, Claire turned to me clearly impressed.

"Wow! You're good. How do you do it?"

I did not know; the words just came to me. How could I possibly explain that? So, I shrugged my shoulders and threw my hands up into the air in a sign of complete puzzlement.

'*Une soirée*', an evening of entertainment had been planned for after supper. Each team took it in turn to sing their signature tune, and I listened avidly, convinced that ours was the best because no one else had thought of mentioning Sister Catherine in their lyrics. A real *tour de force*, I declared to myself with a self-congratulatory smile. I looked across to the nun. She was smiling too.

That summer, we left Sangatte with nostalgic hearts, and from the moment we settled onto our seats in the coach, we began to reminisce over the good time we had been able to enjoy in an unusually relaxed atmosphere. As the engine roared, we sang the few songs we had learned under the guidance of Sister Catherine, and we sang our song, the one with the lyrics that everybody else adopted and sang with real gusto, since we were now allowed, in order to say thank you to Sister Catherine. But as the coach hurtled towards the grey landscape of the heavy industrialised North, it was difficult not to notice that the general mood had become strikingly different, and not just because we were allowed to sing; the lighter more convivial atmosphere was without doubt due to one factor alone: we no longer dreaded going back to *Saint Vincent*.

CHAPTER XVII

Upon our return, the teams were reshuffled with the specific intention to break up any friendships, old or new, that had been formed. Consequently, Annick and I were placed in different teams, which stood us well apart from each other in the stark playground. As the names were called, and the teams gradually reformed, I stood in my line, still wondering what the fuss was all about. Back in Sangatte, Annick had been the captain of my team and we had enjoyed each other's company, talking about various things: her father, her brothers, and how she would like to be a secretary when she grew up because her mother was a secretary, and how she had laughed heartily when I declared that I wanted to become a nun. This idea only came to me because I did not know what else girls could do except work in one of those deafening, back-breaking textile factories.

Rather a saint than a martyr, I had decreed, unable to understand why Annick found it so funny. Anyhow, we had returned to *Saint Vincent* with everyone else declaring us the firmest of friends, and I was more than happy to accept this glorious accolade, mightily proud of my new association, but totally baffled by the strength of it.

*

One day, Maryse ran to me and dragged me towards the pigsty.

"I've got a secret!" She said all excited.

"Oh yeah?" I riled dubious.

There was nothing new about Maryse coming up with some incredible secret; it was one of her favourite games, often revolving around the mysterious lives of witches. Her best secret so far had been that witches could actually communicate secretly among themselves. Yes, she had assured me while desperately trying to keep a straight face, by producing little farts, just like Indians could pass messages to each other by shaping clouds with a blanket and a small campfire. She was always extremely convincing, and sometimes it was hard not to believe her. I waited for her new secret, already laughing at her imminent joke.

"Brigitte Duval's leaving!" She blurted.

"No!" I exclaimed in sheer disbelief.

"Yes, she is!"

Stunned by the incredible news, I lost the urge to laugh.

"How do you know?"

"I can't tell you, but she's definitely leaving."

"Why? Has she been sacked?" I asked, recalling the unexplained departure of Sister Marie-Catherine.

I scrutinised my friend's face, more suspicious than ever. I wanted to believe her. I was desperate to believe her, but I remained cautious. I knew Maryse only too well. I continued to stare at the bright expression on her face, trying to decipher the meaning of her quirky smile and waiting to catch a sign that would betray the whole pretence. The tyrant, the cruel shrew, the monstrous woman with a heart colder than ice, a tongue more forked than the squirmiest cobra and fouler than a cesspit, and a way to hit at her favourite targets with a precision better calculated than that of a laser ray cutting through a sheet of cold metal, was actually leaving? I simply could not bring myself to believe the incredible news, could not take it in; it was far too good to be true. Despite all my doubts, I still felt the irresistible urge to let off screams of huge relief; I wanted to punch the air and shout a resounding, "Yeah!" that would have had all the nuns hanging out of the first floor windows wondering what all the commotion was about. I wanted to grab Maryse's hands and do a little impromptu dance, while I sang my new profound joy, but...was it true?

"When? When is she leaving?" I finally asked, as if coming out of a dream, pressing Maryse for more factual details that would confirm she was telling the truth.

"I don't know...next week? Next month? My dad didn't tell me."

"So, it's your dad who told you! It must be true then," I concluded with glee.

I could not believe it. It sounded too good to be true. Within days, or perhaps less, I would never hear again disparaging insults whistle through her viper's lips. I would never again see her ugly face, with its bulging eyes darting murderous looks at me, and her hands would at last be free of the list of names which she blotted liberally with big black crosses in order to sully our names and blight our humble existence. The tyrant was leaving and the Alsatian cow was about to lose her closest ally. With Sister Marie-Catherine gone, would Brigitte Duval's departure bring, at long last, a little bit of peace and harmony? I smiled at my friend and together we skipped back to the playground where, for once, I readily joined in the laughter and all the games.

I wanted to bounce the ball hard against the brick wall. I wanted to join the queue to skip and chant as two girls swung a long thick rope. I wanted to jump around the elastic that two other girls held around their waist, and I felt so light with joy that I wanted to play hopscotch with my right foot rather than my left. It was all quite unbelievable and for your sake, Maryse, I dearly hoped it was true.

Other more welcomed changes soon followed. We still had to line up, though not in 'ranks' but in our reshuffled teams, because this was the quickest and most efficient way to instil order and discipline, but there would be no more marching on the spot. Instead, Sister Catherine taught us more songs, some of them with actions, which we loved to mime with great enthusiasm and great fun. Now, after lunch, and sometimes supper, instead of having to listen to those self-deprecating, self-flagellating sermons aimed at torturing our poor little souls, she told us stories, sometimes religious ones, sometimes fairy tales like *The Little Match Girl*, and by popular demand, her very own story about how she got 'the call', and we sat on our wooden benches totally transfixed in an enthralled silence, mesmerised by the lively pictures she conjured up in our newly-awakened imaginations. Then, just as she reached the most exciting point in the story, she would declare coolly, in a controlled and calculated move, "that's all we've got time for today."

And, as usual, we would plead and beg her to continue, but none of our loud protests could make her budge from her decision.

"Please, Sister, just tell us quickly what happens next?"

And as always, she would greet our pleas with a nod of the head and a cryptic smile and stubbornly reiterate the same statement she always made when she wanted to dismiss us in a kind, but firm way, "you'll just have to wait and see..."

Having discovered how good we were at listening to her stories, she decided to use the same stratagem to make us listen more attentively to the dominical sermons, thereby improve our behaviour in church. From now on, she told us, she would ask questions about the sermon and whoever could answer the most would have a reward.

"What kind of reward?" A girl asked on behalf of everyone else.

There again, Sister Catherine had no intention of giving the game away. She wanted our undivided attention and the best way to obtain it, she had decided, was to keep us guessing.

I do not think I had ever listened to a sermon as intently as I did that following Sunday, and back in the refectory, each time she quizzed us, my arm shot up faster than anybody else. Thanks to the biblical epics I had reluctantly sat through at the cinema, I could not only retell the parable, I could actually visualise it, which is why I was able to remember so many details about the biblical stories.

The idea of a reward had such an impact on us that Sister Catherine used it liberally: there would be rewards for the tidiest girl, for the best kept dorm, for the cleanest wash-basin, and although the rewards did not always follow, we drew immense pride and satisfaction at being selected the best of something. She even used the large mirror in the refectory as an ocean where each team was represented by a little coloured boat. Ours was yellow, and as points were awarded to teams for good effort, good discipline, and neat presentation, the little boats proceeded laboriously in a colourful wake from one side to the other, until a victorious team was declared. It was huge fun, but extremely effective.

I won the prize for being the tidiest girl, though no reward followed, but when it came to discipline, with Maryse on my team, we were always going to be trailing behind. Yes, I too had the same thought: we were indeed in the same team because, strangely enough, despite our close and longstanding friendship, we were not deemed friends, but rather partners in crime.

Not all the rules were changed, however. Crosses still fell next to our names, which led to more paragraphs to be learnt by heart, more mind-dulling lines to copy and, of course, what every girl dreaded most, no home leave for those who had collected ten crosses or more. And, when our misdemeanours were regarded as too serious, we could still expect to be smacked and Sister Catherine had herself broken a ruler on Annie B.'s thigh, as she smacked the girl for another bout of recalcitrant behaviour. The difference, this time, was that we all felt that the silly girl had wholly deserved it. We even laughed when the nun paraded the two halves of the ruler that had snapped cleanly in her hand.

Despite all efforts from adults to separate us, Annick and I maintained a close association. Girls were sternly warned off by others—if they even thought of coming between us. To tell the truth, the whole idea of a close friendship was beyond me, but the thought of being associated with one of the most popular girls in the Junior Section proved irresistible, and I ambled about the playground, more aloof than ever, cultivating an air of cool arrogance that made me do things I had never dared to even think about before. As for the adults, they could say whatever they liked; we would carry on being 'a team', even if that meant converging two teams into one.

Annick often talked about her dad, but rarely about her mother, only to say that she was a secretary. She had three brothers who were all at a boys' boarding school in the neighbouring town of Roubaix, about whom she rarely talked, except to say, "my big brother would like you".

I used to smile, but never commented, because I did not want to hurt her feelings; the main reason being that, although

I had a jovial bond with Maryse and a certain degree of affinity with Annick, I had always been free from any emotional tie with anyone and that was the way I wanted to remain.

When I was not lock-armed with Annick, I could be seen with Maryse, plotting our next mischief or resuming our silly games. Her favourite taunt was to go and stand in front of Mlle Agnes outside the kitchens and stare. Puzzled, the old woman would ask what we wanted and Maryse would pretend to make small talk while giggling every time the kitchen helper twitched her eyes.

"See," she would whisper discreetly, snagging my arm at the same time. "That's what witches do", and we would both dissolve into an uncontrollable laughter and walk away.

But the game that nearly got us into serious trouble happened during our daily walk to school. A few days earlier, some girls had been reported to Sister Catherine by someone who had caught them looking up naughty words in the dictionary. At the time, I did not even know what a naughty word was and only wished it had been me who had owned the dictionary. The girls were duly punished but, uncharacteristically, the culprits had not been named or shamed. This was most unusual; in fact, it had never happened before which fuelled the incident with a lot of intrigue and mystery. Who were the girls in question and why were their identities kept secret? A lot of the speculations pointed the finger firmly at the group of 'favourites', the rich sisters had even been mentioned and were thought to be in some way implicated. However, the question we all wanted to know was: *what were the words they had looked up?*

Maryse did not know who the culprits were for sure, but she knew the words, oh yes, she knew the words. This gave her an idea.

One Thursday afternoon, during an idle moment which

should have been devoted to making up our lists of sins ready for confession, we stared at each other racking our brains.

"How many sins have you got on your list?" I asked.

"Two," Maryse replied.

"I can't think of any and I can't tell the priest I haven't got anything to confess, he's never going to believe me."

"Make them up then."

"What have you got?"

"I'm not telling, it's supposed to be confidential..."

"It's just to help me...I don't know what to write..."

"Think of the ten commandments."

"I am, I am, but I don't understand half of them...a-dul-te-ry...what's that?"

"Don't worry about it, just write it down..."

"I'm not writing that down, it might be worse than murder!"

"Pick another one then..."

"I don't know which one to pick...I don't really want to pick one that's really bad. Oh God, I really don't know what to confess."

"Well, as I said, you'll just have to make them up."

"OK, what shall I write?"

"It doesn't matter what you write, your sins are gonna be absolved anyway."

"I know what I'm going to do, I'll write ten sins and the very last one will be: I lied. That way, I'll be forgiven for making up all the sins. That's it, that's me done! What are we going to do now?"

"I've got an idea," Maryse whispered. "Get another piece of paper and write '*merde*' on it..."

"*Merde?*" I repeated, pondering over the new word.

"Shush!" She warned, putting her finger over her mouth.

"It's a really naughty word, so don't say it out loud, just write it down and fold the piece of paper so you can't see it, and keep it in your pocket."

"How do you spell it?" I asked in all innocence. Maryse burst out laughing.

"You're kidding me!"

"No," I protested in all seriousness. "I've never heard of this word before."

"I don't believe you," she insisted, "everybody's heard of *merde*! Anyway, write down: m-e-r-d-e…"

"And then what?"

"Keep the paper in your pocket and when we go to school tomorrow, we'll drop it in a letter box."

"What for?" I asked, unable to see what she was getting at.

"For fun! Can you just imagine the faces of the old ladies when they open the piece of paper?"

We had a rough idea of who lived where because in the summer months, the old ladies, usually dressed in black, often used to sit on their old wicker chairs just outside their front doors where they would pass the time knitting or simply staring in sustained beatitude at the passers-by. But, what interested me more than their presumed reaction was to increase my rather limited range of naughty words.

"Do you know any more?"

"Yeah, but I can't say them because they are really too rude…but I'll write some of them down for you."

Upon which, Maryse proceeded to write one word at a time before showing it to me.

"What does that mean?"

And every time, I would put my hand in front of my mouth, half shocked and half giggling. Then, she wrote: '*ferme ta gueule*'.

"What's that?" I asked, my eyes ogling and my lips anticipating another awesome phrase.

"Now, you must never say that! It's really *really* rude. You'd probably get expelled if you were ever caught saying that," she warned sternly.

"*D'accord, d'accord*, but tell me what it means!" I asked impatiently.

"It means 'shut your gob!' but don't ever say it, and if you do, you never heard it from me."

The following day, Maryse and I made sure that we stood right at the back of the crocodile file, and on our way to school, as we looked out for the mail slot on each door, we dared each other to drop our word first, but each time we chickened out, and that afternoon, we returned to *Saint Vincent* with the words still tucked away in our pockets. The same thing happened for several days, until one day, only a few yards away from our school, Maryse took hold of my hand and we dropped back from the group. Then she stopped outside a green door and slipped the piece of paper through the letter box. Immediately after, she rang the bell and we dashed back to our ranks breathless, running like a pair of scared rabbits, giggling all the way. Following this first success, we became more emboldened and a whole row of redbrick terraced houses became victim to our little prank, until one day, our group was gathered by Annie Brenn. There had been a complaint from an old lady who lived in the very house with the green door, and the supervisor wanted to know who the culprits were. Of course, we did not own up to anything until she started to ask each girl individually.

When she interrogated Maryse, my friend adamantly refuted the allegation with a complete look of innocence on her face,

"It was not me, *Mademoiselle*, my piece of paper was blank!"

At first, none of us registered what Maryse had actually said, that unwittingly, my friend had spilt the beans. Annie Brenn laughed like I had never seen her laugh before, then she pointed out to Maryse that she had, effectively, confessed to her own crime. Afterwards, she turned to me. I was always happy to remain silent over a mischievous deed, but if asked directly, I could not bring myself to deny it because Jesus, not to mention my guardian angel, would be so disappointed in me, so I answered truthfully.

We were given hundreds of lines to write, spelling out how we ought to behave in a polite society, but that was all—no screaming, no public beating, nothing that would have thrashed out our inconsiderate behaviour out of our wicked bodies. It was not Sister Catherine's way. She had more clever, more subtle and resourceful means of manipulating our behaviour without systematically resorting to violence, and to our general consternation, she always won. The only trait that aligned her with Sister Marie-Catherine was in their mutual confusion, intended or not, between the words humility and humiliation. Whenever the nuns wanted to instil some degree of humility in us, they invariably resorted to the tactic of humiliation. This was a most hurtful ploy, a ruthless application of cause and effect that was always hard to bear. But as usual, we toughened up, licked our wounded hearts or souls, and carried on as if nothing had happened.

One day, Sister Catherine summoned me. When I saw her in the refectory, leaning against the very same sideboard where Sister Marie-Catherine had stood on that most memorable occasion, when instead of receiving a right old rollicking I had ended up with a new pair of gym shoes, I became tense.

Then I saw the large mirror behind her head with the little boats still plodding along, and that little detail depicting our progress, however slow, encouraged me to think the better of this impromptu meeting. I relaxed a little, but not before wondering: what was it about this time? Sister Catherine did not waste any time in revealing the purpose of her call.

"I think I have found a family for you to go to on leave-out weekends."

"Oh really!" I exclaimed, rather more excited than I thought I would be. After all, it had never bothered me to stay at the orphanage weekends in, weekends out. The food was a lot better when there were less of us around and we could have as much as we wanted, as it was the only time Sister Agatha from the kitchen catered for more than was needed. Sometimes, we even had real cakes with cream and everything for pudding. These were always absolutely scrumptious.

"There are two conditions though…" She continued. "The first is: you must be ten."

I looked at her hesitantly. I knew she thought me clever. Was I about to shatter her illusions by admitting that I did not really know how old I was?

"Er…am I ten yet?" I asked gingerly. "I am…ain't I?" I quickly added, keen to preserve the high esteem she held me in.

"Well, you will be…in October. The second condition is that you will be expected to help with the housework."

"By doing what?" I quickly enquired, my hopes of having fun instantly dashed.

"Well, by helping with the washing up, cleaning the floors, and whatever else needs doing."

That was a real blow to my pride and self-esteem. These people only wanted me so that they could use me as their servant.

"*D'accord,*" I conceded after a thoughtful pause. "I'll do it."

No sooner had I agreed than I began to have second thoughts. Why, in the name of God, was I willing to accept such a poor deal? Why was I letting myself be used and humiliated, and for what gain? I wanted to retract there and then, but it was too late, I had already accepted.

I was now busy reasoning my decision, gauging the good and bad. For one thing, I was already well familiar with all the tedious chores. On the positive side, for the first time ever, I would be able to say, what I had heard the other girls say a hundred of times, "I'm going out this weekend!" I got excited just thinking about it. From now on, I would have to watch how many crosses I would get and make sure I did not notch up ten. That was going to be a real challenge because, up until now, I had not really cared.

When leave-out weekend arrived, M. Langeais came to collect me in his sky blue Simca, which had a cream rooftop. When I first saw him, I instantly felt rather intimidated by his somewhat large frame. He was indeed a lot taller than M. Cateau. I do not recall greeting the new man with a mop of thick dark hair and a dark moustache as I settled in the passenger seat. I just sat resolutely silent, my eyes staring fixedly at the empty street ahead. The man squeezed his large frame into the driver's seat and while I waited for him to start the car, deaf and dumb to his cheerful greeting, my sensitive nose was assailed by the damp smell of leather mixed with cigarette smoke. The car moved, and immediately I flew away, in my head, into a world whose door stood only a few paces away, on the other side of the pavement. I remained silent while I watched the landscape rush past the window. I suddenly noticed that I must have grown, for I no longer needed to stretch my neck to see out of the car window.

Then, while he was driving, I turned my head to have a good look at the stranger, and for a few calculated minutes, I stared at him like a maid stares at a prospective employer—with the best grumpy look I always sported when Maryse was not with me. With his shock of dark hair and square jaw, he looked a lot younger than M. Cateau. Through his dark eyes and thick black moustache, I could not decipher his thoughts, but judging from his initial reaction when he first saw me, I could tell that I was not exactly what he had expected. For a ten year old, if indeed this was my age, I looked rather small.

We came to a modern house situated on a wide street surrounded by wide open countryside. The view gave me an instant sense of light and space, reminiscent of the feeling that overwhelmed me every time we returned to Sangatte, and stood in complete contrast with the tall and narrow lugubrious terraced house of the Cateaus.

Mme Langeais opened the front door with a baby wedged on her hip.

"Come on in," she invited in a rather friendly tone. "You don't have a bag?" She enquired a little surprised.

"No," I replied, wondering why I should have a bag.

After our short introduction, she took me straight to the kitchen where two little girls were sitting quietly at the table. They were drawing.

"Now, this is Sabine, the eldest. She's five. Then, this is Beatrice, she's three. And this is Virginie, just one year old." She declared, taking the baby's hand and cooing at her adoringly. "As you can see, they're all girls."

I stared at the little girls and at the adults for a while, not knowing what I was supposed to do or say. Feeling totally lost, I fixed my gaze on the creamy-white tiles and remained silent. As the pause extended further in an awkward silence, I looked again at the little girls, trying to make out what they were busy drawing, all the time wishing that the woman would get on with it and tell me what tasks she had for me so that I had something to do rather than standing here like a lemon, feeling totally inadequate in front of a bunch of strangers, big and small.

Finally, the woman deposited her infant into the high chair.

"Come with me. I'll show you the rest of the house."

She took me to the lounge, which extended into a dining room with views over the large back garden, then upstairs, to the girls' bedroom furnished with two bunk beds and a cot, past the parents' bedroom, until we arrived into a small room which had, among other things, an ironing board and a whole horde of household brick-a-brack piled up against the wall. Finally, there below the window lay a small camp bed, my bed.

"Right," she said, going back downstairs, talking to her husband. "I have a bit of shopping to do so I'll take her with me; that way, she can explore the neighbourhood."

Then turning to me with a quizzical look as if she had forgotten something, she asked: "Your name is Martha, isn't it?"

"Yes," I replied, already missing my friends back at *Saint Vincent*.

While I pondered over my new fate among these complete strangers, some other thought cropped up in my head. After years of believing that the word 'mother' was a synonym for 'doorwomen'—since the only time I had ever seen them was at the school gate—and that 'father' was a word for all the men in the world, I was slowly coming to terms with the fact that they may not have meant that at all, that their roles were more precisely defined, more individually prescribed, and more specific to each family unit. I was beginning to understand that children had parents, parents had children, and that, somehow, they were tied together by an invisible bond—though what kind of bond, I really had no idea—and the mystery of it all, how each unit fitted together, left me even more perplexed, especially as I did not seem to fit anywhere in the equation at all.

And so, for the first time, I was included in a family routine. I helped bath and dress the girls, but not the baby. I ate with the family, and then did the washing up; then, I was allowed to watch the big black and white television.

In those days, there were two very popular children programmes, '*Bonne Nuit Les Petits*' and '*Le Manège Enchanté*' (*Good Night Children* and *The Magic Roundabout*) shown at around seven o'clock each evening, and at the end of these programmes, children all over France knew that it was time to go to bed. I never once heard the little girls complain, because the sandman himself had said that it was bedtime and the little stars of the show, a brother and sister called Nicolas and Nicolette, always went to bed without any fuss once the magic sand had been scattered all over their bedroom window. What sweet dreams would they be having, tucked up in those beautifully decorated little wooden beds?

Being that much older, I was allowed to stay up a little longer, and when my bedtime came, I went to lie on my little camp bed, thinking about my friends back at *Saint Vincent*. The occasional passing car and the orange glow of the street lights kept me awake for a while. Then, it suddenly dawned on me that this was the first time ever I was sleeping in a room on my own and I began to feel a little uneasy, but somehow, the clutter packed around me acted like a presence, and after looking at what else was piled up, I drifted gently into an uninterrupted sleep. I had never heard of the sandman before and, perhaps, he had come for me too.

*

Another year had passed and now I was ready to move to my last year at primary school. There were two classes; the weaker pupils would be taught by Mlle Jacqueline and the brighter ones by Sister Eugene-Marie.

The first time I met my new teacher was one break time in the playground towards the end of the summer term. As soon as she was spotted, she was swamped by a horde of excited girls, desperate to know which class they would be joining. When I managed to get close enough to the nun, I shouted: "what about me, *ma soeur*, am I going to be in your class?" I asked full of trepidation.

"What's your name?" She enquired, looking at me with a keen eye.

"Martha Bertrand."

"Oh yes," she said with an assured smile, "you'll be coming to me."

Her reaction pleased me. She knew my name and she knew I was fit to be in her class. That was a good start. I was going to enjoy my last year at Notre Dame. I just knew it.

Back at *Saint Vincent*, Sister Catherine continued to observe me, gauge me, and test me to try and get through the implacable wall I had built around myself, in order to unearth the mystery that had baffled everybody. I had once caught her looking at my report shaking her head in disbelief, but nevertheless with a glitter of admiration twinkling in her eyes. She never once complimented me because, as far as she was concerned, nothing could make up for the fact that I was immature, undisciplined, and always messing about with my 'acolytes', a term she loved to use—always in a derogatory manner—to refer to my small cluster of associates. However, although she never expressed a single word of admiration or appreciation, I knew she was impressed, I could see it in her eyes.

I was now spending more and more time with the Langeais family—they must have been impressed with the housework—but the more weekends I spent there, the less I wanted to go. The idea of spending my free time washing up, cleaning floors, and baby-sitting really did not thrill me. To exacerbate the problem, I could not relate to the little girls. I was the house helper, therefore, it did not seem appropriate for me to befriend the children. Throughout my time there, I remained distant and aloof, and stubbornly refused to communicate. The parents tried hard to warm up to me, to discuss things, to try and open up a line of communication on topics that might interest me, but I was not in the least interested, and categorically refused to have anything to do with them. All I was there to do was to carry out my tasks and I did so without as much as a word or a smile, because, quite frankly, I did not care.

Gradually, I began to recognise the same signs of exasperation that I had noticed in M. and Mme Cateau, and I sensed that they were beginning to have misgivings about me. If it had not been for the fact that they desperately needed me, especially as I did not cost them anything except for the food they made me thankful to receive— tripes, please don't anyone mention the word tripes to me —they would have got rid of me ages ago, but unlike in the children's story, they knew better than kill the goose with the golden eggs. So, they persevered.

CHAPTER XVIII

Sister Eugène-Marie's classroom was on the ground floor of the seniors' playground. On that first day, I strolled around the smaller but more prestigious yard feeling ever so proud and ever so grown-up. Here, the segments of the day were punctuated by the enormous brass bell that stood outside our classroom door, and it was always an honour and a privilege to be picked to go outside and shake the bell to announce each break.

The classroom was gleaming with brand new desks and a nice clean tiled floor. There was even a metal basket in between each twin desk where we could store our satchels. Never so bright a start for a brand new beginning: I was ready.

On that first day, I sat full of trepidation, staring at the nun. I had often wondered why women became nuns and, when we had quizzed Sister Catherine, she had described her experience as 'like answering a divine call', and she had left me totally mystified as to how she had known straight away that the call had come from God. Maryse and I had looked at each other and wondered loudly, as we scoured the refectory, which of the girls would be next to get 'the call'.

I was now looking at Sister Eugène-Marie, ogling at her front teeth that jutted out like a hotel canopy hanging over a perilous cliff, and which made it impossible for her to close her mouth properly without having to overstretch her lower lip to seal the wide gap. And, as I continued to stare at her decisively ugly features, I wondered how old she was when she got the call.

If I was busy wondering about Sister Eugène-Marie's motives to become a nun, she, in turn, was trying to match my academic achievements with the notorious reputation I had of being immature, easily distracted, and lazy beyond belief. In her exacting mind, she suspected that something was wrong: the figures did not add up and the equation did not square up. As a stickler for accuracy and correctness, she set about to prove that I had somehow duped all my previous teachers, that I had done a *léger-de-main* under their very eyes in order to claim honours that were not rightfully mine. As a result, from day one, she watched me like a hawk. She marched up and down the wide classroom aisles purposefully, constantly peering at my work with her hands firmly tucked behind her back. After a long spell of astute observation during which every move I made had been tossed and examined several times over, to her chagrin— indeed, with God on her side, she could never be wrong— she found nothing. Still, she remained suspicious.

Eventually, she resorted to one last ploy. She asked a girl who was near the bottom of the class to come and sit next to me, and despite weeks of her plotting and complotting in a vain attempt to see me trip and fall, I continued to flourish. Finally, she gave up, but not before harbouring a huge feeling of resentment against me, a deep rancour that gnawed her to the core, matched only by the profound disdain she held for another girl.

Charlotte was a brash, cheeky girl who had no qualms about lying every time she had to explain why she was late...yet again. Her mid-length mousy hair was always a mess and looked as if she had dried it without bothering to brush it afterwards. Sometimes, she would tie it with an oversize white or pink bow to try and make it look tidier. But the one thing which Sister Eugène-Marie could never forgive, and for which she could not hide her personal loathing, was the well-known fact that Charlotte could never pass a boy without wolf-whistling at him. There were no two ways about it: she was wild and she was loose, and Sister Eugène-Marie could do nothing but wait for the first opportunity to eject the undesirable wench out of her righteous realm. After all, it was not her job to save Charlotte's soul, and as far as she was concerned, the wretched girl could go to hell and be left to rot there, in a festering pool of human decadence. From then on, her morning sermons became more pointed, more vociferous, a sort of public vendetta rammed into our sleepy heads against all carnal sins.

"You mustn't play with yourself! You mustn't play with your body!" She used to thunder with the regularity and frequency of a parrot stuck on one line. "It's a dirty sin and a disgusting habit. If you do, you must confess. You cannot take communion until you have confessed of that filthy debauchery."

While I pondered over what she actually meant, I discreetly shifted my gaze towards Charlotte to study her reaction. Every time, the girl would cross her arms noisily across her chest, stretch her legs with careless abandon—and, purposely or not, wide apart under her seat—and dart a sneering look loaded with breathtaking effrontery and cool defiance towards Sister Eugene-Marie for, if the girl was unable to voice openly her rebellious streak, she was perfectly capable of demonstrating with her blatant lack of respect and nonchalant disposition that she really could not care less about upholding the moral tone of Sister Eugene-Marie's class. I was in awe. I could never have befriended Charlotte—her lax manners and sheer insolence took her too close to the fringe of human decency—but I could not help admiring the courageous, if not foolish, way in which she stood up against Sister Eugene-Marie. I would never have dared...though secretly I wished I did.

Then one day, she was gone. Like everything else in our lives, it was done quietly with no fuss; and while one life took a different direction from ours, more plots and counterplots were being played in the shady background of darkened corridors—all in the name of morality and decency. We did not hear about her again except through the church gossip. There, we listened avidly, and with particular relish, to tales reporting her various misdemeanours and how Sunday mass had become her perfect hunting ground on which she could parade at leisure, and with impunity in front of the boys who were always happy to receive a flirtatious look or a blown kiss wrapped in cheap lavender scent that she dispensed freely to the pubescent congregation. Her slow-paced catwalk down the main aisle, in the shortest skirt she could possibly find, had become legendary and always caused a cacophony of wolf-whistles which were soon followed by short cries of pain as irate mothers all around administrated a swift clip round the ears to their wayward sons. Someone had even intimated to us that, after the bales of hay in the local fields, the church corridors had become her favourite meeting places. Sacrilege! We had exclaimed, as we muffled our giggles in our missals.

At school, her place was soon taken by Benedicte, a plump but very pretty girl with freckles, whose most striking feature was her stunning, thick titian hair which had been coifed into the most beautifully formed ringlets, in a perfect imitation of Shirley Temple's locks. She looked just like one of those little rich girls I had seen in American films, and I simply could not take my eyes of her. I was totally fascinated by the perfection that had gone into styling her hair, by the serene look that radiated through her cute little freckles, and the calm aura that emanated from her, gently permeating through the solid impenetrable wall I had build around myself. To my eyes, she was a vision of beauty, serenity, and harmony, and all I hoped was that one day, we would share a desk together.

CHAPTER XIX

The autumn leaves twisted and fell, torn from the trees by the strong *bourrasques d'automne*, those powerful gusts of wind that shook nature to the core, announcing the approach of winter. The gardener, gesticulating madly in his blue overalls, was often seen involved in a frantic chase to gather the dead leaves amidst our cheerful cries as another gust lifted them and scattered them all over the schoolyard. Irritated by the wind and our ear-piercing squeals, sometimes he would brandish his heavy metal fork and yell at us to go away. On that particular day, after he had regained control of his fugitive clusters, the irascible gardener struck a match and threw it into the pile with a dramatic gesture. Then, with his chin resting on the top end of his rake, he watched the bluish smoke rise from the pyre, until the flames crackled and hissed, releasing into the atmosphere the delicious crisp smell of burning leaves that scented forever the memories of our happy and carefree schooldays.

*

One day, Sister Catherine called me and said as if declaring the obvious: "I expect you know that your birthday's coming soon."

I nodded knowledgeably, preferring to bluff with confidence to looking vacuous and totally ignorant.

"And for your 11th birthday," she continued…

My, I thought, is that how old I am?

"M. and Mme Langeais have organised a little birthday party for you, so you'd better make sure you don't get ten crosses, otherwise I won't be able to let you go."

How kind of her to warn me in advance, I thought, or was she saving herself another embarrassment. Indeed, only two or three weekends ago, M. Langeais had turned up at the orphanage door to collect me, only to be told that I was not allowed out. He had made the trip for nothing, but still had the generous thought of leaving my weekly magazine behind, together with a bar of chocolate. It had never occurred to him to phone beforehand, for he did not know about the system of crosses. On that occasion, Sister Catherine had duly passed on the magazine, but had kept the chocolate bar, because, she chided, since I was being punished, I did not deserve any treat, and far be it from me to protest, for if she had known me better, she would have realised that I valued the magazine far more than a piece of chocolate that was going to disappear within minutes of receiving it. Besides, I probably would have had to share it anyway.

Then, one day in that very same week, Maryse ran to me, all flushed and flustered, and in her most dramatic voice she declared:

"Martha, you've got a parcel!"

"Have I? Are you sure it's for me?" I asked, incredulous.

I was flabbergasted. I very rarely got a letter, so to me, getting a parcel was very much like finding a diamond buried in the sand. Quite simply, a clear impossibility.

"Yeah! I saw your name on it!"

I was mightily excited at the thought that a parcel had arrived for me, but as always when receiving information from Maryse, I held back until I found out for sure whether this was true or not.

I went straight to the small room, right next door to the refectory, where Sister Catherine usually resided, mending, knitting, tidying, and sorting whatever needed sorting like the small bunch of envelops that arrived everyday with the mail.

"*Ma soeur?* Is it true that there's a parcel for me?"

"Who told you?"

"Maryse."

"Right, well in that case, I'm confiscating your parcel for being indiscreet."

"Who is it from?"

"It's from your godmother. You wouldn't be getting it today anyway, because it's not your birthday yet."

"When is it?"

"Thursday or Friday...I can't remember exactly."

On Thursday, after we had completed our cleaning chores and we had all gone outside to play, Sister Catherine called me. She had a small parcel in her hand, the size of a shoebox wrapped up in brown paper tied together with a piece of string.

"I'm going to show you what was in the parcel, but as I said, you're not allowed to have any of it, I shall give it all away to the poor," she said, moving towards the table in the middle of the room.

She lifted the lid and revealed a doll that took up most of the space inside, and some sweets squashed in the pleats of her pink dress. I stared at the content with a cold detached look, my arms tightly folded against my chest to reflect my truculent mood, telling myself that I did not like dolls anyway and wondering why she had even bothered to show me the gift.

"Can I go now?" I asked, showing not a trace of emotion in my voice or on my sullen features because, Sister Catherine may very well have relished the thought that she always had the upper hand, but I was well acquainted with her mind games, and the way she liked to prod our feelings just to see what kind of reaction she could provoke. So, I had taken to adopting an indifferent stance, cold and aloof that revealed nothing of my inner feelings. I left the room without giving her as much as a glance.

"What about saying thank you?" She hailed.

I slammed the door. Outside, Maryse ran towards me.

"Well? What did you get?"

"Nothing...she confiscated the parcel because you told me about it and that made me 'indiscreet'."

Maryse looked at me rather confused.

"Oh, but that's not fair...I should be the one to be punished."

"Don't worry, I don't care...I don't like dolls anyway. OK, what game shall we play?"

*

At the weekend, M. Langeais came to collect me. As far as I was concerned, it was a weekend like any other weekend, except that for only the third time in my short life, I knew exactly how old I was. On Sunday morning, M. Langeais took me to church. Mme Langeais, feeling a little less pious for missing yet again another Sunday service, fretted around the stove and energetically paced every corner of her kitchen. She knew the Lord would not be happy, but what ever could she do? The Lord may grumble up there in Heaven and snag Mme Langeais's conscience, but honestly, did He have any idea how much work was involved in preparing a special birthday lunch? I mean, not counting all the faithful, how many mouths did He have to feed? Well, here today, she had a mountain of things to do, because she had invited other members of the family and there would be at least a dozen mouths to feed, not to mention her own children who would have to be fed in the kitchen because there was simply not enough room around the dining table.

In church, the sight of all those hundreds of people ensconced in dark coats and dark hats unnerved me. I did not like their tenebrous look. Suddenly, a dark vision flashed before my eyes in which they all turned around and looked at me... and I saw the pale faces of the soldiers I had seen dying in my dreams. I froze in terror on the threshold. M. Langeais glanced at me with a querying look. I dug my heels in and refused to go in. My unexpected reaction took him by surprise. What was the matter with me? I had been to this church before, but instead of getting cross with me, he simply took my hand and gave it a gentle squeeze. I looked up to him. He was so tall that his large imposing frame standing right next to me reminded me of the beautiful chestnut tree, and suddenly I felt safe, very safe. The vision disappeared and I dismissed any further thoughts of soldiers dying. Then, I followed him in.

When we returned, all the guests had arrived, and even Grandmamma had been wheeled in especially for the occasion. She was now sitting in the rocking chair, lulling herself gently in a paradisiacal slumber using her walking stick.

Dinner was served. Mme Langeais brought in a magnificent leg of lamb on a large stainless steel tray and smiled broadly in reply to the oohs and ahs rising from the table. No tripes today, then. M. Langeais was, at the time, busy refilling the adults' glasses with more red wine and had even offered to flavour my plain water with a few drops. I accepted straight away. I was eleven now and I felt so grown up. As soon as his wife emerged from the kitchen, he put the bottle of Bordeaux down, reached for the carving knife, and proceeded to slice the joint amidst more enthusiastic cries of delight. From the end of the table, I watched each slice of meat fall into a river of blood. I was horrified. Worse still, being the birthday girl, the first slice landed on my plate. I stared at it, half expecting it to move, wriggle, or do something. I remembered then how Maryse had prodded at her piece of dead fish with an exaggerated flick of the wrist for maximum effect, but I could not do that here; it would have been rude. So, after I had eaten ravenously the roast potatoes, the peas, the carrots, and everything else that had been dished out, using the prongs of my fork, I discreetly slid the nearly dead piece of meat towards the edge of my plate, and left it there.

"Oh?" Mme Langeais exclaimed, surprised. "You don't like it?"

Surprised? She was surprised? The thing was practically moving. How could she be surprised?

After the noisy clatter of cutlery had died down, the women rose up and proceeded to clear the table. The men lit up their cigarettes. I had just begun to roll up my sleeves when Mme Langeais interrupted me on a most authoritative tone.

"No, you stay right where you are. It's your special day today; I don't want you to do anything, just enjoy yourself."

I smiled an awkward, embarrassed smile. How could I enjoy myself amid total strangers? Besides, how does one enjoy a birthday party? I did not even know what I was supposed to do. A few minutes later, the women reappeared singing *Joyeux Anniversaire, Joyeux Anniversaire...*' at the top of their voices while Mme Langeais placed the cake with eleven candles on it, all lit up, in the middle of the table. Everyone clapped and I duly blew out all the candles in one breath. Then, she began the ceremonious duty of cutting the cake, and the minute my share was put in front of me, I chomped on my piece avidly, wondering if and when it would be proper to ask for more. A few minutes later, from the side of her seat, Mme Langeais pulled out this large very flat cardboard box decorated with a big red bow. I was so eager to find out what it was that I practically choked on my last piece of cake. Eventually, I was ready for my big surprise. I got up and walked towards her with extended arms. She delicately placed the box on my arms, undid the knot, and lifted the lid. Something flat was hidden under a pile of thin flimsy paper.

"Oh, wait a minute..." she said hurriedly. "I'll remove the tissue paper for you..."

I was now staring at what looked like a piece of material, dark blue with green and red lines criss-crossing each other.

Mme Langeais quickly confirmed my findings.

"*C'est du tissu écossais*...tartan...You like it? I'm going to make you a dress with it."

Wow, I thought, a dress! I had never owned a dress before and I did like the pattern, though the colour was a little dark. Before that, the only item of clothing I had owned was a tartan skirt, which had been lent to me by Sister Bénédicte to go to the Cateaus' house. I adored it. Now, I was going to have a tartan dress, chic and elegant. I could already picture myself, moving stylishly through my paces, perfecting a grand look, and standing in a sophisticated pose.

More Oohs and ahs rose again from all around the table. The women clamoured: "Come round and show us...Oh! Isn't that beautiful...and the quality...look at the quality! Martine, you surpassed yourself here! This looks like a very expensive piece of material."

"Oh, it's nothing. She's a good girl and she's doing ever so well at school. We're very pleased with her, so she deserves it."

Once everyone had had a chance to admire the expensive

gift, I handed the box back to Mme Langeais and returned to my seat. Then, Grandmamma leant forward and said in a quivering voice, "Did she say 'thank you'? I didn't hear."

Of course I had not said *'merci'*. To me, this uncomplicated little word was like admitting to someone that I liked them, when in fact I did not. It was awkward and embarrassing, almost like telling a lie in public, in front of all these people, but I knew I had to do it, my good manners dictated so. Fixing my gaze on the cream colour tiles, I rose from my chair and stood shyly by Mme Langeais while I mumbled my single word of gratitude.

"Don't forget to kiss!" One of the women hailed.

Seigneur Dieu! As Sister Benedicte used to say. What else would I have to do? I had already said thank you, was that not enough? But I felt obliged, especially as Mme Langeais was already leaning her head towards me. So, I planted a light hurried peck on her cheek and scurried off back to my chair before anyone else had a chance to shout for more.

"Now, would anyone like more cake?"

Early that evening, M. Langeais drove me back to *Saint Vincent*. He wanted to hear how much I had enjoyed myself, and know exactly how excited I felt, but all his probing questions made me feel even more self-conscious and I could only answer back with a brief nod of the head, or a murmured *'oui'* that escaped through my lips like a sigh of relief.

*

At school, my attention was now wholly focused on the forthcoming Christmas exams, which I had been waiting for some time with renewed trepidation, as this was going to be my first chance to prove my true worth to my distrustful teacher. As for the nun herself, she made sure that the girl sitting next to me would be of no help whatsoever.

The only mistake I recall making was in the dictation which began with: *'La brume'*...a word I had never come across before and which left me pondering and dithering whether the 'u' should have a circumflex accent or not. The verb *'bruler'* had one, and the two words seemed awfully similar, so at the very last minute, just as Sister Eugene-Marie was coming round to collect the papers, I placed a circumflex accent above the 'u'. This, I discovered later, was not required.

The wait for the exam results became unbearable. My expectations had run so high that I could barely contain my excitement. I knew I had done well, but I wanted to know exactly how well in the class of forty.

Then, one Friday afternoon, I heard footsteps crunching in the snow and saw Mother Superior approaching our classroom with her arms laden with large sheets of paper. She swept into the classroom with a huge smile on her face, bearing the long awaited exam results. As usual, she gave them out in reverse order of merit. Poor Natasha was bottom again. Mother Superior commiserated with her, reassuring her that it was not her fault, that she had been ill a lot and missed quite a few vital lessons because of her illness.

After an excruciating wait, my name was read out...last.

"Wow!" the class erupted. Above the noise, Mother Superior congratulated me while Sister Eugene-Marie smiled in acquiescence, but said nothing. I returned a timid smile, knowing that the teacher would resent me even more now.

With their preconceived ideas and set expectations, adults always think they know better. However, and that was her gripe, so far I had managed to confound every single adult by performing well above what any snotty little girl from the orphanage could be expected to achieve. And it amused me... no end. It was that *schadenfreude* feeling again, causing me to laugh inwardly at the teacher's general dismay, at her startled look every time she felt she had been tricked, yet again. It was a sweet victory, a delectable triumph, and an unquenchable source of pride. It was the perfect way to get back at those who wanted to see me flounder.

In a similar moment of personal triumph, while the mortally wounded Nelson could only ask for a kiss from his faithful officer Hardy, I, Martha Bertrand, the untouchable, the unpunishable, would have asked the latter to hoist me on his shoulders and parade me around in a triumphant display of fairness against prejudice, love against hatred, and pride against humiliation. My resounding success had put me on a pedestal higher than the teacher's desk itself, turning Sister Eugene-Marie apoplectic with rage.

If my teacher was incapable of sharing my personal pride and joy, at least I was able to console myself with the thought that I had won the respect of my peers. At break, they were more forthcoming and began to talk to me. They gradually included me in their games, and one girl even offered to share her snack with me. If my newly-found popularity meant that someone would give me a biscuit, a piece of cake, or half a ham sandwich, then who cared what Sister Eugene-Marie thought of me? My overriding pride and self-esteem, propped up by the whole class, made me feel strong and invincible against all adult enemies—even against Brigitte Duval, if she was still around, for if she thought that she could treat me like her own personal *souffre-douleur*, I could use my growing arrogance to point out to her that she had stooped so low that she did not even reach my ankle, and that her own conscience was squirming over there…in the scum of an overflowing sewer.

My triumphant thoughts were suddenly interrupted by the Voice of Mother Superior who announced:

"The best results will be rewarded with a prize. The top ten pupils will each receive a leather-bound personal diary."

Gasps of delight. A week later, a nun whom I had often seen around the school and who acted as a general helper brought a large cardboard box containing the prized diaries. Sister Eugene-Marie took ten out and handed the box back to the Sister. Then she proceeded to hand them out, but before she started, she turned to me and said:

"Of course, because you came top, you'll get an even better diary, so I won't give you one just now."

I had no reason not to believe her and waited in good faith for my special prize to arrive. Days passed, weeks passed, and I was still waiting. Eventually, I had to resign myself to the fact that the coveted diary, the unique prize that was rightfully mine, would never come. As the end of term approached, I knew that my wait had all been in vain, and I was reduced to watching with envy my classmates leaf through the pages of their exclusive diaries with great affectation and pride, while I continued to draw neat lines in my little notebook, taking care to write each new date in my best neat handwriting.

The fact that I had shown no reaction increased the nun's discomfiture. She had missed out on an opportunity to hear me whine and to see me flail, but she was not giving up. Somehow, she would find a way to pierce through that resigned look and break through that immovable wall, and whilst in the dark clouds of her ruthless mind she plotted her next move, she smacked her lips even more loudly over her protruding teeth, reeling in advance at the prospect of a well assured victory.

Finally, her chance came. As girls were getting their snacks out for break, the girl who shared my desk reported that her apple was missing. The nun told her not to worry, that somehow she would find it. The brass bell resounded in the small yard and we prepared to file out for the mid-morning break. As I passed the nun, she grabbed my arm firmly and said:

"You! You're staying behind!"

I complied happily, thinking that perhaps she had some interesting task for me. When everybody was out, she closed the door and came to stand in front of me.

Then, without any warning, the storm began.

"You stole that apple, didn't you!"

I was shocked, so shocked that I was, for a moment, thrown off balance by her slanderous accusation. Why would I do such a thing? I had no concept of stealing. In fact, to me, the very act was an absolute aberration which was equalled to saying two and two makes five; it did not add up, and I knew it was not right.

"No, I didn't," I firmly denied with a clear conscience.

"Yes, you did!"

"No, I didn't," I insisted.

Suddenly, she smacked me so hard that I wobbled on my feet.

"You stole that apple, admit it!"

"No, I didn't!"

She smacked me again and again, hitting harder and harder still. I wrapped my arms around my head to shield myself and felt the stinging blows rain on my arms, on my hands, and on my head.

"I'm going to hit you until you admit that you stole that apple...you're the only one from the orphanage in this class... no one else is capable of stealing! And you're the one who was sitting next to Corinne, so it has to be you!" She smirched all in one breath.

I had never been hit at school. It was something that simply was not done, especially not here at *Ecole Notre Dame*, and while I had to submit to the nun's brutal assault, my survival instinct kicked in. I had to think fast: either I continued to tell the truth and accept that I was going to be beaten black and blue, or decide to lie in order to spare myself further painful blows. The decision was not hard to make for I, Martha Bertrand, had always vouched never to become a martyr, so I lied.

"Yes, I did!" I admitted, gritting my teeth. "I took it!"

By confessing, I hoped that this would be the end of the matter and I would be allowed to go out and enjoy the rest of the break like everyone else, but Sister Eugene-Marie had not finished.

Feelings of euphoria wriggled through her entire body and when she smiled, her devil's teeth jutted out even more, practically grinding with pleasure. I could tell she wanted more of my blood and to prolong my misery for as long as possible in order to further gratify her sadistic pleasure. She had cracked the wall; now she wanted to see me squirm. She would force the little angel to lie, over and over again, so as to blacken my soul and make hers appear more immaculate than mine. Suddenly, she lunged forward and rummaged through my empty pockets.

"What did you do with the apple?"

I gave her the only plausible answer, knowing that if she did believe me, it would be virtually the same as her confessing to her own heinous crime.

"I ate it," I replied.

"When did you eat it?"

"When you were talking to the class, first thing this morning."

Her face creased with a sardonic smile. That was all she wanted to hear, admitting her own guilt at the same time, for she, the rapacious vulture who could not help observing my every move in the hope of catching me red handed cheating, had somehow not seen me eat an apple right under her nose. Her vindictiveness had surpassed everything I had experienced before, and I was shocked that a nun could indulge in such a cruel charade. In my eyes, she had put herself on a par with the likes of Mlle Agnès, the teacher from *Sainte Germaine*, and Brigitte Duval, equal in their cruelty as they were in their callous deeds.

Standing in front of Sister Eugene-Marie, I was totally defenceless and at her complete mercy, caught in a plot of Machiavellian proportion, and there was nothing, absolutely nothing I could do about it. I looked at her face and saw a soul blackened with indelible lies. She may have reeled with pleasure at having wounded my heart and sullied my soul, but right now as I confessed to my pre-supposed guilt, I knew I was closer to God than she would ever be.

"Now," she said, her words whistling through her reviled lips. "I don't want you to say a word of this to anybody, do you hear?"

"I won't," I muttered after a long pause.

At that point, she grabbed and snagged my sleeve and said most insistently:

"You promise?"

"Yes."

"No, I want to hear you say it. Do you promise?"

I had no wish to be hit again, so I parroted her words feeling quite sick inside.

"I promise," I finally managed to mumble.

After break, when Corinne settled back next to me, I felt compelled to ask her just to reassure myself that I had not gained a new enemy.

"Did you think I had stolen your apple?"

"Of course not," she replied, shrugging her shoulders almost as if she had forgotten that she had ever mentioned the word 'apple'. Her verdict did matter to me though, and I was immensely relieved.

My remarkable progress continued to bother Sister Eugene-Marie. She would get to me somehow. If she could not take any marks away from my work, there were two areas where she could penalise me at will: punctuality and discipline.

"I wasn't late, *ma soeur*, I was at the dentist," I would argue.

"Yes, but you were not present at two o'clock, were you?"

Or, on another occasion, she castigated:

"Martha Bertrand, you were talking, that's two marks off discipline!"

"I was helping Corinne to find the page...she didn't know which page we were on."

This personal vendetta continued unabated, until it became impossible for me to twitch or sneeze without being marked off. The result was that several times in my reports, I was faced with a line of perfect tens in all the subjects except in discipline when I invariably ended with a big bold 'zero.'

CHAPTER XX

Back at *Saint Vincent*, I would normally throw my report on top of the usual pile of reports and make a quick exit. This time, however, Sister Catherine picked it up.

"Martha Bertrand!" She called out.

I retraced my steps sheepishly, ready to have my ears burnt with a sermon on the importance of good discipline, but all she said was:

"It's leave-out weekend. Why don't you take your report to M. and Mme Langeais for them to sign? I'm sure they'd be very interested to follow your progress at school."

I did not know why they should be interested. However, I did as I was told and reluctantly retrieved my report from the pile.

M. Langeais came to collect me on Saturday afternoon and all I had with me was my report.

"What's that you have in your hand?" He asked curious.

"It's my school report...you've got to sign it."

"Let's have a look," he said as he settled himself into the driver's seat.

I opened the booklet and with his sharp eyes, M. Langeais began to scan every single line until he reached the last one. Discipline = 0. For a moment, I stared at the zero dangling at the bottom of a line of perfect tens and the huge contrast made me snigger quietly to myself.

"There's nothing funny about getting a zero in discipline," I heard M. Langeais scold.

I frowned. Who did he think he was to feel he had the right to reprimand me? As far as I was concerned, this was my business and my business alone. What did it matter to him anyway? He was nobody to me.

"All you have to do is sign my report," I said rather flatly.

"What? And ignore that zero in discipline..."

I crossed my arms and sank into the car seat, watching the road ahead fixedly and closing my ears to his chastising words.

As soon as we got through the door, M. Langeais shouted to his wife:

"She's got her report and you won't believe this; she's got zero in discipline!"

"Has she?" Mme Langeais exclaimed, genuinely surprised. "She never says anything! How come she's got zero in discipline!"

Mme Langeais wiped her hands on her apron and took the report from me to study it more closely.

"But she's got ten out of ten everywhere else...that can't be right...the teacher must have made a mistake."

I was amazed. For the first time in my life, someone was prepared to think the better of me. When Mme Langeais eventually asked: "what did you do to get zero in discipline?", all I did was to stare back at her and said nothing. There was no point; they would not believe me anyway.

That afternoon, we went to the shops as usual, but without the company of M. Langeais. Not for him to be seen asking for a baguette or a kilo of tripes; he would rather stay at home and do what men had to do while the baby slept in her cot upstairs.

Free from the cumbersome pram, we ambled through the busy streets at a good pace. I loved these shopping trips. A whole new world was opening in front of me, full of grown-ups: men sheltering under their trilbies and women protecting their bouffant hairdos or hiding rows of rollers tightly set inside a hairnet with colourful scarves. What's more, I was learning the names of shops like *la crèmerie* and *la mercerie*, and the difference between *la charcuterie* and *la boucherie*, or *la boulangerie* and *la pâtisserie*. Each time I stepped across a new threshold, it was like entering a time capsule, a secluded world with its distinctive smell so powerful at times that it was almost palpable, awakening an irresistible urge to grab and snatch all the tantalising feasts. But, I kept thinking, as I wriggled my nose to see if I could detect the slightest whiff of a pungent stench, spare me *la poissonnerie*, I really could not bear the thought of a *tête-à-tête* with a dead fish.

This thought apart, I thoroughly enjoyed the whole exhilarating and exciting experience, which was something I had not obtained from any books, and I felt alive, part of a world that had so far eluded me. I was a child walking with someone else's mother and I was beginning to think that being part of a family unit, despite all the household chores, was not that bad after all.

A few minutes later, we stopped at the haberdashery. Mesmerised, I ran my eyes over the multitude of wooden shelves running right up to the ceiling and stacked with all kinds of material; I scrutinised the numerous transparent compartments full of buttons, coloured threads, balls of wool spun in all the colours of the rainbow, and lots of other things I did not recognise. Here, the smell was musty, but the atmosphere was warm and cosy.

"*Bonjour*, Mme Langeais," the lady behind the counter greeted.

"*Bonjour,*" She replied. "I need some material today."

"What kind of material?"

"It's for a dress. I'm going to make a dress: *c'est pour la petite.*" Mme Langeais confided with a smile.

"Oh, lucky girl!" Then, lowering her voice, the shopkeeper asked: "Is she the little one from…" She finished her sentence with several nods of the head and an air of quiet understanding.

"Yes, she is," Mme Langeais asserted before turning to me. "Which material would you like?"

I was so overwhelmed that I could feel my little heart pounding inside my chest. A dress? Another dress for me?

After Mme Langeais had given me a dress for my birthday, I had felt quite rich. Now, with two dresses, I was practically a millionaire. I scoured the shelves, unable to concentrate at first. Then, my eyes arrested on a bright roll of pink gingham material. Pink! I had always wanted a pink dress. Excited, I pointed my finger at the roll which was squashed between a multitude of others, halfway up the wall. The shopkeeper wheeled her ladder along the shelves and dislodged the coveted material. Then, she took a tape measure and ran it along my side to see how many metres Mme Langeais would need.

"You won't need much, she's so tiny…one metre should do…that will leave you with plenty to spare to make a nice bow or something…"

The precious material was cut and wrapped up delicately in a brown paper bag which Mme Langeais handed over to me.

"Would you like to carry it?" She asked, knowing what the answer would be.

"Yes please!" I effused.

Outside the shop, Mme Langeais asked:

"Well? What do you say?"

I knew what she wanted, but as usual, I went all shy. I was yet again expected to open my heart and bear my soul, and in front of a stranger at that. Clutching the precious parcel and with my eyes fixed on the tip of my well-worn shoes, I managed to mumble a meek and mild 'merci'.

Back at the house, I stood around the kitchen waiting to get on with my next chore. M. Langeais was reading the newspaper in his rocking chair in the lounge. The girls were upstairs, playing in their bedroom. Mme Langeais was busy darting around the house, directing random comments, sometimes at her absent-minded husband, and sometimes at her daughters upstairs. Then, she turned towards me.

"There's nothing that needs to be done right now. Why don't you go and play?"

Play? I asked myself. With what and whom, and where?

"Oh, I see the neighbours are in their garden. Come along, I'll introduce you to them. They've got twins, a boy and a girl, about the same age as you; you might like to chat to them."

We went out through the kitchen door and stepped into the late afternoon sunshine. Over the fence, a short plump woman was bent over a vegetable patch and nearer the house, two children dressed in identical dungarees played noisily, one sat in an old battered wooden trolley with wobbly wheels while the other pushed it along the uneven flagstones. Which one was the girl, I wondered?

"Hi!" They shouted with youthful exuberance.

Straight away, I felt awkward, inadequate, and unable to think of anything to say. The strict code of conduct that had dictated for so long and so rigorously my every move had paralysed every ounce of spontaneity I might have had and, to my dismay, I found that I could not deal with any situation that required me to get involved with other individuals. I simply did not know what to do.

The children came to the fence, bright eyed and all smiles.

"What's your name?" One of them asked.

"Martha," I replied shyly.

"Well, I'm Jeannette and that's my brother. His name is Jean...We're twins," the girl declared with an irresistible giggle. "Do you have a pet?" She continued with a cheeky grin. "We have two cats and a dog...the dog isn't allowed in the house though...he lives in his kennel over there."

While she pointed at an area beyond the vegetable patch, I was racking my brain, desperate to find something suitable to say, but the only thing I could come up with was to ask:

"How old are you?"

The minute I said it, I cringed. What a stupid question, I thought, but the children did not seem to mind.

"We're twelve," Jeannette replied with that same cheeky smile. "Would you like to come over the fence and have a go in our trolley?"

I smiled at the thought.

"No, thank you," I declined politely. "But I'd like to see your cats."

"I don't know where they are, they're away somewhere," she replied with a distant look while her brother pushed the trolley all by himself up and down the garden path spluttering car noises.

"Oh, look! There's Minou over there walking along the fence at the bottom of the garden."

I looked towards the named Minou and saw a scraggly ginger tom making his way precariously along the well-spaced fencing posts. Then, Jeannette suddenly removed herself from the fence.

"OK, Jean! It's my turn now!"

And, with the self-assurance of a leader always in command, she got into the trolley with the rickety wheels and ordered her brother to push.

I walked to the far end of the garden from where I surveyed the vast open land, the flat deserted countryside skirted by an open road that hummed in the distance, in the same way I had scoured the vast horizon at Sangatte, looking out to the endless sea, and I suddenly felt the same irresistible urge to go and touch the light, feel the space, and lose myself in some distant dream.

At night, from the kitchen window, I watched longingly the yellow beams of the occasional car meandering around the contours of the dark, featureless landscape, and I wished I was over there in control of the lights, on a long, never-ending journey.

CHAPTER XXI

The atmosphere at *Saint Vincent* was still fraught but less tense, and the remaining tension was largely caused by the unwavering behaviour of the supervisors who had not yet learnt to let go of Sister Marie-Catherine's ruthless methods.

A lot of the improvements were brought by Sister Catherine herself. With the approach of winter, she had began to knit dozens of bobble hats and, having noticed the poor state of our second-hand shoes, somehow she had got hold of rubber boots, perfect for the wet season. However, unable to obtain sixty odd pairs all at once, the boots arrived in dribs and drabs, and as soon as we were given a pair, we promptly wrote our uniform number on the inside so that no one else could claim they were theirs. We absolutely loved them: they were white, they were shiny...and for once, they were new.

Another dramatic change occurred that concerned Sister Catherine herself and the rest of the nuns. The rich sisters had started the rumour that the nuns would soon be free of their cumbersome uniforms. Needless to say, no one believed them, but we still had to find out for sure.

As our emissary, we always selected a girl who was rarely in trouble, for we knew that the nun would be more willing to give a proper answer to her question rather than dismiss her outright for being 'nosey'. It was thus that one day, as Sister Catherine was doing her rounds in the dormitory, Chantal was forcibly pushed into the main corridor, and once she found herself alone where she should not be, she was left with no other option but to walk up to the nun and ask:

"*Ma sœur*, is it true that you'll soon not wear a uniform anymore?"

As our courageous envoy stood a little nervously in front of the nun, several of us popped our heads round the doors of our respective dorms, pricking our ears and ready to catch Sister Catherine's answer.

"Who told you this?" The nun asked with a look of slight exasperation on her face. "It's extremely unwise to believe rumours...The devil is often behind them, so beware."

"Is it not true then?" Chantal ventured to ask again.

As we stood in the doorways observing Chantal's heroic effort to gain some truth, we knew we had picked the right girl.

"Well, not quite..." Sister Catherine replied, then she paused and we all expected her to say, "you'll just have to wait and see", but she did not and instead, she smiled and confided: "we'll still be wearing a uniform, but it will be a different one."

"Is it going to be that different that we're not going to be able to recognise you?" Roberte ventured to ask.

"It's going to be very different, but you will still be able to recognise me," she confirmed. "The main difference is that we will no longer have to wear the cornet."

An audible gasp rose in the corridor. Amazed by the news, we gathered around the nun hoping to learn more, and as the news spread whisper by whisper, more and more girls joined in to listen to the incredible news. Swamped by a curious crowd, Sister Catherine was fast disappearing.

"What are you going to wear instead?" Another girl eagerly asked.

"A veil. It will be a short, straight veil that falls just below here," she replied, her hand sweeping the back of her neck.

I could not imagine her wearing anything other than a cornet that stood on her small head like a large paper airplane, and as we pressed her for more revelations about her new appearance, she cut short our impatient questions with the same old statement:

"You'll just have to wait and see..."

Then shortly after this little episode, and without even being prompted, she declared almost out of the blue:

"Tomorrow, I shall be wearing my new clothes."

The following morning, as soon as we heard the rusty doorknob creak open, we jumped out of bed and rushed into the dormitory's corridor. From there, we watched a very slight silhouette advance towards us at a slow pace. All the vast layers of her long dark robes seemed to have been peeled off and without her huge white cornet, Sister Catherine looked a great deal shorter and thinner. She even looked fragile, as if the brace of iron that had so far propped her up to uphold the word of God, had disappeared along with her discarded habit. What's more, the metamorphosis went far beyond the mere physical; without the voluminous dark layers to protect her, she looked so exposed that I could not help wondering whether she suddenly felt cold.

The most welcome change of all, however, was the long awaited departure of Brigitte Duval. She was soon replaced by a young student, tall and round with a jovial smile on her face. What struck us immediately about her, apart from the fact that she had a bit of a moustache covering her upper lip, was that she was soft-spoken and mild mannered. Unlike any of the supervisors before her, she was gentle and kind. We did not know what to make of her at first, or how to respond to her radically different approach. Unfamiliar as we were with a supervisor who, for once, seemed to genuinely care about our welfare, we mistook her intentions and took advantage of her kindness and generous disposition. When she asked us to do something, we began to question her decisions, and in turn, she offered a sympathetic ear and listened patiently to our arguments: why were we not allowed to talk anywhere in the building? Why did we have to go on those endless walks? Why were we made to behave like saints and pray all the time instead of playing? And as she nodded her head with compassion and quiet understanding, she evaluated, adjudged, and sometimes even sympathised with our plight. And every time, we watched her deliberate and dither, astounded that anybody could be willing to listen to us, as she granted that, perhaps, we had a case. There was only one thing to do: she would have a word with Sister Catherine.

The verdict was unanimous. Mlle Marie-José was the best; but in return for her good heart, her good will, and her good intentions, some of us spotted a soft target that we could manipulate at will. Having been controlled for so long by screams, crosses, and beatings, we found we could not obey her commands simply because she had had the kind heart to ask us *nicely*. Coldheartedly and in cold blood, we took advantage. The cruel irony was that after years of suffering at the hands of callous, sadistic, and brutal women, we were turning against the one and only supervisor who had shown real care and compassion. It hurt me tremendously and I told Maryse.

"You can't stand up for her...think of what the others are going to say. They're going to call you a coward and a traitor... and they'll all turn against you."

I sighed in distress at the thought...but what else could I do?

Meanwhile, Mlle Marie-José continued to jolly us along. Rather than trudge through the long boulevards, streets, and canal, she took us to parks, close and distant ones. Sometimes these parks were situated many kilometres away, but the thought, that at the end of the long walk we would be allowed to play and have fun, gave us boundless energy. More than once, we arrived at our destination totally exhausted, but after a few minutes rest, we were hopping around like a bunch of happy little bunnies. To this day, I still remember that first thrill of moving through the warm air on the swing, screaming with excitement as, together with Maryse, we slid out of control on the tall wooden slide, bumped our little bottoms hard on the sea-saw, and fell off the merry-go-round in hysterics. And, once we had tasted those simple childhood pleasures, we wanted more. No longer fearing harsh consequences for small misdemeanours, we became bolder in our demands and somewhat more recalcitrant in our behaviour. We were no longer willing to obey placidly, orders that made no sense to us.

For her part, what Mlle Marie-José soon discovered was that by letting herself be guided by her heart, she was quickly losing control. Often, faced with the inability to retain the upper hand, she was reduced to tears. One evening, Maryse and I went to see her in her little cubicle. She was sitting at her little desk, so we sat uninvited on her bed.

She was struggling to write an essay because she could not concentrate.

"What are you studying?" I asked softly, trying to show her that, despite our belligerence, we were on her side.

"Psychology."

"What's that?"

"It's the study of people."

"Mad people?"

"No, no, not mad people, people in general. It's the study of their behaviour and why they behave in certain ways."

"We are bad, aren't we?" I declared, convinced that I had understood the subject of her study.

"Well...not that bad, but I wish you lot would behave better towards me. It's hard, you know. How can I possibly study when there's mayhem everywhere? It's impossible to concentrate! And anyway...I'm trying to be nice to you, so why can't you be nice to me?"

She took out her handkerchief and started snivelling. Maryse and I looked at each other in dismay. I had never heard an adult plead and it was heartbreaking.

"Don't worry, Mlle Marie-José," I said, tortured with remorse and guilt. "I'll speak to Annick. She'll do something."

Mlle Marie-José's weepy eyes rolled on the blank wall and arrested on the clock.

"Oh my God! Look at the time!" She suddenly exclaimed. "You two should be in bed and I've got to finish my essay for tomorrow."

"Good night, Mlle." We both said as we left.

"Good night...and make sure you go straight to bed," she managed to say with a smile.

Maryse and I walked back to our dorm, but as we passed Annick's dorm, I stopped and told Maryse I would join her later.

Annick's bed was the closest to the door. I tiptoed in and checked to see if she was asleep. She was lying facing the wall so it was impossible to tell whether her eyes were closed, but she was aware that someone was looking at her, so she turned round.

"Who's that?" She whispered.

"It's me, Martha."

"What are you doing here?"

"I want to tell you something."

"Get into my bed then."

That last sentence stopped me dead in my tracks. Get into her bed? I could not possibly do that.

"Come on, get in," she insisted, lifting her blanket. "I'm getting cold."

"But I can't...we'll be in so much trouble if we're caught!" I said, unable to move a step closer to her bed.

"Don't be such a nerd! Everybody does it."

"Everybody?" I gasped in complete disbelief. "Like...like who?"

"Like Marie with Blandine..."

"Marie and Blandine?"

I was stunned. In the eyes of everybody, Marie was the perfect child: she was intelligent, obedient, and kept her nose clean. She had never, ever, been in trouble, so much so that she was constantly being taken by Sister Catherine, and Sister Marie-Catherine before her, as an example of the perfect role model. In their eyes, she was the celestial angel who had been sent among us, little sinners, to help us be good and behave. Now, to my complete astonishment, I was learning that she had her very own protégée, Blandine, who happened to be the cutest girl in the Junior Section, and with whom she regularly shared her bed. *Mon Dieu*, if only Sister Catherine knew, I thought, relieved to discover that really no one, and absolutely no one, was ever perfect.

I slid into Annick's bed and straight away, she wrapped her warm body against mine and yawned.

"Don't take too long," she said, ""I'm tired."

"OK. Do you like Mlle Marie-José?"

Annick replied a sleepy "yeah".

"She's upset because of us and I think we should help her."

"OK, but not now, tell me tomorrow morning."

I felt her arms grip my body firmly as she prepared to go to sleep while I lay, wide awake, my head spinning with thoughts and counterthoughts. My first instinct was telling me that I should not be doing this, that I would get into so much trouble if I were caught, and I wanted to tear myself away, but the exquisite, new sensation of a warm body against mine was irresistible. I wanted to linger in her arms, to feel the soft contours of her body, instead of the harsh coldness of the iron bars of my bed, and at this late hour, there was no one around to stop me from enjoying the most wonderful sensation of having a body close to mine. I let myself drift away in a warm delectable dream and when I felt I could no longer fight against falling sleep, I reluctantly prized her arm off my body and slid out of Annick's bed. When I returned to my dorm, I went over to Maryse. She was asleep.

The next day, just before lunch, Annick came over towards us.

"Sorry, Maryse," she apologised, separating us and dragging me away with her, "but I need to speak to Martha."

"I won't be long," I said before walking away to make sure that Maryse understood I did not want to lose her and hoped she would be able to endure my split loyalties.

We held council near the pigsty. Annick had gathered together her team and I was the honoured guest.

"OK, guys," she began. "We've upset Mlle Marie-José. She can't cope with us and the last thing we want is to lose her, so we've got to do something about it. I want you to get hold of all the team captains and bring them back here."

"Now, Chief?" One of the girls asked, using Annick's sobriquet.

"Yes, now!"

As soon as they departed, I grabbed hold of Annick's arm.

"So, is it true what you said last night?"

"About what?"

"About Marie and Blandine...and the others..."

"Yeah, of course it's true. They do it all the time, but only the senior girls. It's like a privilege. They choose their protégées among the younger girls. What's wrong with that? You can sleep with me if you want."

"Well..." I replied, hesitating. "The only time I'd want to do that is when there's a thunderstorm. I'm scared of thunderstorms, they always give me nightmares."

"Funny you should say that, because that's how Marie started."

"Oh really?"

"Yeah...one night, when there was a big thunderstorm, she heard Blandine cry and she went over to comfort her, but Blandine was so scared that she couldn't stop crying. So Marie took her back with her into her own bed. Now, they sleep together all the time...well...nearly all the time."

"But, I'm amazed they've never been caught."

"Martha!...you know that Marie has always been Sister Catherine's favourite, so she can do whatever she likes."

"Lucky her," I sighed, wishing that I was treated with the same deference.

"So...next time there's a thunderstorm, you won't mind if I come to your bed?"

"Of course not...and you don't need to wait for the next thunderstorm either..." Annick added with a big smile. We locked arms and watched a group of girls advancing towards us.

"Right, girls, this is really important, so you've got to listen well. Mlle Marie-José is really upset because of us and she might leave. She's the best supervisor we've ever had and we want her to stay. So, I want every team captain to pass the word around their team that from now on, they'd better behave or they'll hear from me."

"What about the other supervisors? Do we do the same for them?"

"Who cares about the other supervisors!" She exclaimed with such vehemence that every one present refrained from asking further questions. She had made herself loud and clear: from now on, we would have to make a real effort for the sake of Mlle Marie-José.

In the distance, I could see Maryse standing all by herself and looking intently in our direction. As soon as Annick dismissed our little group, I walked back to her.

CHAPTER XXII

Old habits die hard, and whether this was due to limited cerebral powers or to reflexes acquired without any thought processing taking place, I was not sure. All I knew for certain was that the supervisors found it impossible to shake off the brutal approach they had become so accustomed to. Behind Sister Catherine's back, they had lost none of their zealousness in juxtaposing our names with big black crosses or in smacking hard on our naked thighs. Mlle Roseline, usually meek and mild, had joined in the affray, and for some inexplicable reason, that particular week, she was hitting and hitting hard. It had reached the point where I could not open my mouth without being smacked in return. The pain and the unfairness of it all made me seethe with fury and transformed my normally cheeky, but placid, disposition into a super volcano waiting to explode.

That evening at bed time, Mlle Roseline marched into our dorm, for she had heard voices when we should have been silent. She came straight over to me and smacked me hard. I had not even spoken that time. I rubbed my leg, breathing hard to control the stinging pain, whereupon Annie Brenn turned up on the threshold and started to yell at Michèle whose bed lay by the entrance. The supervisor's inane and stupid bark stirred up the rumbling anger that was effusing inside me; I was growling like a wounded tigress, ready to pounce on anybody that looked a threat. Michèle was one of the seven from that far away country called Indochina. She was so gentile, docile, and so caring of others that everybody called her '*mère poule*'— mother hen. There was not an ounce of bellicosity in her, and when I saw her on the verge of tears, totally defenceless against the barrage of painful insults that Annie Brenn was now throwing at her, I pounced on the insufferable supervisor. I lashed out at her and, suddenly, I heard myself scream, "Brenn! *Ferme ta gueule!*"

The supervisor gasped and froze on the spot as if a bullet had hit her from behind. Her mouth was gaping wide, and for a few seconds, she found she could not move. She stared at me with her hollow eyes, and as I looked at her with pure naked effrontery, the sheer look of utter shock on her face made me feel good, so good, in fact, that I could not even begin to think of the consequences. After a few seconds of this silent duel, she turned her heels and muttered in shock, "I'm going to get Sister Catherine."

I do not know how the news spread around so quickly, but as Annie Brenn's stiletto shoes clacked on the wooden floor, the whole dormitory fell into a deathly silence. What would happen now? Nobody had ever been heard saying a naughty word, let alone swearing at a supervisor point blank, mainly because we knew it was a sin, so grave, in fact, that we put it on a par with the ten others that had been deeply carved into our brains; and it was generally felt that if God had known about the act of swearing, he would surely have made it the eleventh commandment. For my own defence, I had to admit that I did not fully understand how bad the words were. To me, it was just a phrase, a sentence that had been scribbled on a piece of paper for fun, but never uttered.

How would Sister Catherine, who had not yet dealt with a serious offence since her arrival, react and deal with this?

Would we see the first public beating since the departure of Sister Marie-Catherine?

When the door shut noisily behind the supervisor, girls tiptoed to my dorm and soon, I was besieged, with everyone wanting a bite of the story so that it could be repeated and passed on like a good old folk tale to which everyone had been a firsthand witness. I stood in the middle of the rush, my arms firmly crossed on my chest, determined to keep the story to myself.

"What did you say?" Annick asked concerned.

I stared at my friend, but refused to answer.

"My! Are you gonna get it!" Someone else threw in, intent on raising the temperature amongst the assembled horde.

Of course I was going to get it, but the sight of Annie Brenn's face paralysed in shock was well worth the consequences. Hence, standing astride in the middle of the corridor, I waited for my fate. Suddenly, the doorknob creaked opened and all the girls scurried back to their dormitories to wait for the events to unfold.

Sister Catherine advanced calmly towards me with her eyes looking fixedly ahead and her jaws locked in a stiff silence. I stood outside my dorm, in defiant form and petulant mood, but after a few seconds, I felt my arms slowly fall against my sides. The girls watched the long march with their mouths gaping.

"Go inside your dorms," the nun ordered in a very controlled manner. Then she stopped right in front of me and stared at me with her steely eyes. I stared back at her, unwavering, trying to anticipate her next move, but Sister Catherine was in no rush.

"What did you say to Mlle Brenn?" She asked calmly.

I looked at Annie Brenn who, despite towering over the nun, was shielding herself behind the nun's silhouette. The impact of the offending words was slowly sinking in. I was about to receive the worse punishment for being the first girl ever to utter them. No, my mind was made up, I would not repeat them.

Sister Catherine made her final advance and smacked me...once.

"You'll spend the night in the attic to repent on your behaviour," she said afterwards. Then she left.

Was that it? Was this all she was going to do? No screaming, no thrashing, no public condemnation? The whole dormitory stood still, frozen in a stunned silence. The drama had unfolded and Sister Catherine had obviously decided that there would be no martyr today. Murmurs and whispers began to rise again and heads appeared around doorways.

"What did she do?"

"What did she say?"

Annick came and stood in front of me, in complete awe.

"Wow! You're amazing! How did you dare?"

I smiled at her and I smiled at Annie Brenn's discomfiture. Her darting eyes were a clear sign that she had not only lost control of the situation, but also that she would never regain her meek authority. Having witnessed many a beating, she had expected no less for such a serious offence, but none had been forthcoming. Had she lost face? Who had won? Surely, she had, and to mark the point, she dragged me away by the arm and spluttered authoritatively:

"I forbid you to speak to anyone! You lot, go back to your dorms."

Upon these words, the supervisor unlocked the attic and threw me inside.

Once the door slammed behind me, before I grew too scared to climb the stairs, I ran up to the top floor and flicked the switch.

LITTLE ANGELS DON'T CRY

The attic covered a huge area which must have run the whole length of the dormitory at least. It was an enormous place littered with abandoned possessions and ornaments. One of the pane-glass windows was broken and underneath it, rows upon rows of second-hand shoes stood in long neat lines, ready to be used. I looked at them studying their style and mentally picking those which looked more fashionable. There on the front row, I found a pair of brown sandals, still in reasonable condition, which would be perfect for me to wear in the hot summer months. I tried them on, and since they fitted, but only just, I kept them on to walk around and explore the rest of the attic, though I could not bring myself to go to the far end of the attic. I did not like dark corners, because some girl had led us to believe that they were usually haunted by the devil. With its dark sloping ceiling, the attic reminded me of the cave full of lepers that Benhur had to access in order to search for his mother. It was terrifying and I hovered in the centre, carefully averting my gaze away from the dark alcoves of the room.

The dusty floorboards creaked under my feet as I explored all the nooks and crannies, passed the broken wash-basin, the cast-iron bath, the white statue with both arms missing, and there, by the stairwell, a white mattress covered in a thick plastic material, my bed for the night. I sat on it while I searched further in the dark shadows of the exposed beams and dormer windows. As long as I did not look at the far end of the room, it was not that scary, I concluded—except for the broken statue whose ghostly presence kept churning frightening thoughts of lost souls and the devil. I steeled myself to block any thoughts of soldiers or clowns, and in order to keep my mind occupied, I began to search for a blanket or some other material that would keep me warm for the night, but found nothing. Eventually, I huddled down on the palliasse, pulling my nightdress as low as possible so that I could wrap up my feet with it and go to sleep. Needless to say, I could not sleep. The wide open gap from the broken window blew a chilly wind inside and the plastic mattress turned cold as soon as I moved to a different position. That night, the dark creatures that I had dreamt up with Nadine, the red devil with his sharp horns and flaming trident, and all the soldiers that I had seen in my recurring nightmares were not able to invade my dreams for the simple reason that I could not sleep. I was too cold and too tired to be scared. I tossed and turned until the morning came, and when Annie Brenn finally opened the dormitory door to release me, a soothing wave of warm air assailed me as I emerged from my bolthole.

*

We were now in the days leading up to Christmas. If the belief in Father Christmas was a pagan dream, where would the big man with the white beard go when he died, I wondered, though not for too long, as right now I was busy listening to words that this year, for the first time ever, we would be able to choose a present for Christmas. In the dormitory, the atmosphere turned electric as the news, confirmed by the supervisors, spread like wild fire. We jumped on our beds and began to sing and dance.

"Hey! Céleste, show us how to do the twist again!"

And Céleste, whom we all agreed was the best singer and dancer, began to wriggle on her bed to the tune of *'Com' on let's twist again like we did last summer...'* except that the words were in French, and we all joined in, singing with her and twisting our hips the best we could, lost in the new craze that was sweeping the country, bringing a whole generation to fever pitch, as they jiggled their hips on the dance floor which, for us, was our beds.

Annie Brenn and Mlle Marie-José paced up and down the dormitory frantically, shouting and ordering us to be quiet, settle down and go to sleep, but their voices were instantly drowned by the general chorus of girls singing at the top of their voices, ignoring the threats that were now happily mingled with the exciting lyrics.

More excited than ever, we ran up and down the corridors on our way to the washroom, sliding on our carpet slippers, and filling the atmosphere with our shrills of laughter; and since we had loads of energy left, refuelled by the irresistible tempo of the hit song, we played Hide and Seek in each other's dormitories, stopping only to ask: "what are you going to ask for?".

I had not had time to think about it and, still out of breath, all I could do was to reply: "I don't know…"

Eventually, we did calm down and began the serious task of thinking of a present that would surpass all other presents.

"What are you going to ask for?" I asked Annick.

"An umbrella…an automatic umbrella," she replied, throwing her shoulders back with pride at being *au fait* with the latest technological advances.

"What's that?" I queried, ignorant as always of all things that evolved outside the orphanage.

"They're these small umbrellas, and when you press a button, they open automatically."

"Wow! Just like magic? I want one too!"

"Right!" A voice suddenly boomed, "I've had enough. I'm going to get Sister Catherine!"

Annie Brenn slammed the door as she left the dormitory. Quickly, we all ran back to our dorms and dived into our beds, teeth brushed or not, to wait for the arrival of Sister Catherine.

She did not say anything when she first came in, but we could tell she was there, for we could hear her rubber soles squeak on the floorboards. Her slow, calculated steps guided her around each dorm, and every now and again, we could hear her voice rise, always in a controlled manner, as she chastised a girl who had not yet made it to her bed. Our dorm being at the far end of the corridor, she finally breathed in quietly, scouring the room and checking its occupants, and left without saying as much as a word. We were confounded, quite unable to believe that we had got away with it.

Naïvely thinking that all had been forgotten, on Christmas Day in the refectory, we stood up when Sister Catherine made her entrance and we watched her take her usual position in front of the large mirror still adorned with the little boats trudging along painstakingly above her head. She looked at us with a glare full of reproach. Next to her, on the floor, we had spotted two cardboard boxes and concluded that they must contain our coveted Christmas presents. We were about to sit back down again when she hailed firmly:

"No, you can stay standing up! Because I want you all to listen to me and I want everyone to pay strict attention to what I'm about to say. Your behaviour last night was absolutely appalling; it was selfish, inconsiderate, and terribly hurtful to Mlle Marie-José who has done her best to care for you. You don't deserve her and I have the regret to say that after your thoughtless behaviour last night, she has decided to leave…"

Here she paused to observe our reaction and perhaps even catch a look of contrition on some of our angelic faces, but not knowing what else to expect, we stood rigidly and in a deafening silence behind our little benches, feeling too contrite and too guilty to even gasp at the devastating news. Our behaviour was never meant to hurt her, or even Annie Brenn for that matter. We had simply got carried away in a mad moment spurred on by that crazy dance '*le twist*', that had made us forget that Father Christmas did not really exist and that presents, however big or small, were all part of a pagan dream.

Sister Catherine waited a few minutes longer to sustain the guilty silence in order to prod our conscience with her accusing stare and our remorseful thoughts. Then she reached for one of the boxes and lifted several pairs of brand new slippers.

"This," she said dryly, "is what you would have had, had you had the good sense to behave, had you had more thought and consideration for the people who care for you."

And as she proceeded to reveal the content of the other boxes, we stared at her arms dipping into the boxes full of Christmas treasures, feeling more and more wretched for what we had done and what we had lost. Then, she dropped the final bombshell.

"As an extra punishment, no one will be allowed home today...and this time, there will be no exceptions!"

We all gasped in complete shock and dismay. Surely, she could not stop girls going home on Christmas Day. But her word was final, and when the realisation eventually hit us, several girls began to cry. I pressed my nails hard against the back of the wooden bench, disappointed at the thought that I could be wearing those lovely warm slippers instead of those rugged carpet squares. At least, I knew I was not going anywhere that day, so the last punishment left me completely cold...until I looked at Maryse. She had begun to cry and I felt a terrible pain in my heart. All I wanted to do right now was to put my arm around her shoulders and comfort her, and tell her that at least we still had each other, but the stiff silence in the refectory acted like a barrier, isolating each one of us in our own predicament and our own guilt. Alone, we would have to pray to seek forgiveness and the redemption of our souls, because alone we would be when, on Judgement Day, we would come face to face with God to be adjudged of our actions.

After the Christmas holidays, we returned to school. We listened eagerly to what everyone else had had, while we kept quiet about our own misfortune. Unfortunately, Bénédicte with the perfect ringlets of hair asked:

"What did you get for Christmas?"

I shifted uneasily on my chair, still overwhelmed by the sense of guilt that had plagued the rest of the holidays. I fumbled clumsily with my ink pen and threw an awkward glance at her, trying to think of an appropriate answer that would not reveal anything of what really happened.

"Oh, nothing much…sweets and things…" I finally mumbled. "What about you, what did you get?"

Her eyes lit up as she started to tell me about this beautiful doll, huge in fact, with eyes that could open and close, and which could be fed with a baby bottle through the little hole she had in the middle of her bright pink lips.

"Has she got a name?"

"Yes, she's called Bella…that means 'beautiful'."

I did not really like dolls and could not share her enthusiasm. To me, they were nothing but lifeless and useless things that never did anything interesting. Still, watching Bénédicte's round features glow with pure joy made me want to soak up the wonderful aura that emanated from her whole being, and if dolls had that effect on her, then I was perfectly happy for her to own all the dolls in the world. What I was more interested in was the fact that she seemed quite keen to befriend me. We carried on talking outside, in the playground.

"What do you normally do during the school holidays?"

The stigma of being from the orphanage never left me and I loathed talking about it. Now, I was looking at Bénédicte trying to think how I could divert the subject away from it, so I answered succinctly:

"I go to a *colonie de vacances*; it's near Calais."

"Oh really!" She exclaimed all excited. "My parents have a holiday home near Calais too. You could come and spend a weekend with us."

I cringed at the thought. I did not want any of my classmates to see me at the orphanage. It was an alien world closed to happy children from happy families. I did not want anyone to see the starkness of its bare walls and the Spartan conditions we lived in, but most of all, I did not want to spoil her happiness by letting her see the harsh reality of a world devoid of human feelings, human emotions, and human contact. She was beautiful because nothing had ever happened to her that would pop the happy, colourful bubble in which she lived.

"I don't think I'll be allowed," I sighed, convinced that her parents were bound to say no, once they found out that I was from the orphanage. I was only allowed out to clean complete strangers' houses, and somehow I guessed I would not be allowed to go to a girl's house simply because she happened to be my friend.

"Don't worry," she replied cheerfully. "If I want to invite a friend, my parents will do everything they can to make sure that she can come."

I smiled at her gentle determination but dismissed, almost immediately, any possibility of it happening.

*

Just before the Easter Holidays, Sister Catherine called me and, as always, she came straight to the point.

"M. and Mme Langeais want you to spend the Easter Holidays with them."

"What!" I cried out.

The thought of spending the school holidays being used as a servant girl to wash up, clean floors, and baby sit for people who thought they were doing me a favour horrified me.

"I don't want to go...I want to go to Sangatte."

"Well, you can't. It's all been arranged."

My heart sank. Only a few days earlier, Maryse had told me that she had begged her parents to let her go and they had agreed.

"I don't want to go! I want to stay with my friends!" I protested vehemently.

"There's no point in arguing, you're going and that's that," Sister Catherine replied on a dry, detached tone of voice.

Suddenly, it all became very clear to me; for the first time, I saw how cool, calm, and calculating Sister Catherine was, and at that moment, I wished I had never come up with those gooey sentimental verses that praised her kindness and generous heart. She was just as bad as Sister Marie-Catherine, if not worse, because her tactic was to get at us from within, and as such, her psychological wounds left marks that lingered on well after the short, sharp pain of a slap on a naked thigh.

Knowing that nothing would make her sway from her decision, I clenched my fists and walked away in a temper. There was only one thing left for me to do—like I had done so stubbornly and so successfully in the past—I would cease all forms of communication. That way, M. and Mme Langeais might hand me back sooner than they had intended to, and with a bit of luck, they might decide, like M. and Mme Cateau had done before them, that they never wanted me back. That was a good plan, I managed to convince myself, and the thought of a sure victory filled me with immense pleasure, for I, Martha Bertrand, was no martyr, but I did not want to be a servant either.

CHAPTER XXIII

When the Easter Holidays came, Sister Catherine rummaged around to find some clothes to pack into a little suitcase she had borrowed from someone else. I did not know what she had put inside and did not want to know. Afterwards, I sat all alone in the parlour waiting to be collected, dangling my feet in sheer frustration as I pictured Sangatte through the crisp air of a clear blue sky. I could almost hear the whooshing sound of the sea and the strident cry of seagulls, and as I conjured up those wonderful images of past holidays, the characteristic smell of iodine air mixed with that of hot bales of hay and somnolent cows ambling nonchalantly in neighbouring fields filtered gently through my twitching nostrils. And I even smiled as I remembered mooing at the cows as we walked past them in a crocodile file, pinching our noses and laughing when they raised their tails to pee noisily on the ground like a tap in full flow, or ejected with vigour that pestilent brown stuff that flopped heavily on the ground, splashing everything in sight. After we had howled in laughter and in disgust, Maryse, using the slogan of the omnipresent road safety campaign, had wagged her finger and warned on a haughty tone, 'Always keep your distance'.

In a rare show of bonhomie, to prolong the fun, Mlle Pierrette had happily joined in the banter and declared that back in Alsace, 'cowpat cakes' were quite a delicacy. Maryse and I looked at each other, and burst out laughing. Only an Alsatian cow could possibly know this and revel in it.

Alas, right now, I was stuck on my own in the cold parlour, sulking and mulling over my fate. Outside, the boisterous cries of the other girls at play sharpened my sense of isolation and I dangled my feet with renewed vigour, bashing them against the wooden bench trying to create my own noises, for I felt so cold, so sad, and so lonely.

M. Langeais soon arrived and I marched to his car, refusing to even look at him. Perhaps he greeted me, and perhaps he even talked to me, but I heard nothing, except the rumbling furore of my belligerent thoughts. I was locked in a silent protest, determined not to give in. After he had pulled the car into the driveway, I hopped out and waited at the front door, scowling heavily. M. Langeais, ignoring my petulant mood, invited me in. I went straight upstairs to deposit my little case next to the camp bed that would be mine for the next few days and stood at the window in a dream state, wishing I was somewhere else. The deserted street felt emptier and greyer than ever before…and the silence…that dreadful unbearable void full of the echoes of departed or dead souls hung around me like a soundproof bubble outside which nobody could hear me scream.

"Martha!" A voice called.

It was Mme Langeais. I went down the stairs and into the kitchen.

"I didn't hear you arrive, I was in the garden."

I gazed outside and saw the sun shining, but it felt cold. In the dining area, I could hear the little girls playing with their dolls, dressing, feeding, praising, and chastising them in such a convincing pretence that it was hard to believe that these little puppets were not for real.

"Now," Mme Langeais said in a commanding voice, "you can start with the lunch dishes and after that, we'll go to town to do a bit of shopping. You like going to the shops, don't you?"

I gave an indifferent nod of the head, rolled up my sleeves, and started to arrange the dishes neatly in the washing-up bowl, just so that it would be quicker to get through them, all the while ruminating dark thoughts on how unfair my fate was. At least at *Saint Vincent*, we took it in turn to clean and scrub. In the same indifferent fashion, I grabbed hold of the tea towel and proceeded to dry the dishes while staring at the view of the large back garden. In the distance, I spotted Milou. I wished the cat would come close to the house so that I could try and befriend it, but Beatrice had said very firmly that no cats were allowed near the house because they were nasty creatures that loved to bite the hands of little children. I remembered smiling at her vehement statement and wondered which of the two adults did not like cats.

And so, the ordinary routine of this small family unit resumed. Mme Langeais looked after the children while I got on with the house chores. M. Langeais disappeared every day to go somewhere. He was going out to work, whatever that meant, and returned in the evening with the newspaper tucked under his arm, which he read while smoking his pipe, sunk in the rocking chair, oblivious to the noise and clatter around him.

While M. Langeais was wholly occupied with reading the local gazette, Mme Langeais asked me to give the girls their bath, so I went upstairs. At that point, M. Langeais decided to come upstairs as well, in case I ran the water too hot or too cold. While he sat on the edge of the bath, I had my first good look at him. His moustache had always given him a stern appearance, but now that I could look at him at close range, I was surprised to discover a certain warmth hiding behind his strong masculine features. I wanted to ask him questions, but did not know what, so I asked the only question I knew to ask.

"How old are you?"

He looked a little taken aback by the directness of the question, but answered all the same.

"I'm thirty-five," he replied with a smile. "Right, this should do," he added, his hand wading through the warm water.

Thirty-five, I thought, that really is old.

*

On market day, we went to town. Mme Langeais pushed the pram and asked me to hold hands with the girls to make sure they did not run into the path of a car. I was quite happy to oblige and thought I was doing rather well, considering, when Mme Langeais interrupted my trail of thoughts with a very pointed question.

"Why won't you talk?"

I was stuck. Never before had anyone asked me to explain or justify my behaviour, and I did not know what to reply. I racked my brains and weighed each excuse in turn so as to pick one that sounded the most plausible.

"You're missing your friends?" She asked trying to appear understanding. "Of course you're missing your friends, and that I understand, but we're trying to be nice to you and we were hoping that you would be a little more friendly towards us, especially now that you know us better."

Her reply astounded me, not the least because it was loaded with hints about my calculated and stubborn refusal to communicate. So far, they had been very patient, made many allowances while biding their time. Now, it seemed that an invisible deadline had come up and it was time for me to act, but how could I tell her that I strongly objected to spending my school holidays acting as a servant girl without sounding rude. In the end, I decided to say nothing.

Gradually, things got worse. Occasionally, Sabine and Beatrice would have an almighty row and fight over their dolls. Sometimes, it even came to blows with screams followed by tears. Then, Beatrice would run to her mother accusing her big sister of all sorts of demonic things she had carried out on her beloved Fifi, and without bothering to hear what Sabine had to say for herself, mother would barge into the dining area red with apoplectic anger, and lash out on her eldest daughter, screaming and shouting, while poor Sabine tried to shield the blows with her arms, screaming and shouting louder than her mother. Then, when she could not shut up her daughter, mother would throw Sabine into the broom cupboard under the stairs and lock her there for a good hour or two.

Unfortunately, like most children, Sabine was terrified of the dark and the door had no sooner been bolted than she rammed it hard with her little fists and her tiny feet. I could easily imagine why she was so scared for I knew exactly what was in that cupboard: brooms that reputedly belonged to witches, strange noises that were the voices of witches, and worse of all, large cobwebs that told her that somewhere in the invisible corners lurked a great big hairy spider.

Many times, I tried to ignore her hysterical screams and her heart-wrenching pleas by drowning my thoughts with the washing-up clatter, or scrubbing the floor with more energetic strokes, but after a while, after Sabine had run out of tears, everything would fall quiet and Mme Langeais would open the door gingerly to check on her daughter only to find her fast asleep, her head resting on a pile of dusters.

This scenario happened on several occasions during the holidays, and just like the times when we were forced to witness girls receiving a good thrashing in the middle of the refectory, I watched in distress as little Sabine took the blame. I had never thought that children living in a family unit could endure the same kind of treatment as we did. It was a stark revelation that almost made me forget how harsh life at the orphanage was. What made it even more difficult for me to accept was the fact that this treatment was being inflicted by a mother upon her very own daughter. Back at *Saint Vincent*, I had always reasoned that the main excuse for the adults to treat us the way they did was simply because they did not care much for us and that made it, if not acceptable, at least understandable. Here, however, I was witnessing a mother—a word that I had grown to associate with love, gentleness, and beauty nurtured by my belief in the Virgin Mary, Mother of Jesus—hitting and kicking her very own child. I could not stop thinking about it and kept pondering over the real significance and the true meaning of words. I watched and observed adults intently because their behaviour often did not match the words they preached, and I needed to understand why they were so intent on condemning us to a life of damnation and hell for our slightest misdemeanour.

Now here, in this household, I was busy watching and observing Sabine and wondered how she viewed her mother. Was this how people developed the notion of forgiveness? I wondered. Without forgiveness, there is no love, and without love, the individual becomes a mere observer: cold, detached, and never involved. This was not Sabine; she was a warm and caring little girl who liked to please, and for this reason alone, she was extremely forgiving. She loved her mother and I felt sure that her mother loved her in return, but the emotional conflict between the two of them was incredibly painful to watch.

By the time M. Langeais came home at night, the dust had settled, the tears dried, and the moods reverted to calm and placid, and I remember sitting at the dining table at supper time and looking at the father, wondering if he had the slightest inkling of what went on in his absence during the day.

*

Shortly before the end of the holidays, M. Langeais drove me back to Sangatte in his little Simca car. The flat featureless landscape rushed past the window with only the odd church spires piercing through the heavy sky that some power above had darkened with clouds loaded with rain. However, for once, I was able to see beyond the leaded sky and, just like Sister Bénédicte had said, I caught a glimpse of the sun hanging high in the bright heavens. How long would it be before I was back with my little gang? My gang...How I had missed them. What would they be doing now? I tried to guess, but totally enwrapped in cheerful thoughts chequered with colourful pastiches of memorable deeds, every time we passed a church, I kept forgetting to look at the clock.

Of the journey, I remember very little, only that the moment we arrived at the *Colonie Saint Joseph des Flots*, I ran through the building, flew doors open, and squealed with excitement every time I spotted a familiar face from our little gang.

The icy rain fell steadily outside, so we were allowed to spend the afternoon in the vast playroom. On our way there, we passed the cloakroom and, immediately, my nostrils twitched at the familiar smell of damp wool mixed with mothballs. At last, at long last, I was back home.

The cloakroom walls were lined with rows of pigeon-holes, and in some of them, I spotted little fluffy yellow chicks.

Roberte accosted me and asked eagerly:

"Did you get anything for Easter?"

"Of course I did, I had a huge chocolate egg…but the best thing was that after church, we had an egg hunt in the garden; that was great fun!" I boasted, acting as if I had had the time of my life.

"Well," Roberte continued all excited. "You'll never believe this…we each had a little basket with a chocolate hen and little eggs filled with liquor in them…and look…" She added, showing me one of the little fluffy chicks. "We got those as well, they were in the basket with the eggs!"

Typical, I thought, the one time I am away at Easter…they get all those sweets, not to mention the delightful surprise they must have had upon their return from church, when they discovered that they each had one tucked away in their little pigeon-holes.

Suddenly, Maryse appeared in the doorway of the playroom.

"Hi, Martha! Come and see what I've found," she hailed.

Curious, I ran close behind her. As usual when the room was turned into a playroom, all the tables had been pushed against the walls and on one of them, right there underneath the window, Maryse pointed at a record player.

"Look!" She said, picking up a record. On the sleeve, there was a picture of a young girl with pony tails and wearing a pink gingham dress decorated with marguerites. Her name was *Sheila* and the song was *L'école est finie*.

"It's number one in the hit parade," she declared all excited. "Let's put it on."

"Do you know how to do it?" I asked, marvelling at her advanced technical knowledge.

"'Course, I do. I've got one almost the same at home...Hey, listen!" She said, after she had placed the stylus on the black vinyl. Straight away, we were swept away by the very catchy tune; very quickly, we picked up the lyrics and sang them at the top of our voices while dancing the twist energetically on the tiled floor. Soon, other girls, attracted by the music, joined in. For several minutes of pure joy, we sang and danced, caught in the frantic rhythm of the twist, and for once, no one came to silence us. Since the lyrics began: *donne-moi ta main et prends la mienne...*—give me your hand and take mine...—we linked hands together and danced the twist to the words, reeling with laughter. I looked at the impromptu chain and felt absolutely wonderful. It felt so good to be back home.

Alas, I had rejoined the gang at the end of the Easter holidays and soon, it was time to return to Tourcoing, to its grey landscape, slimy streets, and steaming slagheaps.

As the coach spluttered along the cobblestones, I began to think of school. I tried to take in the fact that this was going to be my final term at *Notre Dame* and instead of relishing the thought that I was about to move away from Sister Eugène-Marie's treacherous claws, I could only think of how sad it would be to leave the happy atmosphere of a school where I had been able to forget the bleak existence inside the walls of *Saint Vincent*.

However, even there, at the *Institution Saint Vincent de Paul*, life was about to improve, for at the end of the summer holidays, I would move on to *Le Nid*, the transitory 'nest' snuggled below the nuns' living quarters, a mere few yards away from the Junior Section, and where we would blossom into little women under the watchful eye of Sister Odile. I had often seen her short silhouette waddle across the courtyard and I had noticed then that she always had a ready smile for anyone who cared to say hello.

With my poor sense of time and history, I easily imagined that she had come to *Saint Vincent* straight from the pages of the Bible to look after generations of girls, who had come to her with the ragged and bedraggled look of escaped prisoners, and heal the physical and mental scars left by Sister Marie-Catherine and tend to the psychological wounds inflicted by Sister Catherine.

When we were taken across to visit the premises, we had questioned the *raison d'être* of this cosy little idyll which had a large cuckoo clock chirping cheerfully the hours away on the dining room wall.

Why not move straight to the Senior Section? Sister Odile had replied that here, in her exclusive realm, we would be able to develop the maturity and wisdom necessary to join the Senior Section, and as she repeated the sentence, putting particular emphasis on the key words, she had looked at me gauging that anything to do with maturity, wisdom, and me, Martha Bertrand, would be an uphill task. Nonetheless, she had smiled and a little twinkle had sparkled in her eyes as she enunciated the words clearly to show that this was a tease rather than a put down, and in a flash, I understood why she was the most popular nun around. Unlike other nuns, as we knew only too well, her well known trademark was not based on the severity of her regime, but on one important quality that no other adults I had come across so far seemed to own: Sister Odile not only had a heart, but she also had a sense of humour.

These were the exciting times ahead and for once, I could truly look forward to moving on, for this time I could tell that the facts were not lies.

Then, the question as to which secondary school I would be attending came up. There were rumours that I would be joining Marie, the only girl so far to go to the equivalent of a grammar school, but in view of my immaturity, Sister Catherine preferred to reserve judgement until the end of term.

There were more important things pressing ahead. For a start, it was time for me to undergo my second religious metamorphosis: my *communion solemnelle*, which would involve an overload of prayers and a silent retreat somewhere in a convent or a similar edifice.

At catechism, we studied at length the meaning of the vows we were about to take and rehearsed the ritual procession that would meander through the streets, boys first. I may have shunned God for a while and quietly objected to his choice of representatives here on earth, but when I advanced ceremoniously towards the altar, staring at the cross, at the chalices, at the candelabras, and at the stained-glass windows, I could feel His powerful hold on me and once more I was ready to submit to the power of His love and to the wisdom of His will.

Maryse was not with me when I went through my first religious metamorphosis and she would not be with me for my second one either. She was a whole year behind, which meant that she would not be moving to 'Le Nid' either. I did not want to even think what life would be like without her and her cheeky banter. Sadly, having behaved almost like twins up until now, we were gradually coming to terms with the fact that we were growing up, but we would only grow apart once we had been physically separated. Gradually, our mischievous streak began to fade away. In fact, it had been a good while since Maryse had made a passing reference to 'witches', especially as Mlle Agnès no longer sat outside the kitchens. Indeed, she had removed herself and gone somewhere...wherever witches go. We had seen the last of Mlle Agnès and the last of the witches, and unbeknown to us, the final chapter of our lives together was swiftly coming to an end.

It was while I was lost in deep and serious thoughts, contemplating a very different future away from the Junior Section, from the ghastly supervisors and Sister Catherine and well out of reach of Sister Eugene-Marie's vindictive claws, that Sister Catherine called me.

"Your godmother will be coming to your second communion."

"Oh," I sighed before I could stop myself. "Won't the Langeais be coming too?" I enquired, remembering the fiasco of my first communion.

"No," she replied hesitantly. "In fact, you won't be going there anymore."

"Oh? Why?" I asked, half disappointed, half relieved.

"They didn't say…"

I was back to square one with no one to watch over me and I wondered how many crosses I would have by the end of the week.

CHAPTER XXIV

Back in Sister Eugène-Marie's class for my last term here at *Notre Dame*, the teacher gave me a form to fill in. I had been selected to take the scholarship exam and, although it had been a forgone conclusion, I still felt immensely proud to have been picked for such a high honour, so much so that I wanted to hold the form aloft and shout out a resounding "Yeah!", but the nun was only a step away from a verbose tirade, constantly reminding me that I was after all only a snotty little wench from the orphanage. As a matter of fact, rarely a day passed without some Machiavellian plot being hatched beneath the canopy of her devil's teeth. Satan has many facets, I had been warned, and right here I was seeing one of them.

I had never before filled in an official form and I was rather baffled by some of the rubrics.

Nom du chef de famille:...............

Nom de la mère de famille:..............

I raised my hand to request some help. Sister Eugène-Marie lifted the form and studied it briefly before handing back to me saying, "just write: *do not exist*."

So I did. Hence, the form duly completed, I handed it back.

Then Mother's Day came. In the past, I had always been obliged to make something, a little paper basket or a little piece of embroidery, which invariably ended up languishing at the bottom of some forgotten locker. However, this was Primary Seven; we were the seniors of the whole school. We could not possibly be seen wasting our time wrestling with a messy collage, not in Primary Seven. We would have to make something worthy of our high status, a task fit to reflect the high academic achievement of Sister Eugène-Marie's top class.

"You will make a card," she announced, "...and compose a poem dedicated to your mothers, which you will write inside in your best handwriting. Marks will be awarded not just for content, but also for presentation, spelling and writing."

I bristled on my seat, excited by this new challenge. This was my first chance to align words in order to create an illusion or raise emotions that I had heard about, but never felt inside. Besides, I adored poetry. I loved the way words put together in a certain way could create a harmonious sound, a musical cadence where each verse had its own tune.

During the disciplined silence of study time in the vast refectory, I set about to write my very first verses, but before I started, I thought about the role of a mother, conscious that the only example I had was Mme Langeais. And I thought about the kind of mother she was and decided that perhaps, I should write instead about the Virgin Mary, Mother of Jesus. And I wrote about the bliss and happiness that only she, the most beautiful mother in the world with the radiant smile and pure heart, could spread around the family unit, like a mantel of peace and harmony, which would bring joy and eternal love.

On the card itself, I drew a picture of the Virgin Mary with a bright halo around her head and yellow flowers resting on her feet. Having folded my piece of cardboard paper neatly into two, I drew neat lines with my pencil and, in my very best handwriting, proceeded to write down my very first poem.

The next day, Sister Eugène-Marie collected the homework.

I gave my card feeling hugely satisfied that I had succeeded in writing beautiful verses where all the words rhymed and actually meant something.

Two or three days later, the teacher was ready to hand our poems back. She commented on a few and declared that she was very glad to see the brave effort we had put in to write lovely words dedicated to our mothers. At that point, I stopped listening; I had not written the poem for anybody, it was just a nebulous dream that I had shaped into verses with rhyming words. Then, my trail of thoughts veered back to Sister Eugène-Marie's literary debriefing, for her voice had suddenly adopted a dramatic tone.

"...Yes, I particularly liked this one. This pupil has used heartfelt and moving words, and in this way has captured the whole essence of motherly love, the beauty of her feelings and the wonderful aura she creates around her..."

We all sat, riveted, wondering who this mystery pupil was.

"Yes," she continued, still smiling. "I was very impressed with it...and I have to admit that I was rather surprised, extremely surprised indeed."

She paused yet again to study our expectant faces and our pleading eyes urging her to reveal the mystery writer. Finally, she declared with gusto:

"And the author of this poem is...Martha Bertrand!"

A huge gasp of amazement rose from the whole class and a spontaneous applause followed. I stared at the nun in complete disbelief. Was she really for the very first time ever congratulating me for something I had done? I was staggered, speechless. Despite this, instead of feeling mightily proud, my instinctive reaction was to brace myself for a new wave of resentment that was sure to follow. From the nun's smile distorted by the devil's teeth, all I saw was my pride and self-esteem tumble down into an unfathomable abyss filled with burning resentment and treacherous malice. I did not...I could not get excited. But to my teacher, the poem was a revelation that triggered a complete transformation in her. I was no longer the snotty little urchin, the would-be cheat or thief from that God forsaken place called *Saint Vincent*. In her globular eyes, I was now the star of the class and not a day passed without her finding some excuse to get me to stand next to her at her desk. It was almost like an open confession, a public act of contrition which she was anxious to perform while there was still time to absolve herself of all her sins, her way of telling the class that she, the righteous teacher with a soul purer than most, may have been wrong after all—something that my classmates had known all along, but which in her blind prejudice, she had failed to see. It was now my turn to openly resent her and I made sure that her lecherous hands always remained at a safe distance from me.

Now, she had become the helpful, supportive teacher and the day before the scholarship exam, she gave me a lump of sugar because she had read somewhere that the brain performs better if you take sugar just before a cerebral challenge. I did not want to accept anything from her, but I wanted to be the best, so I reluctantly accepted the small offering.

The scholarship exam took place on a Saturday. It was a beautiful warm sunny day and I had never felt so excited in my entire life. The day before, Sister Catherine had instructed that Marie would take me, as she was the only girl who knew the way. I became even more excited at the thought that, should I pass, this would also be my new school.

The classroom looked old and bare, and smelt of that wonderful mixture of wood, polish, dust and chalk, and the wooden desks with flip-tops stood rather battered, but to me, this was the mark of a good academic school, the definitive proof that knowledge had long inhabited these walls, just waiting to be absorbed by the best brains of the land.

The teacher, a tall thin man with greyish hair, peered at us over his half-moon glasses. Hunched over bits of paper that he held close to his chest, his face radiated with a warm friendly smile. When the crowd got too big outside the door, he began to read out our names in alphabetical order, showing each candidate to their desk. Inevitably, I ended up sitting on the front row and while I waited for everyone else to settle, I looked around at the bare walls, at the high windows stretching all the way to the ceiling and at the blackboard smeared with white chalky streaks, but I felt too shy to turn around to look and see who else was behind me.

Lined paper was quickly distributed and I sat full of trepidation, waiting for the dictation to begin. The man enunciated each word even more slowly and distinctly than my usual teacher and none of the carefully measured paragraphs contained a single ambiguous combination of words that would have made us dither between an agreement and non-agreement or ponder over a spurious verb ending. The maths problems were so simple compared to those Sister Eugène-Marie liked to set that, after I had completed all the tasks, I found it incredible to believe that this straight forward, simple exercise was about to determine the future direction of my academic career.

As soon as we left the exam room, I spotted Annie Brenn waiting for me in the corridor. In my eagerness to know the outcome of the exam, I forgot to greet her and asked:

"When am I going to get the results?"

"Oh, I don't know," Annie Brenn replied. "Your teacher should tell you."

I waited for days and I waited for weeks and still, nobody could tell me whether I had passed or not.

Eventually, one Thursday afternoon as we were lining up in the courtyard of *Saint Vincent* to go to the park, Marie, who had gone home to her foster parents the previous weekend, told me that her foster mother had shown her the newspaper *La Voix du Nord* with printed on it the list of all the successful candidates and…there was no mistake about it…she had seen my name. I screamed and jumped, and I screamed again louder than before. I gripped Maryse's arm and shouted: "I've passed! I've passed!"

I now knew for sure that I would be joining Marie and soon I would be sitting among the elite of Northern France. Annoyed by my noisy display of jubilation and pride, Annie Brenn marched towards me and barked:

"Martha Bertrand! You're not going to the park. Go back inside!"

I could not believe it. I had passed the most important exam of my life, and all I got was a punishment. Now, I would not only miss out on going to the park, but I would also miss out on the ice cream we had been promised. I walked grudgingly towards the refectory dragging my feet. Then I sat on the bench closest to the door and slumped my head on my little fists. I was choking with anger. Nobody had bothered to tell me that I had passed, and now that I had learnt the result from one of my peers, I was being punished. It was so unfair. I really could not wait to move to Sister Odile's nest and get away from these awful people.

In a cloud laden with fumes of anger, I plotted my future. "Don't ever let me grow up into an adult," I muttered to myself with renewed truculence. "They are foul people and I never want to become one of them."

While the cloud over my head grew darker and denser, I heard the familiar squeak of Sister Catherine's rubber soles. I was so furious that I had passed beyond caring. I folded my arms across my chest, stretched my legs under the table, and ignored the nun completely. Determined to remain in this sulking position, I did not even turned my head to look at her when she began talking to me.

"Why have you been punished?" She asked, seemingly oblivious to the imminent eruption of my volcanic mood.

I waited to reply. I had too much exasperated air to expel before I could utter a word without running the risk of saying something I might regret. Finally, I jerked my legs, crossed them and uncrossed them in an exaggerated motion, and grumbled:

"Because I was being too noisy..."

"Why were you being noisy?" She enquired still on the same placid tone.

"Because Marie told me I'd passed my scholarship exam." Then I sighed, a long, belligerent sigh that allowed me to expel the mounting flow of boiling fumes.

Sister Catherine gave me some paper and coloured pencils to keep me occupied, but I pushed the whole lot away with a swift swipe of the hand.

"I don't like drawing!"

She suggested something to read and returned with a picture book.

"I don't want it! It's a baby book!"

"What about the one your godmother gave you...*Thousand and One Nights*, wasn't it?"

I did not dismiss it outright because I rather liked that book. I heard her rummage through a cupboard in the room next door and a few minutes later, she returned with it in her hand. She put it in front of me and said:

"You can never control yourself, can you?"

Then, out of nowhere, she produced an ice cream, a strawberry ice cream. I could not believe it. The unexpected surprise made me raise my head and I saw that she was smiling. So, I smiled too.

CHAPTER XXV

The day of my second communion beckoned. It was not the actual event that I dreaded most, but the arrival of the cantankerous, accident-prone godmother who had problems keeping her little Dauphine on the road. Her past behaviour had suggested that, as a suitable act of revenge, she would not have hesitated to have those responsible for her misfortune hung, drawn, and quartered, had these barbaric practices still been *du jour*. Furthermore, from the way she treated me, I could tell that she was immensely grateful to be able to offload on someone smaller than her, the deep rancour she held against every Tom, Dick, and Harry…and that included me. Fortunately, somewhere over there, may it be in Indochina, Paris or Timbuktu, she had *other cats to whip*, as the French expression goes, and so did I.

By now, the Junior Section was buzzing with excitement. All of us older girls were caught in a swirl of religious fervour as we prepared physically, mentally, and spiritually for our '*grande communion*'. I cannot remember which of the nuns used to tell us this, but one of them used to say repeatedly, "always be thankful for small mercies".

A few days before the big event, I had cause to be grateful and I thanked God profusely because, for once, our hair would not be savagely cut by a blunt razor blade. No, not this time. We were taken to the hairdresser's, no less, and the best of it was that, once we had been sheared in a painless fashion, the hairdresser sprayed us generously with a good dose of cheap eau de cologne. That really was fantastic.

Then I needed a dress to wear, because after the ceremony, we would be allowed to wear our own clothes. I wondered where mine were.

"*Ma soeur*, where are my dresses?" I enquired.

"I've given them away to the poor...you'd outgrown them anyway."

Blast! I thought. She's done it again. She's given my dresses to the poor! What about me, was I not poor too?

"Don't worry," she quickly added, seeing how upset I was. "One of the supervisors will take you to town to get a new one."

I did not want a new dress, I liked the old ones. They were mine...I had earned them.

The weekend before the big day, a taxi drove our little group to town. Sitting with Michèle, Claire, Dominique, and the others reminded me of that first occasion that made me feel so pure, so righteous, and so glad to be on a par with God and Jesus. This time, however, my excitement was mixed with doubts and uncertainties, and I was no longer sure I wanted to take the vows and swear my allegiance to God for the rest of my life. His representatives, here on earth, had shaken our faith and sullied our souls. How could I possibly go along with their cruel and ruthless interpretation of God's Will without being seen to condone their evil deeds?

My contemporaries had no such qualms. All their lively conversations revolved purely around the lavish presents they would receive from various members of their families: a watch was a traditional gift along with a small bible. A gold medal or a gold bracelet was another favoured choice. I had no idea what the godmother intended to bring and even questioned whether she was *au fait* with the kind of present she should bestow upon me to celebrate my ultimate reunion with God and Jesus.

On the day itself, I could not fail noticing that our surplices were very similar to the nun's habit except for the colour, ours being ivory white. Looking like young novices, our procession meandered through the crowded streets and reached the church square amid the loud buzz of excited crowds. As the columns of communicants progressed slowly and solemnly down the church aisle, I could not help looking around to see if I could spot Charlotte from my class, and see if she would have the gall to come and swear eternal allegiance to God whilst, in the eyes of Sister Eugène-Marie at least, she behaved like a proper little pagan.

After the ceremony, we walked back to *Saint Vincent* at a quick pace so that the proud girls could be reunited with their parents. Far from sharing their enthusiasm, all I wanted to do was to disappear so as to delay, for as long as possible, the eventual encounter with the godmother. I decided that the vast dormitory was a good place in which to hide and I was already making my way there when Annick hailed me.

"Hey, Martha!" She called out. "Aren't you going to wait to say hello to my dad?"

I hesitated. I really did not want to hang around and run the risk of bumping into the godmother prematurely, but Annick insisted.

The large entrance hall was soon teeming with parents, while communicants in their ivory habits milled around showing off their presents. I readily gasped in admiration as girl after girl paraded in front of me with their new gifts, but in truth, I was waiting for a propitious moment to dash upstairs and disappear.

"Don't tell anyone you've seen me!" I warned every girl I met on the stairs.

"That's silly," one said rather pointedly. "You can't hide. Wherever you go, they'll find you."

Of course I knew that, just like I knew that Father Christmas and witches did not exist, but sometimes a false belief is preferable to a painful truth. Gosh, I wish I were a witch. I could do with their magic powers just now. If only I could make myself invisible...just this once...until the weekend was over. I reached the top landing just as Maryse was coming out of the dormitory.

"Don't tell anyone you've seen me..." I said, not even taking the time to catch my breath.

"But your godmother's coming..."

"I know! That's why!"

"She can't be that bad..."

"You don't know her!" I retorted.

"Think, though...she's gonna bring you a present. You might get a watch."

"That would be great, but I doubt it!" I replied, resigned and increasingly aware that I was fighting a lost cause. "I wish I could go with you," I suddenly blurted out in desperation.

Maryse raised her eyes and shrugged her shoulders. To her, any mention of 'home' was forbidden territory, out of bounds, and I never asked her why because, between us, we had a quiet understanding that told us never to go there.

The godmother eventually turned up with her hair propped up in an elaborate beehive and wearing the same pink frilly blouse and Chanel suit that she kept for special occasions. When she first saw me, I could tell that something rankled her, and half expected to hear another lengthy tirade on some unfortunate event for which I was personally responsible. I greeted her coldly and accepted her gift awkwardly. With an air of utter indifference, I opened the thin oblong box expecting to find a watch, and emitted a quiet, but clearly disappointed sigh when I saw that it was a little bracelet made of pink coral beads strung together with gold links.

"Put it on, then," she urged, still expecting some kind of enthusiastic response to her most generous gift.

"I don't know how to," I mumbled, fiddling with it.

Her perfectly manicured hands with the longest painted nails I had ever seen could not quite grasp the minuscule clasp, so the bracelet was returned to its box. Then, we went into the garden with its three perfectly clipped lawns bordered by rows of rhododendron in full bloom. She positioned herself carefully to take some pictures, wedged her high heels against the flowerbed and nearly fell into the rose bush. I threw a mischievous glance at my friends who were involved in the same process, and sniggered into my virginal sleeve. The godmother seemed to take a rather long time to focus her camera, and I stood on the same spot for ages, frozen in the cheesiest smile I could manage. Eventually, she blasted out: "Take off your glasses! You look much better without them."

That's it, that's what rankled her, I suddenly realised. She could not get used to the idea that I now wore glasses.

Reluctantly, I took them off and squinted at the camera.

Once she had taken several pictures, she stored the camera back inside its brown leather case and we left.

As we had done all those years ago, we took the tramway to Lille and did the journey in complete silence. I stared out of the window trying to spot features in the landscape I would recognise, wishing all the time that I was already on my way back to *Saint Vincent*. Once in town, we crossed the main town square and made our way to a dingy hotel which had a blue enamel plaque on the wall outside with one red star on it. Inside, the room was draped with long, dark curtains which brushed against the stained wall-paper and dragged along a filthy, thread-bare carpet. Most of the available space was taken up by a double bed and lugubrious dark wood furniture. I wondered whether this was the very same hotel where she had stayed that time when she had worried the *propriétaire* by screaming all through the night. Thinking of bad nights, it suddenly occurred to me that I was having less disturbed nights lately, as my nightmares, for some inexplicable reason, had began to subside. Would the soldiers come and haunt me tonight as I shared a bed with a woman who could not help but list all my faults? To think I always struggled to find ten sins to put on my list before she appeared on the scene...Now they reeled off her tongue as easily as if she were a member for the prosecution.

After the most unmemorable two days during which the godmother and I sat on park benches, in restaurants, or simply ambled in the streets gazing into space in an awkward tortured silence, we finally boarded the tramway. Suddenly, I brightened up. I wanted to speak, to share my enthusiasm, but did not know what to say. The godmother, who seemed to sense my sudden gaiety, looked at me, but did not know what to say either.

The electronic doors clunked heavily and I quickly disappeared. It was the same old ritual: the heavy clunk, the hush-hushed tones, and the quick get away. How good it felt to be back on familiar home territory.

Now that this ordeal was over, I was free to contemplate the new exciting life ahead of me: the long awaited move to '*Le Nid*' and to a new school. However, before the latter could happen, I had to prove that I was not only academically able, but also physically fit to stand up to the rigours of the many challenges that lay ahead. For this, I had to undergo a thorough medical examination. In order to fulfil this necessary requirement, one of the supervisors took me to the doctor's to be checked over.

The doctor was a rotund man with round glasses. He looked very old, very serious, and very grumpy. Anyhow, peering through his thin lenses, he took one look at me and shook his head.

"Strip to your vest, please," he ordered dryly.

As I executed his command, he shook his head again. Then he lifted my right arm, felt the flesh, and immediately hit the bone. After a studied pause, he tut-tutted and dropped it. My arm fell limply back against my side. He repeated the same process with my left arm, shook his head and tut-tutted once more. Then, he lodged the ends of his stethoscope in his ears, grabbed the cold metal disc and applied it to my chest. I took a very deep breath, as he told me to, and practically disappeared.

"*Elle n'est pas bien épaisse...*" He kept muttering.

That was rather stating the obvious. After years of minuscule portions of execrable food, I indeed looked as if I could have done with one or two extra meals a day.

At the end of the thorough examination, the first thing the doctor did was to reach out for his prescription pad and scribble down a whole stack of vitamin pills for me. There was no doubt that I was in perfect working order and that I was generally fit, but the evidence showed that I was in desperate need of 'beefing up'.

*

Several days after the weekend of my second communion, Sister Catherine told me to go to the parlour. Who could it be this time? I wondered.

"Your godmother is waiting for you."

Oh no, she's back! I don't want to see her. Why can't she go away and leave me alone.

Grudgingly, I dragged my feet all the way to the parlour and saw her petite silhouette sitting on the bench, her hands fidgeting with her black Hermes handbag.

After a few minutes of small talk with big blank spaces between each word, she finally dropped the bombshell.

"How would you like to come and live in Paris?" She asked, as if inviting me to go for a ride in the park.

Of course I said yes. I even smiled at her suggestion. Who wouldn't want to go to Paris? I had always wanted to travel and explore and experience lots of new adventures. This was my big chance and I grabbed it, so long as I would be coming back here at *Saint Vincent*.

Having received the answer she expected, the godmother left.

Wow! I could not wait to tell everyone that I was going to Paris; that I was going to visit what I had learnt in Geography was the capital of France. Even Annie Brenn got excited at the prospect of this new wild adventure.

"You're going to '*la ville des lumières*'!" She exclaimed.

The City of Lights? Is that what they call it? I looked at her pondering over the meaning of the phrase: 'The City of Lights', 'the capital of France'? I did not really care what they called it, as long as I was going there.

*

The end of term was nigh. At school, Bénédicte reiterated her promise to invite me to her holiday home near Calais, and I left *Ecole Notre Dame* more popular than ever; and since the prize giving ceremony had been abolished, I was able to leave without feeling guilty about monopolising all the first prizes. Life was simply wonderful.

Back at *Saint Vincent*, it was time to prepare for the summer exodus to Sangatte. Sister Catherine asked us all to empty our lockers, an uncomplicated task that was performed routinely at the end of each academic year.

"What a boring chore," I declared, and decided to leave mine until the very last minute.

"Martha Bertrand!" I heard Sister Catherine hail as we played noisily in the courtyard. "You still haven't emptied your locker. Come and do it at once!"

I looked at Maryse, shrugged my shoulders and said:

"I'd better go, otherwise I'm going to be in trouble."

I ran into the study room and opened my locker still cluttered with all sorts of forgotten work. That should not take too long, I thought, I'll simply throw everything into the bin. As usual, Sister Catherine was breathing down my neck to make sure I did not disappear, leaving a job half done. And as I removed, one by one, the crumpled bits of paper, I could feel my hand moving more and more slowly. Suddenly, a huge sense of foreboding seized me, and at this very moment, everything seemed to be moving in slow motion. Then, I felt a blow hit me inside the head and on my midriff. Instinctively, I put my hand on my tummy, let out a big sigh, and without looking at the nun, I muttered:

"I'm not coming back, am I?"

A tense silence followed. All I could hear was Sister Catherine's slow breathing.

"No," she finally replied on a soft tone.

I stared forlorn at the few remaining bits and pieces that lay at the bottom of the locker and whispered:

"I don't want to go…"

As I turned around to put the pieces of paper in the bin, I caught sight of Sister Catherine's face, and there, in the corners of her outstretched lips, I saw the hint of a smile. At last, the drawbridge had fallen, and for the first time, she was able to see the more serious, deep thinking, fragile soul that had been so carefully hidden behind a cheeky smile. During those few minutes, she had seen the real Martha Bertrand, and at that moment, she must have felt the same way as a psychologist feels after solving a particularly difficult case. She had finally cracked the enigma and caught a glimpse of the deeply concealed emotions that she had always suspected were there, but which she had not quite managed to unveil.

"Well, it's too late now..." She answered with a philosophical shrug of the shoulders.

CHAPTER XXVI

Before we left for Sangatte, I had to pack my own bag so that I had something to wear once I handed back my uniform for the last time. Sister Catherine produced a tiny suitcase, no doubt one that had been donated to her for 'the poor', where I would be able to pack the things I wanted to take with me. There were only three things I wanted: my two dresses—given to me by the Langeais and which she had given away to 'the poor'—and my bracelet, given to me for my second communion. No, the nun had not given that one away to the poor; she had put it in the lockable cupboard for safekeeping, so safe, in fact, that she could no longer find it, or so she said.

In the end, there was not a single item we could find anywhere that belonged to me. So, among the pile of fresh laundry, Sister Catherine dislodged a pair of pink pyjamas and squeezed it inside the tiny suitcase with the words:

"I'm sure so-and-so won't mind if I give you her pyjamas."

Then, she added two pairs of pants, the best she could find in the pile, and socks, unfazed by the realisation that, after spending the first eleven years of my life here at *Saint Vincent*, she had not a single possession to pack that actually belonged to me.

However, no matter what had happened before, it always felt good to be back at Sangatte. With my little hands gripping the wire fence, I filled my lungs with the smell of the sea spray hanging above the seashore, and I filled my eyes with the transparent luminosity through which I could gaze at the horizon, already scribbling away more distant and exciting adventures. I did not know what the future held for me, and did not really know what to aspire for, except for one thing: I wanted to travel.

Now that I was about to leave *pour toujours*, everybody, including the supervisors, treated me differently. Annick and I were no longer seen as a pair, but as a 'couple', and we were allowed to hang out together, locked in arms as always, and give each other pecks on the cheeks at night without anyone tut-tutting over that frowned upon physical contact, and while we indulged openly in a close friendship, all the other girls gaped and sighed with envy at the sudden freedom the two of us were able to enjoy.

Maryse had intimated that she was also leaving *Saint Vincent* and we had parted in an excited state, not able to grasp or understand that we would never see each other again. I do not even recall saying '*au revoir*' to her, because back then, it was never meant to be a farewell.

Bénédicte held her promise and her parents came one Sunday after church to collect me. We played with her dolls and we went to the beach carrying buckets and spades, not forgetting a sunhat for her favourite doll, Bella. And while I gave the impression of being wholly involved in the simple joys of childhood, I was busy watching my little friend with sorrowful eyes, observing how she evolved gracefully in her own surroundings, while secretly mourning the fact that I would never again see those perfect little ringlets and that beautiful freckled face, which radiated with pure bliss and serenity. I wished then that all the clocks would stop and the day would go on forever without anyone noticing, so that I could spend a few more precious minutes with the most beautiful creature in the world.

The end of July was approaching much too fast. Each time I started to think about the fateful day the godmother would come and collect me for the last time, my stomach churned and went into spasms, and I had to find some distraction quickly to stop the pain from growing any stronger.

I do not know which day of the week it was, but the final day brutally fell upon me like a death knell. Soon, I would be taken to the blocks, the Tower or the guillotine, but just like the noble aristocrats did as they met their ultimate fate up there on the scaffolds, I would hold my head up high and look straight with steely eyes at my ineluctable fate.

That morning, I left my uniform at the bottom of the bed, and with my hands shaking with apprehension and fear, I put on the pink dress I wore for my second communion.

After lunch, everybody filed indoors to go for their afternoon nap, while I remained behind, alone in the play area, which suddenly looked like a vast expanse of green empty space. I would have liked to go and stand by the wire fence and take one last long view at the sea, but I was conscious that the girls would be able to see me from their dorms on the first floor and I was determined not to let anybody see me wince as the pain in my stomach grew more and more intense. Instead, I picked up a ball, the one and only ball we used to fight over to have a go at counting how many times we could bounce it against the blockhaus's wall without dropping it. Now that I had it all to myself, the fun had gone and all I could do in this final hour was listen to its bounce echoing in the empty playground that reverberated with soulful memories of days gone by. Just like the happy chatter of invisible people I used to hear at night, I could now hear the excited cries and the incessant laughter of Maryse's voice as she plotted yet another game or a mischievous deed. I broke into a sudden smile as I recalled her obsession with witches and the immense joy she had felt when she had found a 'real witch' in the shape of Mlle Agnès who used to sit in complete ignorance outside the kitchens; and I pondered over the spontaneous friendship that had sprung one summer holiday between Annick and I, still puzzled by the fact that it happened at all.

In the distance, I heard the electronic doorbell tear through the still silence. I dropped the ball and advanced slowly towards the main entrance hall, knowing that the call was for me.

The godmother was standing in the hall, her face partially hidden behind a pair of Chanel sunglasses, and her hair firmly kept in place under a Hermes scarf. Sister Catherine handed me the small suitcase and uttered a brief goodbye. I muttered a faint farewell in return and stepped outside.

We walked to the bus stop, all the while with the godmother moaning and groaning about one thing or other.

"You did not say goodbye properly to Sister Catherine. That was so rude...after all she's done for you...you know... she's looked after you for a long time...you should have shown some gratitude at least. Why can't you ever say goodbye properly? It's just like that time when I dropped you off after your communion, you just ran off and disappeared." Here, she paused to catch her breath. "You didn't even turn around to wave goodbye. I was so upset...after all the money I've spent on you! And what about that parcel I sent you for your birthday, you never wrote to say thank you...didn't you like what I sent you? Was it not worth saying thank you for...? You should always say thank you when people give you things. What about the bracelet? Have you got the bracelet...why are you not wearing it, where is it?"

I stood on the pavement in a stubborn stoic silence, not wanting to look back at the *Colonie Saint Joseph des Flots*, and refusing to pay any attention to the irate woman gesticulating beside me.

The bus arrived. The lady driver, a certain Mme Blanche, blessed with generous embonpoint, asked how many tickets we needed, and after the godmother had shaken the loose change out of her purse, we settled into our seats in the near-empty bus. I picked a seat by the window, looking out at the countryside rather than to the sea for the sight of deserted beaches stretching below the empty horizon sharpened the acute sense of desolation I felt, as the bus started up and began to move further and further away from the white building standing behind me. I let out a long mournful sigh and stared at the golden fields and at the black and white cows ambling along the green pastures. Through a haze of misted eyes, I contemplated new wishes and new aspirations, though at this very moment, I was no longer sure what these were.

The future is a mystery to behold and who knows when the bell would toll, for we, children, would never be told.

THE END